PAISLEY

PAISLEY

Religion and Politics in Northern Ireland

STEVE BRUCE

OXFORD
UNIVERSITY PRESS

OXFORD
UNIVERSITY PRESS

Great Clarendon Street, Oxford ox2 6DP

Oxford University Press is a department of the University of Oxford.
It furthers the University's objective of excellence in research, scholarship,
and education by publishing worldwide in

Oxford New York

Auckland Cape Town Dar es Salaam Hong Kong Karachi
Kuala Lumpur Madrid Melbourne Mexico City Nairobi
New Delhi Shanghai Taipei Toronto

With offices in

Argentina Austria Brazil Chile Czech Republic France Greece
Guatemala Hungary Italy Japan Poland Portugal Singapore
South Korea Switzerland Thailand Turkey Ukraine Vietnam

Oxford is a registered trade mark of Oxford University Press
in the UK and in certain other countries

Published in the United States
by Oxford University Press Inc., New York

© Steve Bruce 2007

The moral rights of the author have been asserted
Database right Oxford University Press (maker)

First published 2007

British Library Cataloguing in Publication Data

Data available

Library of Congress Cataloging in Publication Data

Data available

Typeset by SPI Publisher Services, Pondicherry, India
Printed in Great Britain
on acid-free paper by
Biddles Ltd., King's Lynn, Norfolk

ISBN 978-0-19-928102-2

1 3 5 7 9 10 8 6 4 2

Contents

Preface

This is the second time I have written at length about the Right Honourable Ian Richard Kyle Paisley MP, MLA. A few words explaining how the first book—*God Save Ulster!*—came to be written and how this differs from its predecessor might help the reader judge it. Much of my early work was a product of frustration with British social science in the 1970s. I have a very clear recollection, as an undergraduate at Stirling University, of one of my sociology lecturers advancing an evolutionary view of human development in which religion and nationalism, such powerful forces in the past, had been displaced in the modern world by social class. That was a widely held view, even among those who were not committed to the Marxist version of that story (and there were plenty who were). The sentiments and romantic loyalties that drove simpler people had been superseded by material interests. Although I had no more than a few impressions on which to base my reservations, I was sure that my social theory teacher was wrong. Although not personally religious, I was fascinated by religion and, after a first degree that combined religious studies and sociology, I wrote a doctoral thesis in the sociology of religion. When my supervisor, Roy Wallis, was appointed to the chair of sociology at The Queen's University of Belfast, I followed, and under his guidance I developed two interests. In one strand of work I tried to explain the decline of religion in most modern industrial societies over the twentieth century. In the other I studied examples of the enduring salience of religious ideas and identities. And living round the corner from Ian Paisley's church on the Ravenhill Road in Belfast I had a prime example within walking distance.

Through a happy accident I became known to some of the staff of the BBC in Northern Ireland and in 1984 I was commissioned to research a film biography of Paisley. I imagined that it would be largely a matter of reading the official histories of the Free Presbyterian Church of Ulster (FPCU) and the Democratic Unionist Party (DUP), and finding a few representatives of church and party to add personal colour to the story. I discovered that there was no official history and little or no serious commentary and was forced to collect my own primary material. Arranging filming brought me into contact with Dr Paisley and his colleagues, whom I discovered to be quite happy to talk about their movement to anyone who took the trouble to understand their religious beliefs. Once I had made the film, it seemed sensible to continue the research in order to fill a significant gap in our knowledge of the conflict in Northern Ireland, and in 1986 *God Save Ulster: The Religion and Politics of Paisleyism* was published.

Dr Paisley and his associates have produced a considerable amount of documentary material. The *Revivalist* appeared as the official organ of the FPCU fairly regularly from 1951 to the 1980s and since then there has been *Truth for Youth*. Since the mid-1960s the *Protestant Telegraph* (replaced for a time by the *Voice of Ulster*) has acted as a record of the political campaigning arm of Paisleyism. Almost complete sets of these publications were made available to me by Free Presbyterians and by the Linenhall Library, whose staff were extremely helpful. I was able to collect some simple information about the ministers and their congregation from a brief questionnaire. Twenty-seven FPCU ministers were interviewed and I interviewed Dr Paisley on a number of occasions. Over a period of two years I attended many church services and other religious meetings. Leading party activists were interviewed at length. During the course of the research there was the 1984 European Parliament election and the 1986 Westminster by-elections and I was able to talk to many DUP activists during those campaigns. Although few opinion poll data were directly cited in *God Save Ulster!* I benefited greatly from the survey work done by my colleagues at Queen's University and from access via the BBC to commercial polls.

Four things persuaded me to write a follow-up to *God Save Ulster!* First, and most obviously, a lot has happened in Northern Ireland since 1986. In the 1990s the major terrorist organizations called a halt to the most disruptive of their activities; with considerable assistance from the USA, the British and Irish governments crafted a political settlement that, at the time of writing, has not fully taken hold but still seems set fair to produce a long-term solution to the Ulster crisis; Sinn Fein displaced the Social Democratic and Labour

Party (SDLP) as the main voice of northern nationalism; and the DUP overtook the Ulster Unionist Party (UUP).

A second stimulus was the publication of a large amount of biographical material. Partly as a result of many of the protagonists reaching old age and partly because the ceasefires have radically changed the climate, a large number of biographies and autobiographies that cast new light on the Troubles have been produced.

Thirdly, and this explains much of the difference in emphasis between this book and *God Save Ulster!*, what is interesting about Paisleyism has been markedly altered by a change in real world and a change in opinion. The real change was the rise of what is loosely called 'fundamentalism'. The success of the New Christian Right in America brought Protestant fundamentalism to the fore. And changes in the Muslim world made us all familiar with Islamic fundamentalist or 'Islamist' movements. Increasing awareness of what a real *jihad* looks like made me much more aware of the relatively constrained nature of Paisleyism. As I have learnt more about the character of such theocracies as that imposed by the Taliban in Afghanistan and the Ayatollahs in Iran (and intended by the Muslim Brothers in Egypt or Hizbollah in Lebanon), the liberal critiques of Paisleyism that were commonplace in the 1980s have come to seem hysterical. Dennis Cooke, for example, entitled his biography of Paisley *Persecuting Zeal*. Compared with the ecumenical Protestant's desire for greater inter-church cooperation, Paisley's unkindly critical opinions of Catholicism (and of his Protestant rivals) might seem 'persecuting', but, when compared with the Islamic *jihadi* view that defection from the true faith of Islam should be punished by execution, Paisleyism appears in a very different light: *Nagging Zeal* would have been a more appropriate title. My views of Paisleyism have also been changed by my increasing knowledge of the loyalist paramilitary world with which Paisley is (mistakenly) associated by his critics. After *God Save Ulster!* I spent many years cultivating paramilitary contacts and eventually wrote *The Red Hand: Protestant Paramilitaries in Northern Ireland*. The changing realities have also brought a change in perceptions that has made some of my 1986 concerns somewhat redundant. In writing *God Save Ulster!* I felt obliged to stress the impact of Paisley's religion on his politics because so many people then shared the view of my inadvertently inspiring social theory teacher: that religion did not matter. Twenty years on, few readers will have trouble accepting the general principle that religious ideas and identities can be powerful drivers of social action and so I can concentrate on a more detailed consideration of just how and in what ways religion matters. The point can be made in terms of contrasts. In 1986 I wanted to stress how Paisleyism differed from secular politics; twenty years on I want to show how Paisleyism differs both from secular politics and from Islamic fundamentalism. A great deal has been written about Paisley since 1986, some of it critical of my work. Some insights I have incorporated; others I have rejected. Rather than dot the text with petty points of self-justification, I will permit myself just this one immature observation. A common theme of criticism is that I misrepresented Ulster unionism by giving too much weight to Paisleyism and underestimating the new liberal and secular Ulster unionism that was based not on religio-ethnic identity but on a philosophy of equal citizenship, the philosophy promoted by Robert McCartney at the start of his political career and David Trimble at the end of his. That the new unionism has been thoroughly beaten by the old does not prove I was right but it does suggest that my critics were wrong.

Acknowledgements

God Save Ulster! was my third book; this is my twenty-second. In producing both, and all the words in between, I have acquired innumerable debts. The British Academy, the Leverhulme Foundation, and the Economic and Social Research Council have periodically funded my research, as has the American philanthropist Tom Tracy. My employers—The Queen's University of Belfast from 1978 to 1991 and subsequently the University of Aberdeen—have given me the time to pursue my work. By inviting me to take part in the seminal 1980s American Academy Fundamentalism project, the American historian of religion Martin Marty stimulated me to broaden my research field from Paisleyism to religion and politics more generally.

Ann Brown, Evelyn Hunter, Margaret Drumm, and Margaret Mullany of Queen's University assisted in the production of the pre-word-processor *God Save Ulster!* Karen Stewart word-processed the original text and notes in preparation for this text.

The staff of the Northern Ireland Census Office and the Northern Ireland Statistics and Research Agency were kind enough to produce a detailed breakdown of statistics relating to Free Presbyterians, and my Aberdeen colleague Professor Bernadette Hayes was helpful in interpreting those data. The various election studies produced by Professors Rick Wilford and Sydney Elliott of Queen's University were extremely helpful. Professors Paul Bew, Arthur Aughey, and Henry Paterson have also been a considerable source of insight into Northern Ireland politics.

By their example and by their comments on my work, Professor David Martin, formerly of the London School of Economics, and the late Bryan Wilson, of All Souls College, Oxford, were of considerable assistance in my general intellectual development. I also owe a lifelong debt to the late Roy Wallis, who taught me when I was an undergraduate at Stirling University, supervised my doctoral research, appointed me to a lectureship at Queen's, and laid the foundation for all my later work with his insightful direction.

I also owe an enormous debt to John Douglas, the Clerk of the Presbytery of the Free Presbyterian Church, who gave me considerable assistance with contacts and with historical information about the church, to Ian Paisley Jnr, who played a similar role with regard to the party, and to the very many Free Presbyterians and Democratic Unionists who have put up with my intrusions over the last twenty-five years.

List of Abbreviations

CLMC	Combined Loyalist Military Command
DOW	Down Orange Welfare
DUP	Democratic Unionist Party
ECONI	Evangelical Contribution on Northern Ireland
EEC	European Economic Community
EMU	Education for Mutual Understanding
EPS	Evangelical Protestant Society
FPC/FPCU	Free Presbyterian Church of Ulster
IPC	Irish Presbyterian Church
IRA	Irish Republican Army
LPP	Liverpool Protestant Party
LTBS	Let the Bible Speak
LVF	Loyalist Volunteer Force
MLA	Member of the Legislative Assembly
NILP	Northern Ireland Labour Party
NUP	National Union of Protestants
OO	Orange Order
OV	Orange Volunteers
PUP	Progressive Unionist Party
RHD	Red Hand Defenders
RUC	Royal Ulster Constabulary
SDLP	Social Democratic and Labour Party
TA	Territorial Army
UCDC	Ulster Constitution Defence Committee
UDA	Ulster Defence Association
UDP	Ulster Democratic Party
UDR	Ulster Defence Regiment
UKUP	United Kingdom Unionist Party

UPV	Ulster Protestant Volunteers
UUC	Ulster Unionist Council
UUP	Ulster Unionist Party
UUUP	United Ulster Unionist Party
UVF	Ulster Volunteer Force
UWC	Ulster Workers Council
WCC	World Council of Churches

List of Tables

xvi   *List of Tables*

1

Ulster Protestants

INTRODUCTION

Ian Paisley is unique. No other person in modern Europe has founded a church and a political party. There was nothing unusual about senior church officials also wielding great political power in early modern societies: Cardinal Wolsey in England in the sixteenth century or Cardinal Richelieu in France a century later are well-known examples of church leaders who ran their countries. In times when the Christian Church provided the main nationwide social organization and had a near-monopoly of literacy and bureaucratic expertise, it was common for the monarch to draw advisers and administrators from the ranks of the clergy. But modern democracies assume that religion is a private matter and that the price for the state no longer interfering in matters of faith is that the churches no longer manage the state. Apart from Ian Paisley, the only founder of a political party in western Europe who was also a senior churchman is Abraham Kuyper, who founded the Dutch Anti-Revolutionary Party and became Prime Minister in 1901. But, although a widely respected and innovative theologian, he did not lead his own church.

That there is no model for Paisley's twin career shows us how unusual for modern democracies is the interaction of religion and politics we find in Northern Ireland. This chapter is intended to provide sufficient background for us to make sense of the environment that created Paisley.

PRESBYTERIANS IN IRELAND

Without Martin Luther there would have been no Ian Paisley. Since 1054 Christendom had been divided into two: the western church centred on Rome and the eastern church based in Constantinople. When in October 1517 the German priest Martin Luther nailed his list of complaints to the front door of the church in Wittenberg, he set in motion a series of doctrinal and organizational upheavals, retrospectively dubbed the Reformation, that split western Christians into Protestants and Catholics. By different routes the majority of the English, Scots, and Welsh people became Protestant; the Irish did not. The competition between the two very different visions of Christianity amplified their differences, and the greater political and military power of Britain laid the foundation for the enduring conflict that eventually created the Free Presbyterian Church of Ulster and the Democratic Unionist Party and made the career of their founder.

The Protestants in Ireland come from two sources: England and Scotland.[1] While most of the English and many of the Scots were deliberately planted in Ireland, the majority of the Scots settled in the north-east of the island before the plantation of James VI or in the period after the Williamite revolution of 1689. What makes the religious history complex is that the current threefold division of Roman Catholic, Church of Ireland (or Anglican or Episcopalian), and Presbyterian is a relatively late development. The British government and its agents in Dublin were generally concerned to create a national state-supported Church of Ireland but they largely failed to recruit the native Irish to such an organization: they remained Roman Catholic. The Presbyterians had a shifting relationship with the state church because the doctrines and practices of the church were in flux. The first Presbyterian ministers in Ulster actually held parishes of the national church and were for some years tolerated, even though their rejection of government by bishops—episcopacy—brought them into conflict with their local bishops. The first Presbyterian

---

[1] See, e.g., L. M. Cullen, *The Emergence of Modern Ireland, 1600–1920* (Dublin: Gill and Macmillan, 1983), and J. C. Beckett, *The Making of Modern Ireland, 1603–1923* (London: Faber and Faber, 1969).

clergy came to Ulster between 1620 and 1630 from Scotland because they could not accept James VI's attempts to reimpose bishops in the Scottish Church. As they established themselves and began to mobilize like-minded dissenting clergy, the Irish bishops increased their persecution, and Archbishop Laud in London instructed his agents to have them suppressed. Driven out of the province, the Presbyterians tried first to sail for America but were driven back by the seas and retreated to Scotland. The collapse of the monarchy of Charles I saw Charles, Laud, and his agent in Ireland, Wentworth, executed, but this gave little immediate advantage to the Presbyterians. The native Irish rose in rebellion in 1641, and many Protestants, both Episcopalian and Presbyterian, were killed. A large Scots army was sent to Ireland to crush the rebellion and it gave a considerable boost to the Presbyterians by bringing its own chaplains, who created the framework for the revival of a Presbyterian ministry.

However, the Presbyterians continued to be caught between the Irish Roman Catholic natives and the English. Although persecuted by the Stewarts, they remained committed to the idea of a legitimate monarchy and so were seen by Oliver Cromwell as a threat. Only towards the end of his Protectorate were they accepted and given government financial support. The Restoration of the Stewart monarchy brought a restoration of persecution. Sixty-one Presbyterian ministers were expelled from their parishes, and the arrival on the throne of James VII in 1685 only increased their problems. When the Dutch Protestant Prince William of Orange was invited to take the throne and James fled from London to Ireland, the battle lines were drawn. James's largely Catholic army quickly took most of Ireland. The gates of Derry City were only closed, against the advice of the local bishop and civil leaders, by a group of apprentice boys, whose action immortalized them in Protestant mythology. Then came William and the battles of Aughrim, the Boyne, and Enniskillen, and the establishment of a Protestant monarchy.

If the Presbyterians thought that the expulsion of the Stewarts had finally stabilized their position in Ireland, they were mistaken. As so often happened when religion was regarded as a tool of foreign policy and a device for ensuring loyalty, Presbyterians found that even Protestant princes were more interested in stable government than in religious orthodoxy. William endorsed the episcopalian Church of

Ireland and left the Presbyterians in the awkward position in which they had been caught since their migration from Scotland: sandwiched between the native Irish and the Protestant Ascendancy. The isolation of the Scots Presbyterians from the Ascendancy made it possible for the more liberal and affluent Presbyterians to consider alliance with the Irish.[2] A number of Belfast Presbyterians were active in the United Irishmen movement and in the 1798 rebellion, but they were the minority. The rising failed, and the majority of the Presbyterians threw their lot in with the British government. For all that they had been excluded from political power and suffered such periodic insults to their religious culture as the refusal to recognize Presbyterian marriages as binding on a non-Presbyterian partner, they were persuaded that their best interests lay with their fellow Protestants rather than with the Catholic Irish. The increasing politicization of the Irish produced a strong conservative movement within Presbyterianism. The combination of an increasingly confident Irish nationalism and a strengthening of the power and claims of the Catholic Church were enough to fuel the reciprocal development of a shared Protestant identity. In the 1830s we find Henry Cooke, the leader of the conservatives in the Irish Presbyterian Church (IPC), taking the side of the Episcopal Church when there was pressure to disestablish it by removing its legal superiority and its claims to income from rents. Cooke argued that a state Protestant church, even if it was the wrong one, was better than a free market system that Catholics would dominate by virtue of numbers.

Rank-and-file Presbyterians began to join the Orange Order(OO), the fraternal Protestant society that had developed from early agricultural vigilante groups and that had previously been predominantly Episcopalian.[3] By the time of the Home Rule crisis at the start of the twentieth century, the Anglo-Irish were returning the compliment

---

[2] R. F. G. Holmes, 'Eighteenth Century Irish Presbyterian Radicalism and its Eclipse', *Bulletin of the Presbyterian Historical Society of Ireland*, 3 (1973), 7–14.

[3] H. Senior, *Orangeism in Ireland and Britain, 1775–1835* (London: Routledge and Kegan Paul, 1966); T. Gray, *The Orange Order* (London: The Bodley Head, 1972); H. Senior, 'The Early Orange Order 1795–1870', in T. D. Williams (ed.), *Secret Societies in Ireland* (Dublin: Gill and Macmillan, 1973), 39–45; R. Dudley-Edwards, *The Faithful Tribe: An Intimate Portrait of the Loyal Institutions* (London: Harper Collins, 1998).

and borrowing symbols from Presbyterian culture. To display their implacable hostility to a united and independent Ireland, the Protestants modelled their protest on the old Scots covenants: petitions couched in the form of a legal contract between the people and the state, with God as the third party.

DOCTRINE AND DIVISION

In a largely secular society, in which religion plays little part in public life and is largely relegated to Sundays and the family home, it is sometimes difficult to appreciate the importance of religious beliefs for social identity. One way to grasp the significance of religion in Ireland is to try to imagine its history if the Scots and English settlers had also been Roman Catholics (or if Ireland had become Protestant). Differences of power, status, and wealth between settler and native would have remained, of course, but a common culture would have encouraged intermarriage and eroded ethnic boundaries. It is because the settlers were of a different religion to the natives and because settlement took place in an era when people believed that churches controlled access to salvation, and hence that adhering to the correct one was vital, that mixing was rare. Add to that the fact that religion played a major part in politics and foreign policy and we can see why the three ethnic groups remained divided and were able to develop competing political agendas. We should also recall, for it is crucial to the rest of this book, that Protestantism and Catholicism are not any two different religions. They stand in opposition to each other. The former began as a protest against features of the latter, and after they had separated, each developed those elements that most clearly distinguished it from the other. So long as each took seriously its claims to unique insight into the will of God, they were irreconcilable.

The points of dispute were many and are not easily summarized without caricature, but I will outline enough for the gravity of the disagreements to be appreciated. The Protestant Reformation can be seen as a simplification of the previous dominant tradition. Man is sinful. God gave his only Son so that his death would wipe away our

sins. Believe that and you will be saved. We know this to be the case
because the Bible says so and the Bible is the word of God; everything
that we need to know is presented in the Bible, most of it in terms
plain enough for ordinary people to appreciate. Hence there is no
need for professional priests to act as mediators between man and
God. In contrast, the Roman Catholic doctrine of the Mass, as it was
understood in the seventeenth century, almost argued that Christ's
sacrifice had to be repeated and that, by taking the consecrated
bread and water, the believer was, in some mystical sense, replaying
Christ's sacrifice. In addition, the Roman Catholic tradition had
added a variety of events and activities that, if not absolutely essential
to salvation, were held to be extremely useful aids. In particular, the
Protestants objected to the addition of confirmation, confession and
penance, extreme unction, holy orders, and matrimony to the two
sacraments of baptism and the Eucharist (or communion).

The major disagreement about necessary beliefs and actions has its
counterpart in a fundamental disagreement about organization and
authority. In the sphere of religion at least (it took some time for the
implications to spread wider) the Protestant Reformation was profoundly democratizing in that its assertion of the sole authority of the
Bible removed the need for ordained priests and reduced considerably
the clergy's role.[4] Protestants argued that the Holy Spirit working in
us to allow us to understand the words of the Bible was sufficient:
religious professionals might have been useful as preachers and
teachers of the Word of God but they were not essential. The Roman
Catholic Church accepted the Bible as central but argued that it
must be understood within the historical traditions of the organized
church. Although most Protestant traditions evolved some sort of
structure to settle doctrinal disputes and preserve the faith, such
structures were matters of convenience and gained little weight from
core beliefs. The authority of the organization came from the bottom
upwards: the people chose their ministers, who chose their representatives. The Catholic Church maintained a hierarchical form of
authority in which spiritual and bureaucratic power came downwards

[4] For a detailed discussion of the role that Protestantism played in the rise of
liberal democracy, see S. Bruce, 'Did Protestantism Create Democracy?', *Democratization*, 11 (2004), 3–20.

from the Pope and his cardinals to lesser functionaries. Bishops imposed priests on the people: the people did not choose their priests. A third general principle of the Reformation was the rejection of the idea that religious merit was transferable. Many religious traditions accept a division of labour in which the majority of the people do very little religion but financially support an elite that acquires religious merit and transfers it to the secular mass of the population. Varieties of Buddhism allow a transfer of credit from those who feel assured of their salvational status to others who are in need of some bonus points. Catholicism, in permitting the living to act on behalf of the dead by, for example, saying Masses or offering prayers that hasten the dead's move from purgatory to heaven, operated a transfer system. The Protestant Reformers found any such system to be profoundly abhorrent because it reduced the necessity for each and every individual to recognize his or her religious and moral responsibilities.

We could continue to list differences. The above points are made, not because they exhaust what separated Protestants and Catholics, but because they are enough to show the fundamental nature of the divide. The fact of conflicting religious allegiances added to and cemented other differences of language, status, and wealth between the populations.

Being Presbyterian was important for the Scots who settled in Ireland. So was being Calvinist. John Calvin made a number of contributions to Protestant theology, but the doctrine most associated with him is that of predestination. Although he defended the doctrine by reference to Bible texts, it is perhaps easiest explained by logic. Imagine that God is all-powerful. If that is so, he is hardly likely to be impressed by anything that we do, especially given the state of utter sinfulness we have been in since Adam turned his back on God in the Garden of Eden. As Paisley put it: 'If God gave me the due reward for my deeds, he would send me to hell. I am a sinner. There is nothing good about me. From the sole of the foot to the crown of the head there is no soundness in man, but wounds and bruises and putrefying sores.'[5] We are incapable of winning God's favour through our own efforts. If we are to be spared eternal damnation, it can only

[5] I. R. K. Paisley, *Paisley: The Man and his Message* (Belfast: Martyrs' Memorial Publications, 1976), 158.

be as a result of a gift from God; we can have done nothing to earn or deserve it. So whether we are to be saved or damned is in God's hands, not ours. So far, so good. But God is not only all-powerful; he is also all-knowing. And, if he knows everything (which seems like a sensible attribute for a divinity), then he knows the future as well as he knows the past and present. He thus knows whether we are damned or saved in advance of our being born and becoming moral actors in the world. These ideas should make it possible to see how Calvin could argue that we are *predestined* to salvation or damnation by God.

Although there are many problems in the working-out of the implications of this line of thinking, one consequence is to suppose that some of us have been chosen for salvation, are part of the elect, and others are not. Calvin himself and strict Calvinist theologians have always argued that only God knows who is part of the elect and that, for all practical purposes, one must suppose that all humans living at any particular time might be saved. The evangelist preaches the gospel to all people because he has no sure way of knowing who is a member of the band of saints. But the social scientist is usually more interested in what ordinary believers make of a set of doctrines than with the refined clerical version, and there has always been a strong tendency for popular Calvinism to slide into a form of racism. Calvinist peoples have tended to suppose that their children have a better than even chance of being part of the elect and conversely that people of other races, especially those who reject the gospel and oppress the godly, are unlikely to be part of the elect. It is easy to see how Calvinist Presbyterians can turn inwards and concentrate on preserving their own religion rather than trying to convert as many of the heathen as possible. As one Presbyterian historian puts it: 'Congregations could easily identify with Israel, taking possession of the promised land, threatened by the hostility of its fierce inhabitants.'[6] Such a tendency becomes especially strong when the non-Calvinists, instead of being disorganized followers of a variety of folk religions, are organized into membership of a disciplined anti-Presbyterian organization. When the heathen act badly towards the Calvinists, as

---

[6] R. F. G. Holmes, *Our Irish Presbyterian Heritage* (Belfast: Presbyterian Church in Ireland, 1985), 9.

some native Irish did in the rebellion of 1641 or the Scullabogue Massacre of 1798, the Calvinists can read such acts as confirmation that the natives are not part of God's chosen people. All religions give believers the chance to think of themselves and their descendants as God's favourites. The point about Calvinism is that, compared with other variants of Protestantism, it offers a ready justification for the believers to refrain from even trying to convert the heathen, and hence for the shared religion to create a further barrier between one ethnic group and another. The Scots Presbyterian settlers would probably have failed, even if they had tried to convert the native Irish, but they hardly tried. It is noticeable that when the Presbyterians divided into two competing camps, with followers of the Seceder Church in Scotland starting to recruit in Ireland, the recruitment was directed almost entirely to the Scots settlers. The competition was confined to the ethnic Scots and there was little attempt by the Seceders to expand by taking in the native Irish.[7]

Paisley and others who call themselves Calvinists now make considerable efforts to convert Roman Catholics, but this is a modern development. The Presbyterian settlers became committed to evangelizing the natives only once their own ethnic identity had become secured and once other differences between the competing populations had become firmly established. There is a good socio-logic for this. Let us suppose that all people have an interest in belonging to some social group with a shared history, shared traditions, and a worldview that makes sense of their position in the world and creates a social identity. Such identities require that some other people be excluded. Nationalism, for example, is concerned not only with who we are but also with who we are not. Our superiority depends on some other group's inferiority. When two or more ethnic groups inhabit the same geographical boundaries, every shared identity is precarious unless the boundaries between the groups can be established and maintained. The initial dimensions of conflict in Ireland were laid out in an era when worldviews were heavily informed by religion. For

---

[7] D. W. Miller, 'Presbyterianism and "Modernization" in Ulster', *Past and Present*, 80 (1978), 74. For a general history of the Seceders, see D. Stewart, *The Seceders in Ireland with Annals of their Congregations* (Belfast: Presbyterian Historical Society, 1950).

the Scots settlers to have succeeded in sharing their religion with the natives (either by converting them or by defecting) would have removed a crucial dimension of difference. Because they wished to maintain their own identity and to be able to explain and justify their claimed superiority, this is not something that the settlers would have welcomed. Hence it was only relatively late in their sojourn in Ireland—once it was clear that for Catholics to become Protestants would also mean giving up their Irishness and national identity—that Protestants engaged seriously in missionary activity. The Methodists began an Irish mission in 1799. Magee threw the Episcopal Church into the 'Protestant crusade' when he became Archbishop of Dublin in 1822. But 'the Presbyterians were not in the vanguard of the crusade', and they were not heavily involved in evangelism until the 1840s—almost 200 years after their arrival in Ireland.[8]

A similar pattern can be found in another Presbyterian settler country: South Africa. There the Dutch settlers, united by, among other things, their reformed Protestantism, did not initially seek to convert the natives and were opposed to English missionaries who did. It was only when social boundaries were firmly established that the Dutch undertook missionary activity, and the extent to which the boundaries were fixed can be seen in the fact that, when the natives did begin to convert in large numbers, they were segregated in black churches and not brought into the main structure of the Dutch Reformed churches.

A final preliminary point can be made about the consequences of the Scots' Presbyterianism. Presbyterian Church government is a compromise between congregational independence and centralized government. Although Presbyterians share the cardinal Protestant principle that all people can know the will of God, they have always tempered this democratic principle with a healthy suspicion of the anarchy that would ensue if every group of believers was allowed to make its own decision about what God was telling them. So Presbyterianism groups congregations together in presbyteries, collects presbyteries in synods, and then brings all synods under the control of a General Assembly composed of representatives from all the congregations. The pyramid of democratic centralism prevents anarchy.

---

[8] Holmes, *Our Irish Presbyterian Heritage*, 111.

But the centralization is not strong because there is no doctrinal support for an authoritarian hierarchy. Unlike the Catholic, Orthodox, and Episcopalian systems, there is no notion that Christ's authority had been delegated to any one office, the holders of which have the power and authority to instruct the lower levels. In practice, Presbyterianism permits local autonomy. Individual congregations do go their own way, and there are no sanctions equivalent to the Catholic Church's power to excommunicate deviants.

This has a very important consequence for Presbyterians who leave their mother country to settle in some foreign part. The clergymen who were sent as missionaries to southern Africa by the Anglican Church were controlled by the Anglican hierarchy in England. Their values and interests remained those of England and, if they 'went native', they could be recalled. But when Presbyterians left northern Europe to settle in other countries, they quickly developed local interests. Apart from anything else, they were paid by the local settlers and not by the sending church. The Seceder Presbyterians in Scotland were in fierce competition with the national Kirk, but when their missionaries went to America and Canada they cooperated with other Protestant churches and simply ignored the instructions from the Seceder Synod in Scotland to break such contacts. The centre could not control the outposts. The fact that the Scots who settled in Ulster were Presbyterians is thus important, because it explains why their religion could be readily adapted to suit the social and political conditions in which they found themselves.

These points have been made to establish the combination of religious and social factors that led to their shared faith remaining a vital part of the ethnic identity of the Scots settlers in Ireland. The Scots arrived with a religious culture that gave them good reason for feeling superior to the Irish natives and that separated them from the native population. Their very presence caused social conflict as the natives resented and attacked the status advantages of the Scots settlers. Those settlers in turn interpreted the conflict as proof of the godlessness of the natives. That interaction of religious ideology and social conflict established the foundations for later political developments: when the native Irish adopted a nationalist ideology, the Presbyterians became fully committed to union with the country, which not only guaranteed their political position but which was also, in rhetoric at least, Protestant.

This last point, like so many things in this introductory history, has to be stressed, because it has become buried by the subsequent changes in British culture.[9] British civil society of the eighteenth and early nineteenth centuries was deliberately and self-consciously anti-Catholic. The rising bourgeoisie that had invited back the Stewart monarchy to re-establish order after the chaos of the later Cromwellian period had concluded that papist monarchs could not be trusted to rule in the manner in which the new elites wanted; hence the invitation to William of Orange and the development of the idea that basic civil liberties and good government could be preserved only by a Protestant monarch. Until the Catholic Emancipation Act of 1829, Catholics were excluded from most parts of civil society, and, under that Act, Catholics continued to be excluded from many senior and influential political offices. The Irish setting raised the conflict between Protestants and Catholics to a level not known in the rest of Britain, but most Britons shared a similar commitment to anti-Catholicism. Rhetorical devices such as the Coronation Oath, which requires the monarch to promote the Protestant faith and reasserts the perils of Catholic rule, had deep resonances in Ireland, where they could be translated into judgements on the political conflict between unionists and nationalists, but such devices were fabricated in London and had a similar, albeit attenuated, resonance in the rest of the realm. If this point seems to have been laboured, it is only because it is very easy for modern commentators to suppose that Irish evangelical Protestants such as Ian Paisley have somehow invented a new set of religious beliefs to justify their political postures.[10]

THE ORANGE STATE AND RELIGIOUS REVIVAL

The late-nineteenth-century popular agitation in Ireland for Home Rule persuaded the Liberals under Gladstone to free themselves from

[9] S. Bruce, 'The Strange Death of Protestant Britain', in E. Kaufmann (ed.), *Rethinking Ethnicity: Majority Groups and Dominant Minorities* (London: Routledge, 2004), 116–35.
[10] This error is made by J. Brewer and G. Higgins, *Anti-Catholicism in Northern Ireland 1660–1998: The Mote and the Beam* (London: Macmillan, 1998).

the disputes of the Irish. The Protestants organized their resistance to any breaking of the Union and in the first decade of the century demonstrated their opposition to a united and independent Ireland by joining Sir Edward Carson's potentially revolutionary Ulster Volunteer Force (UVF). The onset of the First World War postponed the need for rebellion. The Ulster Volunteer Force was recruited into the British Army as the 36th (Ulster) Division and decimated in the Battle of the Somme. However, Protestant opposition to 'Rome rule' was not eradicated. If anything, it had been reinforced by the Irish Republican Easter Rising in Dublin in 1916 and the violent struggles that followed it. For the Protestants, the rising was proof positive of Catholic treachery: their opponents waited until Britain was occupied in a bloody struggle for democracy and freedom and attacked from the rear.

Ireland was partitioned.[11] The Protestants of the north-east were given six of the nine counties of the province of Ulster, the demand for the other three having been dropped once it became clear that the inclusion of all nine would have threatened a unionist majority, and the state of Northern Ireland was born. Partition had the effect of increasing the importance of Presbyterianism in Irish Protestantism. Although many Presbyterians were stranded on the wrong side of the border (especially in Monaghan), the majority were in the new state of Northern Ireland and a large part of the Church of Ireland Protestants were in the Free State. And the Church of Ireland people in the new state were well organized into a working alliance with the Presbyterians through the Orange Order and the Unionist Party.

The period after the foundation of Northern Ireland as a political unit was a time of considerable Protestant unity. The Catholics had been given the Free State so Ulster would be a Protestant country for a Protestant people.

Not all religious revivals are reactions to social or political unrest, but, in religious cultures, such stresses do often produce popular movements of increased religious commitment. Collective recommitment to the shared tradition is one way in which people can bolster their sense of community and reaffirm those values that they hold to

---

[11] For a brief history of the foundation of the Northern Ireland state, see D. Harkness, *Northern Ireland since 1920* (Dublin: Helicon Books, 1983).

be central to their identity. With a degree of exaggeration, a historian of Protestant crusades in post-partition Ulster explains their success as a reaction to civil strife.

Ulster has undergone many changes during the past four years. Its boundaries have been modified, and its Government recast.... Four years ago, the North of Ireland was in a state of chaos. Fears and uncertainty filled the minds of people. Politicians were at their wits' end. Murder and destruction, for the time being, seemed to be on the throne. No one could possibly describe the hopelessness of the situation, as things continued to travel from bad to worse... [but] man's extremity is always God's opportunity and in the day of trouble He never fails those who call upon Him.[12]

What God provided was William P. Nicholson, an Ulster-born evangelist who was at home in Bangor recuperating from an illness contracted while working in America. He was asked to address a local meeting of Christian workers. The crowds attending the meetings grew and many were converted. Nicholson's fame soon spread, and he was invited to preach at meetings in Portadown, Lisburn, Newtownards, and Dromore. The services held in the Albert Hall on the Shankill Road in Belfast were conducted against a background of rifle and machine-gun fire. In his blunt and sometimes vulgar manner, Nicholson preached the message of eternal damnation, repentance, faith, and salvation, and thousands responded.

What is significant about these revival meetings is that they were sponsored by clergymen of all the major Protestant denominations and attended by sizeable numbers of working-class people. Shipyard workers marched from the yards to the services in the Presbyterian church on the Ravenhill Road in East Belfast:

It was in one of these services that about 200 men openly came out for Christ, many of them publicly destroying their betting books, cards, etc. Salvation became epidemic and on the street and the car, the topic was either Nicholson or the work he was accomplishing. Tramwaymen, railwaymen, postmen and policemen were all roped in.[13]

[12] J. A. Gamble, *From Civil War to Revival Victory: A Souvenir of the Remarkable Evangelistic Campaigns in Ulster from 1921 to December 1925 Conducted by Rev. W. P. Nicholson* (Belfast: Emerald Isle Books, 1976). See also S. W. Murray, *W. P. Nicholson: Flame for God in Ulster* (Belfast: The Presbyterian Fellowship, 1973), and J. Barkley, *St Enoch's Congregation, 1872–1972* (Belfast: St Enoch's, 1972).
[13] Gamble, *From Civil War*, 6.

It is this unusual appeal to working people that makes these meetings interesting. By the 1920s the major Protestant denominations had lost contact with most of the lower classes in the British cities. What made the Belfast situation different was the importance of religion in establishing the social identity of Ulster Protestants. To make sense of their opposition to the Home Rule movement, and of the crisis from which Ulster was just emerging, they had to retain at least a nominal attachment to Protestantism. Nicholson was then able to use the sense of crisis to call large numbers of these people from their nominal Protestantism to a serious personal commitment.

The strong sense of Protestant denominational cooperation was short lived. Nicholson's first campaigns between 1920 and 1923 had been integrating; his second series of meetings three years later was supported by a much narrower evangelical base and tended to be divisive. There were two general reasons for this shift. From the point of view of the audience, the crisis had passed. The civil war in the Free State had taken the pressure off Ulster, and the world appeared to be settling down. With the external threat removed, the overwhelming pull to dramatic commitment to a shared religious ideology was attenuated, and people could return to their own denominational attachments. The second general reason concerns a shift in the religious climate most easily described as the rise of 'fundamentalism'.

MODERNISM AND FUNDAMENTALISM

The end of the Victorian era had seen some significant developments in Protestant religious thought. Perhaps the most important was the popularity of what was rather arrogantly called 'the Higher Criticism'.[14] German scholars had begun to search for the historical Christ: the real figure who had been buried under the various myths of the early gospel writers and the early Christian Church. The logic

---

[14] For brief accounts of the Higher Critical method, see R. Grant and D. Tracy, *A Short History of the Interpretation of the Bible* (Philadelphia, PA: Fortress Press, 1984), and E. Kretz, *The Historical–Critical Method* (London: SPCK, 1975).

was this. Every civilization has its own worldview, its own set of background beliefs expressed through its language, and the early Christians were no exception. Christ was a real person, but what we know of him has been heavily overlaid with the worldview of the people of this time. In order to discover what God really intends for us we must strip away the Hebrew and Aramaic myths and get to the real heart of the Christian message. The same scholars were drawing on recent historical and archaeological discovery to dismantle the Bible. It was no longer to be regarded as the revealed Word of God but as a collection of writings put together by a variety of authors who borrowed from and embellished various ancient texts to make sense of what they saw and experienced. The Higher Criticism was coupled with a desire to remove the miraculous and supernatural elements from Christianity in order to produce a rational version of the faith that would be acceptable to a culture that knew about science and technology and that, so the higher critics reasoned, could no longer believe that the Red Sea really parted or that Jonah lived inside a big fish.

This rationalism gradually permeated all the major Protestant denominations and it was not only a theological movement. Its proponents tended also to be socially liberal and politically progressive. They believed that the gospel entailed Christians being socially reformers because the improvement of people's material conditions would make them more receptive to the preaching of the Word. The conservatives tended to the view that man was beyond redemption and that only religious conversion could improve anything. Hence they thought that one should preach the gospel, get men saved, and then social and economic reform and prosperity would follow naturally from a saved population acting righteously.

Fundamentalism as an organized movement had its origins in America, although the controversy that produced it was to be found in all the Protestant churches.[15] The title of the movement came from

[15] For excellent accounts of the origins of fundamentalism, see M. Riesebrodt, *Pious Passion: The Emergence of Modern Fundamentalism in the United States and Iran* (Berkeley and Los Angeles: University of California Press, 1993), G. M. Marsden, *Fundamentalism and American Culture: The Shaping of Twentieth Century Evangelicalism, 1870–1925* (Oxford: Oxford University Press, 1980), and B. B. Lawrence, *Defenders of God: The Fundamentalist Revolt against the Modern Age* (London: I. B. Tauris, 1990).

a series of pamphlets called 'The Fundamentals: A Testimony of the Truth' published in America between 1910 and 1912. The fundamentalists argued that the Bible was the divinely inspired and revealed word of God. It was infallible. If there was a conflict between science and religion, then science was wrong. There was a Trinity of God the Father, the Son, and the Holy Ghost; it was not just a case of Jesus being a particularly inspiring and holy man. And he was born to a virgin, as the Bible said.

W. P. Nicholson was a fundamentalist, and he brought to Northern Ireland an aggressive critique of liberalism in the Protestant churches. By 1925 he was being seen, not as a man who united Protestants, but as a sectarian whose preaching against the evils of modernism and liberalism would split the denominations. The anti-modernist Nicholson struck a chord with some Irish Presbyterians. An initial skirmish in the inevitable war between the liberals and conservatives came with a split in the Scottish Free Church. Although the Free Church had been formed in 1843 by conservatives who left the national Kirk because it was unable to divorce itself from the civil state enough to purify itself, the Free Churchmen (especially those of the growing urban middle class) had quickly become advocates of liberalism and modernism. In 1900 the majority of them united with another organization of Presbyterians that had grown from earlier splits from the national Kirk. A rump refused to accept the merger and claimed that, as they were continuing in the beliefs of the original Free Church, they were entitled to all the property of the Free Church. At the end of a bruising legal battle, the House of Lords found in favour of the small conservative remnant. The Irish Presbyterian Church was a sister reformed church and in its early difficult years it had been supported by the Scots. Hence there was considerable interest among the Irish in the Free Church's battles. The leading spokesmen of the Irish Presbyterian Church supported the main body of the Free Church in its desire to unite with the United Presbyterians. James Hunter, a leading conservative in the Belfast Presbytery, proposed a motion supporting the conservative rump. He was heavily defeated.

With the legal disputes in Scotland and the fundamentalist movement in America, it was inevitable that the Irish Presbyterians would eventually turn from taking sides in other people's controversies to

staging their own version of the dispute, and it was in this context that
Nicholson was influential. Although he did not openly argue that the
conservatives should abandon the Presbyterian Church, he was increasingly aggressive in his preaching against the liberals in the Irish
Presbyterian theological colleges. One consequence of his preaching
was the formation of the Bible Standards League to maintain 'the
infallible Truth and Divine Authority' of the whole Bible against
liberals such as Professor J. Ernest Davey, who wished to argue that
one could select from the Bible certain general principles that were
infallible and dismiss other sections as wrong or mythical.[16] Although
the Bible Standards League attracted only a handful of ministers, it
did draw a lot of grass-roots Presbyterian support, and under James
Hunter's leadership it organized a major campaign of publicity for
the notion that true Protestantism was under attack from within.
Hunter 'regarded it as his supreme task to stem the tide of theological
liberalism, and he now became confirmed in his opinion that the
Church was less than loyal to her creedal statements'.[17]

As formal statements of what their forebears believed, the creeds
were a major rhetorical obstacle for liberal Presbyterians. Although
Presbyterians took the Bible as the only standard of authoritative
knowledge, they accepted the Westminster Confession of Faith and
the Longer and Shorter Catechisms as subordinate standards. These
were documents drawn up in the 1640s and accepted by the Church
of Scotland in 1647. They had long been an embarrassment to
liberals, and in 1820 a group led by Henry Montgomery was driven
out of the Irish Presbyterian Church when Henry Cooke persuaded
the majority of the church that all ministers and elders should
subscribe their name to the Confession. In the last quarter of the
nineteenth century, liberals in the various Scottish Presbyterian
churches had modified their commitment to the Confession with
Declaratory Acts that claimed to interpret the Confession but that
actually undermined it. By the 1920s there was pressure in the Irish
Presbyterian Church for a similar relaxation of commitment to the
Westminster Confession. Conservatives such as James Hunter and

---

[16] J. Austin Fulton, *J. Ernest Davey* (Belfast: The Presbyterian Church in Ireland,
1970), 12.

[17] R. Allen, *The Presbyterian College, Belfast, 1853–1953* (Belfast: William Mullen
and Son, 1954), 256.

other members of the Bible Standards League were naturally firmly opposed to any such move. The simmering dispute in the church was brought to a head by liberals. In 1924 thirteen college students petitioned the Belfast Presbytery to know exactly what obligations would be imposed on them by their subscribing to the ordination formula, which included the Westminster Confession. The General Assembly established a commission to consider the matter. Hunter issued a series of pamphlets criticizing the theological teachers. The Belfast Presbytery replied by censuring Hunter for pursuing his campaign outside the church. He appealed against the censure and was defeated in the Assembly by 499 votes to 115—a fair reflection of the balance of power in the church. Hunter and supporters then pursued two leading theologians for heresy and were again defeated.

The arguments are worth describing in some detail because they are precisely those that motivated Ian Paisley forty years later. J Ernest Davey, Hunter's main target, was a good representative of the liberal tradition in theology and the Higher Critical tradition in biblical criticism. He wanted to modify the traditional Protestantism of the seventeenth and eighteenth centuries to something that could encompass the new ideas of science and Freudian psychology. He was a believer in 'new light'—the idea that God's revelation was not fixed but was always changing (and improving). We knew more about the world than did the Divines who wrote the Westminster Confession and we certainly knew more about the way in which the Bible texts were constructed, so why should we be constrained by the categories of thought they used? A subsidiary element in the controversy concerned professionalism. The liberals, though they were hardly aware of it, were snobs. They slid very easily from arguing that new forms of scholarship were useful tools for understanding the Christian message, to suggesting that they were, in some sense, essential, and that only professional theologians who understood the new German rational philosophy or Freudian psychology could speak with authority on matters of doctrine. The conservatives were extremely bitter at this shift from the basic tenet of reformed Protestantism that all that was necessary for salvation was in the Bible and available there for any normal person to comprehend. One of the conservative protagonists summarized the liberal view of the Bible thus: 'a discredited scrap-book that requires a Professor at your elbow to tell you how much or how little it is worth, either for reading or believing.'[18] This was a little harsh but only a little. A biography of Davey, written forty years after his trial for heresy, begins by denigrating the conservatives for a lack of scholarship: 'The people whose antipathy to Professor Davey was aroused had, for the most part, little qualification, if any, for forming theological opinions and less for pronouncing theological judgements.'[19] This tension between the professionals and the democrats was to be found in the fundamentalist controversies in Scotland, England, and America, as well as in Ulster. Conservatives saw the theologians advocating a new priestcraft. Liberals saw the fundamentalists hiding from the modern world with their heads in the sands of seventeenth-century dogma.

THE FAILURE OF THE SCHISM

In July 1927, twenty-seven years after he had first protested against the lack of orthodoxy in the Irish Presbyterian Church, James Hunter quit the Belfast Presbytery, but very few others went with him. Most of the supporters of the Bible Standards League remained in the IPC, arguing that they could best defend orthodoxy from within, and public interest in the controversy evaporated. By the 1930s the new Irish Evangelical Church had recruited only nine congregations, six of them in the Belfast area.

As the failure of the 1927 schism provides a useful contrast with Paisley's later success, it is worth making a few general observations. Hunter and his supporters were working in an environment that had not been prepared for schism. Although many in the IPC were unhappy at its direction, there were few organized networks of disaffected Presbyterians. By the time Paisley led his movement, a considerable infrastructure of mission halls and evangelistic organizations had been created by small groups of people gradually distancing themselves

[18] J. Edgar, *Presbyterianism on Trial: An Answer to 'The Record'* (Belfast: James Edgar, 1929), 8.
[19] Fulton, *Davey*, 33.

from what they saw as increasing apostasy within the Presbyterian Church. Hunter was trying to do too much too soon.

A second problem was the new church's identity. Omitting the word 'Presbyterian' from the title 'Irish Evangelical Church' was, in a culture with such a strong Presbyterian heritage, a tactical mistake. The confusion of name reflected deeper uncertainty. Within five years of its foundation, some leading men were expelled for deviation on beliefs about the 'second coming' of the Lord. Only then did the church clarify its doctrinal basis and signal its commitment to a Presbyterian sort of orthodoxy rather than to conservativism generally.

Thirdly, the dissidents did not work hard to recruit a following. They set out their stall and waited for customers to turn up. Having been members of a large national organization of congregations, they were not prepared for the arduous task of selling their product.

Fourthly, a small point with profound implications: the new church decided to have its students for the ministry trained by the Free Church of Scotland in Edinburgh. In many ways this was sensible, as the two churches were extremely close in doctrine and practice and the Free Church of Scotland was well staffed with able teachers. But this made it difficult for a clear Irish Evangelical Church identity to develop among the ministers, who instead saw themselves as being simply evangelical Presbyterians.

But by far the most important difference between this schism and Paisley's movement was the general climate of the times. I have already mentioned the tenor of the early Nicholson crusades with their appeal to social cohesion and the way that harmonized with a very general desire of Ulster Protestants to pull together after the crises that accompanied the formation of the Ulster state. The 1920s were a period of consolidation. The Unionist Party was firmly established as the political voice of the Ulster Protestants, and people who had just come through a major crisis had little appetite for creating further divisions. What handicapped Hunter's revolt was the absence of any major threat to Protestant identity in the political sphere. In a later chapter we will see how Paisley's fledgling Free Presbyterian Church benefited from political instability. Here it is enough to note that, because their critique of liberalism was confined to the religious sphere, the schismatics of the 1920s were denied an important aid in the promotion of their conservative views.

2

Early Years

THE FAMILY BUSINESS

James Kyle Paisley was born to staunch Protestant parents in County Tyrone in 1891. Apprenticed to the drapery trade in Omagh, he was converted at a YMCA meeting and he began to preach. At that time many pious families in the country areas of Ulster held prayer meetings in their kitchens. Recent converts were encouraged to talk about their experience and those who showed a gift for witnessing to what the Lord had done for them would be encouraged to speak at more formal, larger meetings such as open-air rallies. Kyle Paisley followed such a route into evangelism:

As I look back upon those days I can see the guiding hand of the Lord upon my life. He led me to conduct monthly meetings at Grangemore, a short distance from Armagh and this meeting continued with great blessing for approximately four years...The Third Armagh Presbyterian Church Hall was opened for me for the preaching of the gospel...for young men thirsty for the Water of Life...This was really the foundation of a great work of God in the city of Armagh and led finally to the commencement of the first Baptist church in the Mall.[1]

The Baptist assembly in Armagh asked Paisley to become their pastor, and he trained at the Baptist College in Dublin. While pastoring in Armagh, Paisley met and married a Scots girl from a Covenanter background. The Reformed Presbyterian Church, to give the Covenanters their formal title, was the most conservative of the various

---

[1] R. J. Beggs, *Great is Thy Faithfulness: An Account of the Ministry of Pastor James Kyle Paisley and a History of the Separatist Testimony in Ballymena* (Ballymena: Ballymena Free Presbyterian Church, n.d.), 12.

Scottish Presbyterian churches. It was not some late schism but
had always been outside the national Church of Scotland because it
believed the state church had been set up on terms that gave too much
influence over religion to the monarch, without the monarch making a
matching commitment to impose the true faith on the populace.

Although almost extinct in Scotland, the Covenanters have to this
day maintained a conservative theology and an old-fashioned style
of worship: they sing only the metrical Psalms of David and those
unaccompanied.[2] Their rejection of the state has been diluted from
open warfare to mild abstention. They generally do not vote or hold
public office (though even this very limited withdrawal of consent is
often now compromised).

It was to these parents—an evangelical Baptist and a Covenanter—
that Ian Richard Kyle Paisley was born in 1926. Shortly after his birth,
the family moved to Ballymena in County Antrim, where Kyle Paisley
became pastor of the Hill St Baptist Church.

The desire to maintain religious purity, so strong in the younger
Paisley's ministry, was inherited from his father. Shortly after going to
Ballymena, Kyle Paisley quit the Baptist Union. Although most Irish
Baptists were solidly conservative, many English assemblies were
adopting modernist ideas, and some pastors were, albeit tentatively,
becoming involved in the various interdenominational meetings
and associations that were later collectively dubbed the 'ecumenical
movement'. With a few of his flock, Kyle Paisley started services in a
disused carpet warehouse. He then 'trusted in the Lord to provide'
and acquired a building site by the railway lines. A plain single-storey
building—the Waveney Road Tabernacle—was erected, and the small
congregation set out in its Covenant its firm opposition to 'the anti-
super-naturalism of modernism, and the deceptions of fanaticism,
and the formality of a dead and defunct orthodoxy'. In a 'day of
apostasy, declension and compromise', the remnant would maintain
a faithful witness to the belief that the Bible was 'the whole Word
of God... verbally inspired by God the Holy Ghost... the final
authority on all matters of Doctrine, Faith, Practice'.[3]

[2] The FPCU does not support exclusive psalmody. For its justification, see 'Exclusive Psalmody—is it Commanded by God?', *Burning Bush*, 35 (Feb. 2005), 2–3.
[3] Beggs, *Great is Thy Faithfulness*, 17.

Although Paisley was a Baptist, his small church drew disaffected members of the Irish Presbyterian Church (IPC). The parents of William Beattie, who became one of Ian Paisley's early colleagues, were Antrim farmers, the descendants of the old Scots settlers and Presbyterian since their arrival in Ireland. But they were opposed to the modernism of Professor Davey and other leading figures in the church and they wanted to hear orthodox preaching. The Irish Evangelical Church had no congregations in the Ballymena area and there was no Reformed Presbyterian Church nearby and so they found themselves drawn to the Baptist congregation led by Kyle Paisley.

The foundation of a small independent Baptist work in Ballymena was a matter of little significance even in Ulster, but it was part of the wider fundamentalist controversy and that was signalled by Dr. T. T. Shields, one of the leading North American fundamentalists, laying the foundation stone for the Waveney Road Tabernacle.

Ian Paisley's childhood was unexceptional, except perhaps in the rigour of his religious socialization and the decor to which that gave rise. The words 'Salvation to the Uppermost' (now on the wall beside his church pulpit) were a text fixed to a large portrait of General William Booth, the founder of the Salvation Army, that adorned his bedroom wall. When other children read Enid Blyton, Paisley's favourite books were Foxe's *Book of Martyrs* and Wylie's three-volume *History of Protestantism*. By his own account his schooling was perfectly normal and his family life happy. After a brief period working on the farm of a family friend near Sixmilecross in County Tyrone, Ian began to preach at small meetings and felt a call to full-time Christian work.[4] He was sent for a year to Barry School of Evangelism in South Wales, a non-denominational college that offered practical training in the skills of open-air preaching and door-to-door visitation, and rigorous Bible study. In 1943 he returned to Ulster and he enrolled as a student with the Reformed Presbyterian Church in Belfast, although he had no intention of becoming a minister in that denomination. There he acquired a thorough grounding in Calvinist

---

[4] It is an interesting sign of the extent to which critics of Paisley will go to uncover anything to his discredit that biographers have tried to make something of the fact that he did not enlist, and one potential author asked me if it was not the case that he had been sent to college to avoid the call-up! He was only 14 in 1940.

theology and biblical scholarship and acquitted himself well enough
to win a prize in each of his three years of study.[5] He also began to
make contacts in the evangelical milieu. In addition to the Reformed
Presbyterians who taught him, he became acquainted with W. J. Grier,
who, since the death of James Hunter in 1942, had become the leading
figure in the Irish Evangelical Church and on occasions he acted as a
supply preacher for Grier.

On Christmas Sunday 1945 Ian Paisley preached an invitation
sermon to a small congregation in working-class East Belfast that
called itself the Ravenhill Evangelical Mission Church. His performance was acceptable and he was invited to become its pastor.

PAISLEY'S FIRST CONGREGATION

The history of the small Ravenhill congregation is worth detailing,
because it shows the fine threads that linked the world of evangelical
Protestantism in Ulster. It had been formed as a result of a schism in
the Ravenhill Presbyterian Church, the building that had been
packed in 1922 by the shipyard workers coming to hear W. P.
Nicholson preach against modernism. The minister of that church
and his elders had been signatories to the heresy charges laid against
Davey, and the congregation was generally very conservative. The
occasion for the division was almost trivial and involved a large
amount of personal friction in addition to the basic tension between
theological positions. Some members took strong exception to modern dress and hairstyles. In particular they wanted the kirk session to
censure some girls for having their hair bobbed in the fashion of
the day. One of the girls was the daughter of the minister, John
Ross. Despite the fact that Ross was himself deeply conservative
and had been a signatory to the charges against Davey, the issue
divided the kirk session against him. In March 1935 a small number
of conservative members left to meet in a building 300 yards down
the Ravenhill Road.

---

[5] I am grateful to Prof. Adam Loughridge, a former Principal of the Reformed
Presbyterian Theological Hall, for making these details known to me.

Most schisms involve arguments about which side best represents the tradition. In some disputes, real estate is at issue. In others, it is the *symbolic* estate that is fought over. The formation of Ian Paisley's Free Presbyterian Church in 1951 began an argument, which still runs, over the propriety of the label 'Presbyterian'. Such arguments are not trivial: they have major implications for the ability of contending parties to recruit others with the claim that they represent the heritage. The people who moved down the Ravenhill Road to form their own congregation were Presbyterians, and the leaders of the schism were ordained elders of the IPC. When Ian Paisley accepted their call, he was stepping into the Presbyterian tradition. However, by the time he was called, eleven years had elapsed and some of the original Presbyterians had left and been replaced by evangelical Protestants drawn from across the denominational spectrum. There were Methodists, Baptists, and Brethren, and, for eighteen months prior to Paisley's call, the congregation had been led by a Brethren evangelist. Nonetheless, Paisley was consolidating the foundations of the Presbyterianism he had acquired from his mother's influence, his own training with the Reformed Presbyterians, and his connection with Grier's schismatic Presbyterians, when he accepted the call of a secession Presbyterian church.

Different denominations have different notions of how someone is called to the ministry. The Catholic, Orthodox, and Anglican churches have a high theory of ordination. They believe that the ability to interpret God's will correctly and to perform religious rituals was passed from Christ to his Apostles, and from them to a succession of office holders. Only people in the correct succession have a valid calling. Reformed denominations have no such magical conception of the ministry—there is no mystical quality that is passed from one generation of priests to the next—but most still have some ceremony in which representatives of the church test and endorse aspiring ministers. At the low end of the spectrum, denominations such as the Baptists and the Brethren hold that whether someone has been genuinely called to lead a community of Christians is known only by the fruits of his ministry.

Ian Paisley himself tends to the low position, while the traditional Presbyterian view has usually been somewhere between the high apostolic succession notion of Catholics or Anglicans and the free-for-all of the independents. For this reason, the Irish Presbyterians have been keen to show that Paisley was not properly ordained.[6] The bare facts of the ordination service in the Ravenhill Evangelical Mission Church are as follows. Professor T. B. McFarlane, a Reformed Presbyterian minister who had taught Paisley, offered a prayer. Revd Thomas Rowan, an old Irish Presbyterian minister who had worked with the American evangelists Moody and Sankey in their missions at the end of the previous century, 'brought the charge to the congregation'—the part of an ordination in which the congregation are reminded of their obligations, especially to pray for their new minister. W. J. Grier, one of the founders of the Irish Evangelical Church, preached and charged Paisley 'to be faithful in contending for the faith that was once for all delivered to the saints'.[7] Paisley's father and a number of the elders of his new church, in his words, 'laid their hands upon me and set me aside for the preaching of the Blessed Word of God'.[8] The elders had been ordained into the Presbyterian ministry (which makes no radical distinction between the minister and his elders) when they had been in the Ravenhill Presbyterian Church. Of the four ministers who took part in the service, three were Presbyterians. The only non-Presbyterian involved was Ian Paisley's father. Thus, unless one takes a rather high view of ordination, and reformed Protestantism does not do so, Paisley was validly ordained.

However, to treat the question in this way is to discuss it only in the terms set by Paisley's critics. Paisley himself had no great commitment to a specifically Presbyterian style of ordination: 'I don't think that the emphasis is on denominational ordination. I think the emphasis is on a *Christian* minister.'[9] I asked him if the service had not been rather cynically designed to appear Presbyterian, to lay claim to a particular heritage: 'Well, I mean, that was the people I was moving among and I was going to minister to: a secession Presbyterian church.' The

[6] J. H. Withers, *Our Past Years: Fisherwick Presbyterian Church, 1823–1973* (Belfast: Fisherwick Church, 1973), 172.

[7] I. R. K. Paisley, *These 28 Years* (Belfast: Martyrs' Memorial Publications, 1974), 2.

[8] I. R. K. Paisley, *Life's Four Windows: A Sketch of my Life Story* (Belfast: Martyrs' Memorial Publications, 1983), 7.

[9] This and all subsequent quotations that are not followed by a reference to a published source come from interviews conducted either between November 1984 and January 1986 or in 2005. The context makes it clear which.

service took its form, not from a clever anticipation of the day when he would have to defend his credentials, but rather from a combination of his own inclinations and those of the congregation that had called him. Paisley was more interested in establishing his evangelical credentials than he was in laying the foundations for an argument that had not yet started.

This can be seen in the attention that Paisley devotes to two other elements of his entry to the ministry: encouragement from a great revival preacher and a profound spiritual experience that followed a number of years of little success. In most of his accounts, he gives as much space to Nicholson's presence at his first Sunday service as he does to his actual ordination. He is fond of repeating Nicholson's remarks to him after the service.

After I had finished Mr Nicholson got up, walked forward to the Communion Table, rapped it and said to me: 'Young man, have you ever seen a cow's tongue?' I said 'Yes, sir'. 'What is it like?' I said 'It is like a file'. Then he lifted his hand and prayed, 'Lord give this young man a tongue like an old cow.'[10]

A good example of Paisley's often neglected ability to laugh at himself was given when he told the story during a BBC television interview. After he had delivered the punch line, he paused and added: 'And

[10] Paisley, *Four Windows*, 8. To put oneself in the tradition of which Nicholson was part is to claim an important resource. Paisley wishes to claim it—the Bangor Free Presbyterian Church was named the 'W. P. Nicholson Memorial'—and his opponents, especially conservatives within the IPC, are keen to deny his inheritance. In a radio documentary I wrote for the BBC, I presented Nicholson as a forerunner to Paisley. Sidney Murray, an admirer of Nicholson, wrote to *Evangelical Voice*, a magazine of a pressure group in the IPC, to contest my analysis and save Nicholson from Paisley by showing that Nicholson was not a separatist. Murray is correct that Nicholson, although highly critical of its liberals, continued to support the IPC. He did attend Paisley's Ravenhill Mission Church, but he also worshipped at the Ravenhill Presbyterian Church when he returned to Belfast in the early 1950s. Nicholson's lasting impact on Ulster religious life came through the Christian Workers Union: a ginger group *within* the church rather than a separatist movement. But I would argue against Murray's conclusion that Paisley was motivated by beliefs that Nicholson did not hold. Paisley and Nicholson were very close in theology. What had changed between the world of the late 1920s and 1930s, and Paisley's world of the 1950s, was the degree of 'apostasy' in the IPC. Nicholson was concerned to stem and reverse an emergent trend. Paisley had come to the conclusion that the rot had set in so firmly that only radical separation would do. I see nothing in Nicholson's beliefs that would have led him to act in a manner different from Paisley had he been faced with the same circumstances.

some people would say perhaps that prayer has been answered far more abundantly than we can ask or even think,' and burst out laughing.

The next few years of Paisley's ministry were trying but outwardly uneventful. In October 1949 he had a profound religious experience. Feeling a definite weakness in his ministry, he called three friends to a late night prayer meeting. They prayed through the first night, the next day, and into the second night. By the close, Paisley felt himself to have been 'filled with the Holy Spirit' and possessed of renewed evangelistic power. This new phase in his ministry brought him into some conflict with some congregants who expected to be consulted about his work. For example, they were offended when he saw Rico's Circus tent in the grounds of the Ormeau Park and persuaded Rico to let him use it for an evangelistic rally. Without consulting his committee, he had posters printed and handbills distributed advertising the meetings and drew a crowd of almost a thousand people. Like many a group formed as a schism from a larger body and convinced of its own possession of the saving truth, the Ravenhill congregation had turned inwards. Some members drew such satisfaction from being part of a select band that knows something the rest of the world does not know that they had no great desire to see the band extended. While Paisley worked the doors of the small working-class streets of East Belfast and held tent missions on cleared ground, resentment grew and Paisley fed it by frequently preaching against those members of the congregation whose religion was more formal than real.

Well, if my preaching lacked fire it now caught the fire, but I tell you when that happens in a Church you are in for trouble, and I was sure in for trouble. When you meet the Devil in trousers he is very vicious, but when you meet the Devil in a skirt, then you are for it! I met the Devil in a skirt. There was one woman in that congregation and she vowed that she would finish me for good.

Of course that sort of thing has to come to a head and it came to the head one night when I preached a sermon on Hell. Her unconverted father was in the meeting and she was entirely upset that I would dare to talk about Hell and offend her father. Going out she said to me 'I want to talk with you.' I said 'All right, in fact I would like to talk with you.' So we went into the little room and we shut the door and she started on me. She said 'Your ministry is finished here.' I said 'I'm glad to know it. I would like to get away, there are wider places than this, but I can't get away for the Lord has told me I'm going to be around here for a very long time.' She said 'You are mistaken, my husband is on the church committee, my father-in-law is an elder, we control this church, and young man, you are going.' I said, 'Isn't that strange, because I wanted to tell you for a long time that you were going. Now tomorrow night the elders will meet, and the trustees will meet, and they will make a decision and it will be very simple. They will either say 'Preacher, you go' or they will say to you 'Go'. She said, 'Right!'

So the night came and I walked into that Church. I had perfect peace. I wasn't afraid of losing a pulpit, for if I hadn't that pulpit I would have preached on the Ravenhill Road. It would not have made any difference to me. We might have had this Church built 20 years before it was. I walked in, and she had her armour on. The greatest weapon a woman has is tears, and she was there weeping. She said , 'Oh Mr Paisley, do we need to have this meeting?' I said, 'We certainly do, and either you are going or I'm going.' She said, 'Could we not come to an agreement?' I said, 'I'm sorry'. I said, 'You know what you have done? You have criticised every person I have led to the Lord in this Church, and I want to tell you, the little ones will be offended no more. It is now or never.' I walked into that room and I said to the elders, 'Gentlemen, I'm just a boy, a stripling, but I believe the Book, and I want to tell you men, I'm going to preach this Book. I'll either preach it in here or out there. Make a choice, I don't want to be hard, I don't want to be cruel but this woman has got to go.' I left and in a few minutes I was recalled, and they said, 'She has gone, and you are to stay.' I said, 'Gentlemen, you have made the right decision, let us get down to prayer.'

Of course she didn't go on her own, she visited every member of the congregation, she took a lot of people with her. There was I with more empty seats. So I decided that instead of having a prayer meeting sometimes, we would have a night of prayer every week and we would pray on the seats that nobody sat in. We went up into the little gallery and you could have written on the dust that had accumulated on those empty seats and we prayed at every one of them. It was a dusty prayer meeting I can assure you, but as we prayed at every seat, things started to move. Then, of course, the Lord opened the doors.[11]

Important for Paisley's later success was making contacts. The world of evangelical Protestantism existed outside and beyond any particular denomination. There was a milieu of conservative members of

---

[11] Paisley, *Four Windows*, 12–13.

It is noticeable that the press statement released by the elders of the new congregation made no mention of Ian Paisley.[13] His name was first brought into the public parts of the controversy by the Down Presbytery in their repudiation of the schismatics. In their view, the 'Free' in the title meant anarchic and the 'of Ulster' signified a parochial vision. 'Presbyterian' it would not be. Thirteen column inches down the Presbytery's press release comes the mention of Paisley, and he is introduced only so that his credentials as an ordained minister can be disputed.[14] The new congregation's coyness about their inspiration was in part a deliberate attempt to minimize Paisley's role in the dispute, but it also reflected a desire to establish the general principles on which they had seceded. Obviously Paisley was central to the controversy, but it would be a mistake to imagine him plotting and planning it. Like so many crucial events in Paisley's career, the Crossgar split and the subsequent founding of the FPCU was an affair with complex roots in which others played a large part in producing the outcome, and Paisley seized the opportunity

From March 1951, Paisley was committed to active competition with the IPC. For the Crossgar split to be anything more than a commonplace congregational spat, it would have to be followed by others, and, from that point on, Paisley's preaching tours of the province took on a new meaning. He was no longer a preacher holding 'undenominational' rallies. He was the leader of a new sect that aimed to attract other dissident Presbyterians; and it did. In the summer of 1951, two more groups of Irish Presbyterians were added to the Free Church.

Ballymoney is the main market town between Coleraine and Ballymena in North Antrim. The Drumreagh Presbyterian Church, which covered the farming area south of Ballymoney, was attended by Alexander McAuley and his family. After his conversion in a small country gospel hall, Sandy McAuley came into conflict with two successive ministers: he thought John Barkley a liberal and William Hyndman a libertine. When he asked Barkley if he could continue to smoke now that he was saved, Barkley told him to smoke two pipes a day and not worry. When he challenged Hyndman about his personal life, Hyndman hit him.

---

[13] *Belfast Telegraph*, 13 Mar. 1951.   [14] Ibid., 15 Mar. 1951.

In the summer of 1951, McAuley invited Paisley to conduct a series of meetings in the Cabra School House. In addition to promoting the virtues of salvation, Paisley criticized the apostasy of the IPC—something readily accepted by the McAuleys—and, at the end of the mission, a handful of Presbyterians decided that they could not go back to an apostate denomination. So another Free Presbyterian congregation came into being, meeting first in the upstairs of a barn, and later erecting its own building right next to the Cabra School, the site of the mission, which had been closed to them from the moment they had announced the formation of their own congregation.

Of the first three congregations, that of Rasharkin, 10 miles south of Cabra, was least inspired by doctrinal disputes. What divided the Presbyterians of Rasharkin was their minister's divorce and accusations of ill-treating his wife. Paisley was preaching in Cabra at the time of the dispute, and the conservatives went to hear him. They were impressed enough to create a Free Presbyterian congregation.

The formation of the new denomination at Crossgar and not at Ravenhill put Ian Paisley in a rather awkward position: his own congregation had not yet signed up! The debate about whether to join exacerbated the tension that had been there since Paisley's ordination. Paisley finally convinced the management committee to affiliate, and his critics withdrew.

The plan for an extension of the Ravenhill Church into the Mount Merrion housing scheme that Paisley had proposed to Cecil Menary in the summer of 1950 then went ahead.

In order to build up a congregation an attack was made on the battlements of hell, sin and apostasy in the neighbourhood: an old time Gospel campaign conducted by the Rev. Ian R. K. Paisley, was held in a large tent. Here God the Holy Ghost was seen in dynamic soul-saving power and seventy-six souls hit the cinder track for salvation. Glory to God! Having received such blessing from the hand of Almighty God in this, our first Gospel attempt in Mount Merrion, the Spirit led us again in another hell-shaking, sin-smashing, Holy Ghost mission conducted by a special commando team from Ravenhill Free Presbyterian Church, when over a score of precious souls sought and found God. Hallelujah! From victory to victory Jesus leads us on, and another milestone was passed when on Saturday 2 August, 1952, this building was opened to the glory of God, the quickening of the saints, the salvation of souls, the denunciation of sin, the exposing of modernistic teachings and soul-damning heresy, and the defeat of the old serpent.[15]

Mount Merrion gave the Free Presbyterians five congregations. The sixth was novel in that Paisley acquired a building before he had the nucleus of a congregation. In 1952 Cecil Harvey, a founding elder of the Crossgar church, suggested that a vacant property in Whiteabbey, just north of Belfast, might be suitable. The former police station and court house was nothing like as grand as its former purpose suggests, but it was solid and had a large meeting room. It never prospered. Despite the best efforts of lay preacher George Hutton, the founding membership of 5 grew to only 30 after five years. Ivan Foster, who was responsible for Whiteabbey while he was training for the ministry in 1965, recalls that the sight of his church always gave him a 'sensation of dread and fear in the pit of my stomach. Whiteabbey was known amongst the ministers and students as a spiritual Siberia, a wilderness of apathy and darkness.' Evening meetings in Mossley Orange Hall Tent, about 5 miles inland, were much better attended, and one tent mission in that area 'was very well attended ... particularly on the Lord's Day. Thirteen souls professed faith in Christ at those meetings but nothing could persuade them to come to the meetings in Whiteabbey.'[16] Eventually Whiteabbey was abandoned in favour of a site in Mossley.

A year after the Whiteabbey building was leased, a more promising work began in Ballyhalbert, a small village on the Ards peninsula. A small group of people broke from the local IPC and applied for admission to the Free Church. As if to atone for the Whiteabbey mistake, the Free Church hesitated to accept this group because the reasons for the secession were not obviously theological, and there was considerable doubt that the Ballyhalbert people were 'saved'. So the group was accepted, on probation, for preaching, and not as a full congregation. John Douglas, the first of Paisley's Ravenhill converts to train for the ministry, was given oversight of the group. In circumstances that were similar to those of Paisley's first years at

[15] *Revivalist* (July–Oct. 1952), p 1.
[16] Brian McClung, *These Fifty Years: A History of Newtownabbey Free Presbyterian Church Marking Fifty Years of the Congregation 1953–2003* (Belfast: Quinta Press, 2004), 47–8.

Ravenhill, some of the audience came to regret their request for preaching offices and drifted away, but others, mainly from Portavogie, a few miles down the coast, joined, and in 1958 a church was built in Portavogie.

The year 1957 saw two further branches added: at Coleraine, a small town in the eastern and Protestant part of County Londonderry, and at Dunmurry, a southern suburb of Belfast. I will explore this point in more detail later, but it is interesting to note here that the Mount Merrion and Dunmurry congregations were always small. Although set in dormitory areas with growing populations, they made few inroads into the local council estates. In part this was because potential Free Presbyterians could easily travel to hear Paisley. In part, it reflected the relative lack of interest in evangelical religion among the urban working class.

The tenth Free Presbyterian congregation was short-lived. A Church of Ireland curate in Antrim and some of his parishioners seceded from the Church of Ireland and were admitted to the Free Presbyterian Church. Harold V. Magowan shared Paisley's dislike for modernism and for the ecumenical movement, but they had little else in common, and four years later, in 1963, Magowan resigned at the same time as the Free Church Presbytery sacked him, and the work in Antrim dried up.[17]

Only three other congregations were added in the period before 1966: Sandown Road in East Belfast, Limavady in County Londonderry, and Armagh City. The Sandown Road congregation, like Mount Merrion and Dunmurry, was an extension of Ravenhill. Armagh was a congregation formed after a successful tent mission, but, although it was not a schism from a Presbyterian congregation, like most Free Churches, it mainly attracted Presbyterians. The Limavady church was fairly typical of later congregations in the method of its formation. A local farmer who had been a keen Irish Presbyterian left the Dungiven congregation because its minister was a liberal, became interested in the Free Church's separatist stance, and

[17] In an advertisement placed in the *Belfast Telegraph* (4 Jan. 1964), Magowan's supporters gave as his reasons for leaving the absence of annual elections for moderator, the preponderance of a political element to the detriment of spiritual life, and, somewhat implausibly, 'the recent growth of modernism in Presbytery'.

travelled first to Cabra and, when it opened, to Coleraine, to attend the services. He also started holding small meetings in his own house. He soon found that, although the distance to Coleraine would not put off any committed Free Presbyterian, it made it hard for him to invite local people to 'come to the Free Church', and so he determined to promote a meeting in Limavady.

To summarize: in 1965 the Free Church had twelve congregations. Although Paisley and his aides were leading evangelistic crusades all over the province, the Free Church had been built up only to the same sort of size and presence as the Irish Evangelical Church, which seemed thin reward for fourteen years of endeavour. The time had not been entirely wasted. The years of evangelism had brought Paisley to the attention of many evangelical Protestants and created a network of contacts that would prove invaluable once the political climate created the 'showers of revival rain' for which Paisley so earnestly prayed, but in 1965 there was little sign of any impending great deliverance.

THE PERSONNEL PROBLEM

Paisley's greatest problem in the early days was finding enough suitable men to pastor his new congregations. Menary had turned down Mount Merrion. Stears was an old man and obviously only a stopgap in Crossgar, and there were three empty pulpits. In July 1951 Paisley again approached Menary and asked him if he would serve Rasharkin and Cabra. This time he accepted and was ordained in August. Three months later, he passed Cabra over to John Wylie.

Like Menary, Wylie was a disenchanted Presbyterian. He told me: 'I was brought up in the Presbyterian Church. I went to church and so on and learnt my catechism. When I got converted—now I had a very Presbyterian life, keeping the Sabbath day and so on—when I was nineteen, this was a real work in my heart.' Once people heard of his conversion, he was invited to address farmhouse meetings and he also attended the Knock Church formed by James Hunter after the Davey heresy trial. There he heard 'a real firey old preacher and I enjoyed him and I got a real grasp of what had happened and how they [the Irish Presbyterians] had drifted from the principles of

Presbyterianism, from the principles of the word of God'. In his own Presbyterian congregation, Wylie tried to engage his minister in argument during a Bible class. The minister refused to be drawn into debate and asked Wylie to leave.

I became a sort of wandering Jew for a while and went here and there. I went to the Methodist Church and then I used to go to the Baptists and I went here and there. Then when we got married we went to the Presbyterian Church in Gransha where the minister was an evangelical. I got to know Ian [Paisley]. We were involved in Protestant rallies. The church was formed in 1951; I must have met him in 49. I got to like the fellow. He was very sincere and he appealed to me.

Although his electrician's business in Dundonald was thriving, Wylie felt a distinct call to the ministry. He was accepted by the Free Presbyterian Church and called to take over Cabra from Menary.

The first minister of Mount Merrion differed from Menary and Wylie in not having been a Presbyterian. Robert Coulter had trained at the Faith Mission College in Edinburgh and was working as an evangelist for the Faith Mission when Paisley, who had shared a platform with him in Ballymena, invited him to take over Mount Merrion. Finding ministers was so difficult that Paisley could not be fussy about denominational background. As Coulter put it: 'I don't think he was all that worried at the time. I think he wanted the help; people to come in and take charge of these churches that were springing up.' Coulter did not last long in Mount Merrion, largely because he was unhappy with the aggressively controversial style of preaching that was expected. He was himself conservative in his theology but he had little taste for denouncing the apostasy of others.

I was later summoned for not preaching against individuals like Dr Davey and so on. My reply was that my first priority was to preach the gospel and, if I had any time left over after preaching the gospel, I would preach against heresy. They had to agree with it. The gospel had to come first in their thinking.

The Presbytery gave him a month to adopt a more aggressive attitude but Coulter had already decided to accept an invitation to work in America and he left the Free Presbyterian Church.

The American invitation came from an eccentric individual who played a very minor part in the early days of the Free Presbyterian

Church: Hugh Johnston. In October 1952 the Free Presbyterian Church announced the opening of its own training college with lectures from J. K. Paisley, Ian Paisley, H. H. Aitchison, and Hugh Johnston. This was Paisley's second choice scheme for staffing his church. Initially he had intended to follow the Irish Evangelical Church model and send his students to the Free Church of Scotland College in Edinburgh, but there were doubts on both sides. Paisley felt that the Scottish Free Church, although itself orthodox, was keeping bad company by associating with other denominations that were not entirely sound. The Free Church for its part consulted one of the theologians of the IPC and was told that Paisley's denomination was not genuinely Presbyterian. The failure of this scheme had long-term advantages but it immediately left Paisley with a problem that forced him to the unhappy expedient of taking any help he could get.

Aitchison was a Scottish Presbyterian minister who had come to Ulster in 1931. After serving two Presbyterian churches in Belfast, he fell out with his kirk session and defected to pastor a Congregational church. His fourth congregation, which he was serving when he met Paisley, represented yet another link back to the Davey heresy trial. When Whitehead Presbyterian Church chose as its minister a vocal Davey supporter, a conservative faction withdrew to form its own congregation and called Aitchison to minister. Although no great intellectual or preacher, Aitchison had the paper credentials and the right associations to be at least a symbolic asset to the new Free Presbyterian theological hall.

Johnston's failings may have been exaggerated in the innumerable retellings, but Paisley remembers him as a charlatan: a serious drinker who managed to disguise his vice from Coulter and Paisley (who shared lodgings with him) by keeping his whisky in a hot water bottle. He was a reasonably talented preacher and for a few months he had made a living from collections taken when he preached before returning to America.

The short career of Harold Magowan in the Free Church has already been mentioned. Another man who came to the Free Church with experience of full-time work was Victor Burns, a pastor in an independent evangelical church in England. He lasted only a year before returning to England. David Leatham, who ministered in

Whiteabbey and Dunmurry, also left the Free Church for the Baptist ministry.

What is clear in hindsight is that the expansion (and even the survival) of the FPCU was threatened by Paisley's inability to find enough men who shared his vision. Until his movement began to produce its own clergy it would not be able to supply the nascent demand, let alone stimulate more.

WHY DID PEOPLE JOIN THE FREE CHURCH?

A brief account of the key points of Protestant belief, particularly those that most radically separate Protestants from Roman Catholics, has already been given. But to explain what attracted people to Paisley, we must consider what distinguished his preaching from the Ulster Protestant mainstream and what distinguished his movement from the already extensive world of undenominational meetings and gospel halls.

People such as Sandy McAuley and Bob Wilson's father were not just swapping churches; they were also being converted. Their newfound faith was qualitatively different from their old religion. Evangelicals believe that salvation requires more than just intellectual assent or the correct performance of religious ritual. No amount of faithful attendance at church will win salvation. What is required is a 'born-again' experience. It is difficult to compress a complex faith into a few propositions, but the core of evangelicalism can be summarized in this way. Since Adam's rejection of God's will, man has been in a state of sin. God sent his only Son Jesus Christ to suffer and die as an atoning sacrifice for our sins. His death pays off our debt. But we have to accept that sacrifice and take it into our hearts. God has chosen some of us for salvation; nothing of our doing saves us. God's offer of salvation is a free gift—an idea commonly expressed in the term 'sovereign grace'.

Becoming saved is a two-stage process. God has laid the foundation by calling some of us, but we still have to respond to that call. The job of the preacher is to make that clear to us; we then respond. We should appreciate our sinfulness (or 'come under conviction of sin'), appreciate Christ's sacrifice, and take the gospel into our hearts. This then makes effectual—or cements—the foundation laid by God in our being called. Being saved is similar to those adhesives, such as Araldite, that come in two tubes. Neither element on its own is a glue, but mix the two together and one has a fast hard-setting adhesive. The analogy is a good one because another element of evangelical Protestantism is the certainty of salvation that follows conversion. Being born again brings the security of knowing that one is saved.

The evangelical emphasis on a personal response to Christ's sacrifice distinguishes it from more liberal interpretations of Protestantism. There have periodically been movements that openly assert that all of God's creation will be saved and that differences in doctrines between this or that church are, in the final outcome, unimportant. More common than such overt universalism is a general tendency to think that way. Evangelicals insist that only those people whom God has called and who respond to the gospel message will be saved from eternal damnation and hell fire. Things such as behaving well all one's life or performing religious rituals will not do it: 'Being a real Christian is not ultimately a matter of things that you do. It is a relationship that you enter into, between a holy God and a broken sinner, saved not by anything that he or she can do but only by the blood of Jesus Christ, shed on the cross at Calvary.'[18]

Free Presbyterian converts often described their lives in two epochs. In the first period, they were good Presbyterians and went to church regularly and lived moral lives, but were not saved. They blamed this firmly on the unsaved Presbyterian ministers who did not preach the whole gospel to them. In the words of a working-class Belfast man who later became a Free Presbyterian minister: 'I was completely ignorant of what not only Presbyterianism was but also what the gospel was. I had no idea. Sunday School boy all my life. Youth fellowship all my life. Went to church every Sunday practically. Never, never, was confronted with the fact that the Bible condemned me as a lost sinner.'

Bob Wilson was converted at the same time as his father who had been an elder in the Rasharkin IPC:

---

[18] W. McCrea and D. Porter, *In His Pathway: The Story of Rev. William McCrea* (London: Marshall, Morgan and Scott, 1980), 15.

It wasn't until February 1952 that I answered an appeal being made in the church to trust Christ as my saviour. I answered that appeal, went through to the enquiry room...I discovered that Dr Paisley was talking to my father, and to his son, at the one time. He wasn't aware of it at the time, but when we had a prayer together after I trusted Christ in that prayer, he asked me to shake hands with the person beside him. Here was my father!

This fundamental difference over the meaning and necessity of conversion explains the desire for a separate organization. Nicholson, an encyclopaedia of couthy proverbs, used to say 'you never get live chickens under a dead hen'. Sandy McAuley's son uses the same theme to describe the need for the formation of a new church.

I never heard the Gospel really preached in the Presbyterian Church that I went to. Many of the others were the same. They were modernistic in their views and they didn't preach the new birth, that you had to be saved. And we felt, well, to send young converts to churches such as this, well, it would be wrong, so that's why we considered this with much prayer and at the end of the day we felt led of the Lord to commence a Free Presbyterian Church.

The above describes a common core of conservative evangelical thought. What distinguishes Free Presbyterianism are the following additions: a vigorous anti-Catholicism, the insistence on separation, a suspicion that we live in the end-times, and an unusually tolerant attitude to the baptism argument and other minutiae of conservative debate.

Anti-Catholicism

The sensible observation that theological objections to Catholicism chimed well with the political circumstances of Ulster Protestants is sometimes stretched to imply that they invented antipathy to Rome.[19] They did not. The Reformation was 'anti' what we now call the Catholic Church; the Catholic Church was subsequently anti-Protestant. The Westminster Confession of 1646, the codification of British reformed belief, referred to the Church of Rome as the 'anti-Christ', 'anti' here meaning 'taking the place of'. The Church of England's founding Thirty-Nine Articles contains similar language.

---

[19] See, e.g., J. Brewer and G. Higgins, *Anti-Catholicism in Northern Ireland 1600–1998: The Mote and the Beam* (London: Macmillan, 1998).

The FPCU is being old-fashioned but it is not innovating in reading chapter 17 of the book of Revelation, of which the following is part (verses 1–6), as a description of the Roman Catholic Church.

And there came one of the seven angels which had the seven vials, and talked with me, saying unto me, Come hither; I will show unto you the judgement of the great whore that sitteth upon many waters: With whom the kings of the earth have committed fornication, and the inhabitants of the earth have been made drunk with the wine of her fornication. So he carried me away in the spirit into the wilderness; and I saw a woman sit upon a scarlet coloured beast, full of names of blasphemy, having seven heads and ten horns. And the woman was arrayed in purple and scarlet colour and decked with gold and precious stones and pearls, having a golden cup in her hands full of abominations and filthiness of her fornication: And upon her forehead was the name written, Mystery Babylon the Great, the Mother of Harlots and abominations of the earth. And I saw the woman drunken with the blood of the saints, and with the blood of the martyrs of Jesus.

If this text is an allegorical reference to a person or organization, then Rome seems a plausible candidate, especially given other references to sitting astride seven hills. Those who wish a naturalistic interpretation for this and other references to the 'Mother of Harlots' suppose it to be a veiled denunciation of the Roman Empire, written in allegory to safeguard the author from the wrath of the occupying imperial power. Largely because they take biblical prophecy to be enduringly applicable (and hence having current and future referents), Free Presbyterians follow the conservative Protestant tradition of taking this and other passages to refer to the Roman Catholic Church. In their eyes Rome goes beyond offering false teaching. It is actively evil in that it has a history of persecuting true Christians. It has also opposed liberal democracy, which Free Presbyterians believe is a result of the Reformation and which they value as the system that offers the best conditions for maintaining and promoting the true religion.

There is no problem in finding evidence of Roman Catholic persecution of Protestants in the seventeenth and eighteenth centuries. These were times when few thought there was anything wrong with coercing religious conformity. More recent examples can be found in Franco's oppression of Protestant missionaries in Phalangist

Spain.[20] And Free Presbyterians suppose that the Roman Catholic
Church is quietly supportive of 'physical force' republicanism, the
statements of the Irish Catholic hierarchy to the contrary notwith-
standing.

But even lack of evidence is no problem because one can always
posit a secret conspiracy. If the Jesuits, the storm troopers of the
Vatican, are not apparently conspiring to subvert Protestantism and
democracy, that is just because they have become more devious. At
first sight, clinging to theories for which there is little evidence by
invoking a conspiracy may seem like evidence of the irrationality of
Free Presbyterians, but such reasoning is commonplace. Free Presbyterians believe that there is a God and that all that occurs in the
world happens ultimately at his behest. The Bible is the word of God
and contains his plans for the world. Suppose one finds in the Bible
the prophecy that Rome will grow in power and, as the end of the
world approaches, will actively persecute the saints. If there is a
temporary shortage of evidence that Rome is actually doing this,
then one can conclude that the word of God is fallible (in which case
he is not much of a God), that one's interpretation is mistaken, or
that Rome is engaged in secret conspiracy.

This faith in the power of Rome leads Free Presbyterians to
attribute most things they do not like to its influence. They do not
see the ecumenical movement as a genuine, if misguided, attempt to
create a Christian movement that is sufficiently united to be able to
stand against secularization. They do not believe that ecumenical
Protestants have promoted reconciliation for their own reasons.
Instead, the ecumenical movement is seen as Rome-inspired and
Rome-led. Some Free Presbyterians were so firmly convinced of the
hidden hand of Rome that they claimed that Michael Ramsay, leader
of the Anglican Church in the 1960s, was not really an Anglican
archbishop seeking better relations with the Roman Catholic
Church; he was actually a Roman bishop, having secretly been
ordained by the Pope.[21]

Free Presbyterians discover unity in ancient enemies of the true
religion and some argue that Rome is actually Babylon. After all, the

[20] S. Bruce, *Politics and Religion* (Cambridge: Polity, 2003), 95–111.
[21] *Revivalist* (Jan. 1970), 1.

verses of Revelation quoted above tell us that the Mother of Harlots had 'Mystery, Babylon the Great' written on her forehead. Hislop's *The Two Babylons*, which is on sale in Free Presbyterian bookshops, lists hundreds of similarities between Babylonian worship and the practices, beliefs, and symbols of Roman Catholicism. Thus Rome is seen, not just as being like Babylon in that both religions are wrong, but as actually being the continuation of Babylon, which *explains* why Romanism is wrong. In his pamphlet on the Jesuits, Paisley argues that the Order is not even Christian. Although the Jesuits claim that their sign—IHS—stands for 'Jesus Hominum Salvator (the Latin 'J' being written as 'I'), Paisley believes that it actually stands for 'Isis, Horub, Seb': the pagan Egyptian trinity of the Mother, Child, and Father of the Gods. 'IHS pay the semblance of a tribute to Christianity, but they are in reality the substance of devil-worship. The cloven hoof is upon them.'[22] Thus Rome is not a permitted variant of Christianity. It is not Christian and never has been.

As well as linking together all the enemies of the true faith in a grand and ancient daisy chain of Antichrist-led error, Free Presbyterians like to expand the vices of their enemy. They take real cultural differences (which often have social-class origins) and amplify them into positive and negative stereotypes. So they will claim that Protestants are self-reliant, hard-working, diligent, honest, loyal, responsible, and temperant. In contrast, Catholics are discouraged from thinking for themselves by priests who wish to keep their people in a state of dependency. They are slothful, dishonest, and untrustworthy. Because they owe a higher loyalty to Rome than to their own country, they are politically disloyal. They are sexually irresponsible and produce large families that they cannot support. They fritter away their earnings in gambling, smoking, and drinking alcohol. Because their religion allows them periodically to wipe clean the moral slate through confession, penance, and repentance, Catholics are not encouraged to accept responsibility for their actions.

The authority of the priest, the requirement for priestly celibacy, and the nature of confession are taken to combine to encourage sexual perversion among the Catholic clergy. Because they are not

---

[22] I. R. K. Paisley, *The Jesuits: Their Start, Sign, System, Secrecy and Strategy* (Belfast: Puritan Printing Co., n.d.), 6.

inclined to believe any of the positive claims made by the Roman Church, Free Presbyterians scorn the notion that the repression of sexual urges leads to a state of enhanced spirituality and suppose instead that priests regularly exploit those to whom they minister.

In sum, Free Presbyterians view Catholicism as both false religion and the source of a wide range of social vices.

Separation

What marked Paisley's preaching from that of many who held similar evangelical beliefs was his insistence not only that his people must not be in error but that they must also avoid associating with those in error. 'Throughout its history, the Free Presbyterian Church, in obedience to the word of God and by the grace and help of God, has sought to adopt a separatist position in matters personal and ecclesiastical.'[23] This position is based on Paul's instruction in his Second Letter to the Thessalonians (5: 22): 'Abstain from all appearance of evil.' 'He did not say abstain from all evil but took it one step further by advising that if something be perceived as evil, refrain from it. We should resolve to jealously guard our Christian witness if we are to be effective instruments used for extending God's Kingdom.'[24]

Separation can be presented either in positive terms—as the requirement that God's people be 'separated unto the Gospel of God'—or negatively, as a wish to avoid contamination and confusion in the mind of any audience. In practice, separatism can often appear as an ill-tempered refusal to accept the humanity of those with whom one differs on matters of substance, and the Paisleyite separatism often went further: to require the regular denunciation of those who held very similar views on matters of substance but who refused to distance themselves sufficiently from those with erroneous beliefs. In the ecclesiastical climate of the 1950s and 1960s, with the ecumenical movement in the ascendancy in mainstream Protestant churches, this 'double separation' meant that the attacks on Protestant ministers who remained in the mainstream churches were often more

[23] J. Greer, 'Why We Stand: Biblical Separation', *LTBS Quarterly* (Apr. 2001), 22.
[24] Sandown Road FPC Sunday School and Bible Class, *These Forty Years* (Belfast: Sandown Road FPCU, 2004), 11.

animated than the criticisms of Catholicism that all 'true Protestants' knew to be profoundly wrong. As is common in left-wing politics, those claiming the same ideological ground fought with each other more bitterly than they fought with those on the other side of the hill.

Eschatology

Eschatology—knowledge of the impending end of the world—is a profoundly difficult subject, and, unlike sects such as the Seventh-Day Adventists, which were created specifically to embody a particular view of how and when the world would be brought to a close, the FPCU has always been careful to avoid making any one particular theory a test of the faith. In his *Dictionary of Theological Terms*, Alan Cairns asks 'each believer to hold his views in humility and with due love and regard for the equally sincerely held views of differing brethren'.[25] Harry Cairns, an early FPCU minister, said: 'There are some things I am not dogmatic about because I am not settled in my own mind.' Stanley Barnes, the minister of Hillsborough, one of the largest congregations, advised caution: 'I always think it is a danger to try to interpret situations around us into the scriptures because they had Hitler as the Antichrist, they had Henry Kissinger as the Antichrist at one stage in a book I read, and there was Mussolini and looking back it was ridiculous.' Nevertheless, there is considerable agreement about certain points that I will introduce in the context of Ian Paisley's views on the European Community.

In the 1984 election campaign for the European Economic Community (EEC), Paisley denounced British membership. He shared the common concern that membership would entail a loss of sovereignty. The Christian moral standards of Ulster were already threatened by unrepresentative and undemocratic rule from Westminster. To subordinate Britain to the European Community with its Court of Human Rights and law-making powers would further reduce the ability of Ulster people to control their own future. There had already been a case in point. In deference to Ulster conservatism, the 1960s

---

[25] A. Cairns, *Dictionary of Theological Terms* (Gilford, Co. Down: Whitefield College of the Bible, 1982), 92.

Westminster legislation that had legalized consenting adult male
homosexuality was not extended to cover the province. In 1981 the
European Court of Human Rights judged Britain to be in violation
of basic freedoms by permitting this exception. The government
bowed to the Court and passed an Order in Council extending the
law to Northern Ireland.

But Paisley had a particular reason for opposing continued mem-
bership: the countries of what was then the European Economic
Community were overwhelmingly Catholic. The legal basis of the
EEC—the aptly named Treaty of Rome—was drafted by Konrad
Adenauer, Jean Monnet, and Robert Schumann: all Catholics. The
Roman Catholic Church has diplomatic representation at the EEC,
and Pope John Paul II had expressed a desire for European unity.
Thus the general threat to sovereignty was compounded by it also
being a Catholic threat. These considerations were offered by Paisley
to the electorate in his election literature.[26] In a series of sermons in
Martyrs' Memorial, he presented a complementary analysis that
examined the place of the EEC in Bible prophecies about the end
of the world. In brief, the creation and then-impending expansion of
the EEC was a sign that the end of the world has fairly well nigh.

Those Christians who believe that Christ will return, that there will
be a Day of Judgement, and that there will be a thousand years of
righteous rule on earth, may disagree about the order in which these
things will occur. One school expects the judgement to come before
the thousand years of righteousness and is sensibly called 'pre-mil-
lennialist'. Others expect the millennium, seen as a period of unprecedented success for the Church, to be followed by the judging of the
quick and the dead; hence the title 'post-millennialist'. A third view,
amillennialism, either denies the reality of the millennium as it is
depicted in the other two schools or is deliberately agnostic, and a
large proportion even of conservative Protestants have no firm views
about this.

The majority of Free Presbyterians in the church's first two decades
were pre-millennial, which is something of a departure from the
dominant Presbyterian position of the nineteenth century, although
it is not unprecedented and is part of the general decline in the

[26] I. R. K. Paisley, *The EEC and the Vatican* (Belfast: DUP, 1984).

popularity of the rather optimistic post-millennialism.[27] What is important for understanding Free Presbyterians is the role that Roman Catholicism is supposed to play in the approach to the end-times. Elements of Revelation and the books of Daniel and Isaiah are taken to prophesy the rise of an 'Antichrist' who will not only dominate the Church but who will also be a major political force in the 'tribulation': the period shortly before the Second Coming when the Jews and the Christians will be persecuted for not worshipping the Antichrist. There is some difficulty with the figure of Antichrist, who can variously be seen as an individual or a system. When someone such as Paisley calls the Pope the Antichrist, he is applying that designation to all popes and not just to the current holder of the office. It is the office of the papacy that usurps the place of Christ in the Church. Some pre-millennialists expect two Antichrists: one in the Church and one in politics. Others see just one, with two spheres of influence, but, whichever view is taken, Rome and the papacy are still taken to be the driving force: an identification that is defended by arguing that there is no worldwide organization other than the Roman Catholic Church that has the power, influence, and reach to be the sort of comprehensive anti-Christian force suggested in prophecy. Interestingly, Catholics themselves have at times fuelled Protestant fears by making grandiose claims for authority over all peoples and all spheres of life. For example, in the 1930s, Monsignor Ronald Knox addressed meetings in Edinburgh on the subject 'Wanted: a world leader! Why not the Pope?'

Most contemporary Protestants dismiss these eschatological speculations as misplaced fantasies, and many of those who trouble themselves with the interpretation of the relevant scripture passages explain them as covert references to the original Roman Empire. Free Presbyterians need not deny such naturalistic interpretations. One minister suggested that Bible prophecies have the peculiar quality of being able to refer to more than one event in more than one era so that any particular prophecy could be a veiled reference to something in the writer's time, in his future but our past, and in our future. Thus the Whore of John's Revelations could be the original

---

[27] For a good survey of such beliefs, see A. A. Blaising and R. B. Strimple, *Three Views on the Millennium and Beyond* (Grand Rapids, MI: Zondervan, 2001).

Roman Empire, the present Roman Catholic Church, and the future world Church created by the return of the ecumenical Protestants to Rome.

Baptism

Considering how aggressive the FPCU has been in pressing its distinctive beliefs, it is interesting that it has been able to avoid some of the most divisive arguments in Christianity, and there are few issues more contentious than the baptism of infants. What is at stake is simple. Those who see the churches possessing some sort of magical power regard the baptism of babies as an important act that changes the salvational status of the child. In the Middle Ages this was held to be sufficiently important for midwives to be taught a simple formula for baptizing babies thought unlikely to live long enough for a priest to arrive. At the other end of the theological scale we have those who regard salvation as being given only to those who consciously accept Christ as their saviour. This clearly requires a degree of consciousness that a baby or even a young child cannot possess. Hence the preference for adult baptism (which is generally taken to mean full immersion after the manner in which John baptized people in the New Testament book of Matthew 3).

The FPCU does not have an agreed position on baptism. Some congregations practise infant baptism, some do not, and most avoid the issue by having a service of dedication for infants. That the church has not divided over this is explained by some critics as resulting from Paisley's awkward relationship to Presbyterianism. Presbyterians generally accept infant baptism, but Paisley himself comes from an adult baptizing tradition. This seems too cynical and misses the more obvious point that what is worth fighting over always depends to some extent on the context set by external threats. If everyone accepts the basic Christian doctrines, they are free to squabble about other differences. In an increasingly secular world, where the mainstream Protestant denominations are abandoning even the few tenets listed in the Apostles' Creed, it seems more sensible to concentrate on preserving the truly central beliefs and allowing liberty of conscience on the rest.

ARE FREE PRESBYTERIANS MAD?

To the liberal Christian or the atheist, conservative evangelical beliefs seem so strange that it is easy to suppose that those who hold them must have come to them by some strange route. Many commentators imply, even if they do not openly state, that Free Presbyterians are not only mistaken in their beliefs but flawed in the ways they have arrived at them. One wrote of the 'weak and wanting minds' who are attracted to Paisleyism.[28] Clifford Smyth describes Paisleyites as 'closed-minded' and 'anti-intellectual'.[29] A Church of Ireland rector wrote that Paisley's gospel has

commanded wide acceptance among the grass-roots Unionists and the near-illiterate Protestant element of the population ... A close acquaintance with Paisleyism confirms the credibility of brainwashing: nothing short of a mental, emotional and spiritual upending could account for the oddities of thought, speech and behaviour it can bring about.[30]

More often the same point is implied by using words to describe Free Presbyterian thought that the author would not normally use to describe his own beliefs: Gallagher, for example, uses the term 'mentality'.[31] Elaborate social-science versions of such a dualism (I have beliefs; you have a mindset) were popular in the 1950s and 1960s,[32] but were largely given up, mainly because of the circular nature of the evidence. You explain why someone becomes a fascist by saying he has an 'authoritarian personality', but the only evidence for his possession of such a personality is the very thing you wish to explain: the fact that he is a fascist. What at first sight looked like an explanation turned out to be just renaming. But that serious social science has abandoned the search for types of minds does not prevent it being widely supposed

[28] D. Boulton, *The UVF, 1966–73* (Dublin: Torc Books, 1973), 31.

[29] C. Smyth, *Ian Paisley: Voice of Protestant Ulster* (Edinburgh: Scottish Academic Press, 1987), 137.

[30] *Irish Times*, 19 Feb. 1971.

[31] T. Gallagher, 'Religion, Reaction and Revolt in Northern Ireland: The Impact of Paisleyism in Ulster', *Journal of Church and State*, 23 (1981), 427.

[32] T. A. Adorno, E. Frenkel-Brunswick, D. J. Levinson, and R. N. Sandford, *The Authoritarian Personality* (New York: Harper, 1950); M. Rokeach, *The Open and Closed Mind* (New York: Basic Books, 1960).

that people who believe strange things must be odd beyond just the strangeness of their beliefs.

If we are to take this seriously we must clarify the problem. First, we should note that Free Presbyterians beliefs are not in any obvious sense odder than those of liberal Christians who deride them. If, as all Christians do, you can believe in an omnipotent divine being, there seem few grounds for dividing subsequent minor propositions about the actions of God into those that are more or less plausible. If God can create the world, there seems no reason why he should not preserve Jonah in the belly of a large fish. Secondly, we can somewhat reduce the apparent credulity of Free Presbyterians by noting that some of their assertions about Catholicism are not as ill-founded as is commonly supposed. While critics of Catholicism (and many of those are Catholics) are obviously making political capital out of the Catholic Church's opposition to liberal democracy, they are not entirely wrong. Until the 1960s, the Church's own social teachings were firmly opposed to representative democracy, to the separation of church and state, and to the idea that freedom of conscience was an inalienable human right. Where Free Presbyterians are wrong is in failing to recognize the extent to which the Vatican has come to accept that which it could no longer effectively oppose.[33] To take a second example, Paisley's claim that the Vatican supports European integration because it wishes to re-create a political entity that it could dominate is not his invention. Because he presents them in extravagant and archaic language, his views are dismissed as para-noid fantasies, but Catholic academics have said much the same (but without the apocalyptic gloss).[34] Even the accusations of clerical sexual perversion that were the staple of Victorian anti-Catholic street theatre no longer seem quite so ill-founded. The torrent of convictions for sexual abuse that rocked the Catholic Church in the 1990s has caused many neutral observers to argue that insisting that

[33] The extent to which the Catholic Church has since Vatican II been on the side of democratization is detailed in J. Casanova, *Public Religions in the Modern World* (Chicago: University of Chicago Press, 1994).

[34] M. Hornsby-Smith, 'The Catholic Church and the European Project: Catholic Social Teaching, Roman Realpolitik and Lay Practice', Religion, Culture and Ideology paper given at the conference, BSA Sociology of Religion Study Group, St Mary's University College, Strawberry Hill, April 1996.

clergy remain celibate inadvertently encourages harmful and oppressive sexual practices.[35] My point is not that Free Presbyterians are right; it is the more general one that they are not so glaringly wrong that we must suppose them to be feeble-minded.

A third observation may set us in a more useful direction: much of what Free Presbyterians believe now was commonplace in mid-nineteenth-century Protestantism.[36] Claiming to occupy the same ground as their forebears is an important part of Free Presbyterian self-image (and is common currency among conservative unionists), but it has a basis in fact. Before I consider why conservative evangelicals in Northern Ireland have been unusually resistant to change, it is worth briefly describing the major changes in British religious culture.

THE DISTINCTIVENESS OF NORTHERN IRELAND

Over the course of the twentieth century the Christian churches in Britain declined drastically. In 1900 almost all the population had some familiarity with Christianity and about half the population attended church at least once a month. By the end of the century a majority of Britons had little or no contact with Christianity and less than 10 per cent attended church. Associated with that general pattern of decline are two important and related minor trends: the mainstream churches became increasingly liberal and church members become more selective about which of their churches' doctrines they would accept. Even those who continued to attend church regularly

---

[35] A draft survey prepared for the US Conference of Catholic Bishops said that more than 11,000 complaints of sexual abuse had been made against 4,000 priests between 1950 and 2002: www/cnn.com/2004/US/02/16/church.abuse.

[36] Liberal Christians such as Dennis Cooke want to contest the Paisleyite claim to be in continuity with Reformation teaching. Cooke is correct that FPCU views of the Catholic Church are more thoroughly condemnatory than some of the sentiments to be found in Luther and Calvin, but the hardening of ideological differences long pre-dates Paisleyism and can be found in the Westminster Confession of Faith of 1646 (the subordinate standard of Presbyterianism) and the Church of England's Thirty-Nine Articles. See D. Cooke, *Persecuting Zeal: A Portrait of Ian Paisley* (Dingle: Brandon, 1996); *The Westminster Confession of Faith* (Glasgow: Free Presbyterian Church of Scotland, 1967), and B. J. Kidd, *The Thirty-Nine Articles* (London: Rivingtons, 1899).

became increasingly consumerist about their faith. Their church involvement was no longer a taken-for-granted expression of loyalty but a matter of personal preference. What had once been a powerful social institution became an impotent collection of small voluntary associations.

That the decline of Christianity in Britain is mirrored in almost all modern liberal democracies is good reason to suppose that it has been caused by general social forces. I have explained the process of secularization at great length elsewhere.[37] Here I want to mention just those parts of the process that are particularly relevant to understanding Northern Ireland.

Religion is most persuasive when a single faith is shared by an entire people. Then it can be supported by the state (for example, funding the church from taxes and promoting the faith through a national school system). It can also be routinely affirmed and reinforced through the church celebrating the agricultural seasons (as we see in harvest festivals). The church can link individual biographies to the life of the community by managing such rites of passage as birth, marriage, and death. And most importantly religious beliefs can be expressed and reinforced in the conversation of day-to-day life. There was a time when the common parting expression 'Goodbye' was known to speaker and hearer to be a contraction for 'God be with you'.

There are a number of ways in which a religion consensus can be weakened. Migration may bring religious innovation, and the expansion of the state may bring into its boundaries different Gods. A third, and potentially more potent source of diversity, arises from within a modernizing economy. Protestant cultures have a natural tendency to fragment. Because they reject the idea of a hierarchy of enlightenment, with an apex that is closer to God than is the mass of the people, they are vulnerable to schism. That potential is turned into a reality by two common features of modernization: the gradual division of a population into competing classes and a growing sense of egalitarianism. In simple societies where there are few significant differences in life circumstances and styles it is possible to maintain a common religious culture that overarches and encompasses the entire people.

[37] See S. Bruce, *Religion in the Modern World: From Cathedrals to Cults* (Oxford: Oxford University Press, 1996), and *God is Dead: Secularization in the West* (Oxford: Blackwell, 2002).

In more complex and economically developed societies such as those of medieval feudal Europe there could be great differences of wealth and power but there was still considerable closeness between all 'stations'. Differences in station were accepted and the masses so little regarded that such disquiet about the propriety of the dominant religious images generated little dissent. But, as economies grew, social structures became more complex. New classes began to develop versions of the dominant religion that better suited their social situations. The elites who controlled the religious establishment were for a time able to suppress dissent, but economic modernization, especially when it was associated with the growth of nationalism (which encourages members of the putative new nation to see themselves as brothers and sisters in a common enterprise), also brought an increasingly egalitarian ethos. This gloss simplifies enormously, but we can say that the Reformation, with its assertion of individual rights in the narrow sphere of religion, inadvertently laid the foundations for a slow but gradual expansion of the idea of personal liberty. In the seventeenth century, the British state was willing to use force to coerce religious conformity. By the end of the eighteenth century the constraints on dissenters had been reduced to some financial penalties and exclusion from certain offices of state. By 1851 Baptists, Presbyterians, Methodists, Independents and Quakers had become so numerous that the Census of Religious Worship showed that more people in England worshipped outside the state Church of England than attended its offices.

The proliferation of religious diversity, when it is accompanied by an increasingly egalitarian ethos, has two sorts of consequence. First, the state has to become increasingly neutral. If it regards social harmony as more important than religious rectitude, it must reduce its active support for the dominant religious tradition and allow religious affiliation to become a private matter. The newly formed United States in the first amendment to its constitution announced the new settlement: 'Congress shall make no law respecting an establishment of religion, or prohibiting the free exercise thereof.'[38] The British state got to the same end point by slow accommodation.

---

[38] E. S. Gaustad, *Proclaim Liberty throughout the Land: A History of Church and State in America* (New York: Oxford University Press, 2003).

The state churches (and there was already a large dose of diversity in the fact that Britain had three state churches rather than one) were allowed to retain a few symbolic advantages but gradually lost all real power. While this allowed dissenting sects to flourish, it removed central state support for religion. As the modern state developed its complex apparatus of social welfare, education and social control, these systems became increasingly secular. Precisely because the changes were gradual, their importance was often not perceived clearly at the time. For example, in the late nineteenth century, the two main Presbyterian churches in Scotland handed their schools over to local government control. Because they were then popular organizations that could count on the at-least-nominal attachment of the vast majority of the population, they did not seek any legal protection for specifically Presbyterian forms of religious education. They took it for granted that the schools would remain Presbyterian. Within fifty years they had become largely secular.

In brief, the proliferation of competing religions gradually creates a religiously neutral public sphere and hastens the acceptance of the idea that the rights of subjects or citizens should not be conditional on them worshipping the correct God in the correct way. Religion becomes a matter of personal preference.

Diversity changes the formal operations of the state; it also changes the way that ordinary people hold their beliefs. It is easy to believe that your religion is the only true faith and that all others are dangerous falsehoods when your religion is so thoroughly dominant that others are known only in the abstract and through invidious stereotypes. Some novelty may pose no threat if the new religion is the preserve of a minority that can be dismissed as a lesser form of life. But when your own neighbours and kin, people whom you like and who are like you, promote an alternative religion, then the taken-for-granted certainty of your own beliefs is inevitably undermined. When it becomes clear that good men can differ, it becomes hard to avoid the suspicion that you have chosen God, rather than the other way round.

To put it rather formally, there are two possible responses to diversity: avoidance and toleration. Either you try to insulate yourself from alternatives or you scale down the claims made by your religion. The majority of British Christians followed the second route. The mainstream churches gradually reduced their exclusive claims and came to accept an ever-broader range of alternative faiths as being almost as pleasing to God. Most Christians became in effect relativists and universalists. Instead of seeing their interpretation of God's will as binding on all his creation, they supposed their faith was right and proper for them but need not apply to others. And, instead of supposing that only they were going to heaven and everyone else was going to hell, they supposed that all decent people would be saved. While this had the great benefit of allowing harmonious relationships with those of other faiths, it had the debilitating consequence of reducing the impetus to ensure the survival of any particular religion. If there are many ways to God, why work hard to ensure that your faith survives? If we are all God's children and nothing very bad will happen to those who do not worship in the correct manner, then why work hard to raise your children in your faith?

In brief, pleasant and rewarding interaction with those of other faiths weakens commitment to one's dogmas and doctrines. Religion ceases to be a necessity and becomes a matter of taste. This effect is much amplified when attachment to any particular religion becomes so weakened that people are willing to marry out. Where religions are strongly embedded in group identities, intermarriage is rare and it results in one partner changing sides. Where religion is seen as a matter of personal preference, intermarriage becomes common, and, instead of one partner shifting, both partners loosen their attachments. The odds on their children keeping the faith of either parent are much reduced. A large body of recent survey evidence allows us to be fairly specific about this: the odds on the children of a mixed marriage having any active involvement in organized religion are only half those for the offspring of a same-religion marriage.[39]

Northern Ireland is both more Christian than Britain and more conservative in its Christianity. In 1998, 88 per cent of survey respondents in Northern Ireland described themselves as Christian; the same figure as for 1991.[40] For Britain the 1991 figure was 56 per cent.

[39] D. Voas and A. Crockett, 'Religion in Britain: Neither Believing nor Belonging', *Sociology*, 39 (2005), 11–28.

[40] These data are taken from S. Bruce and F. Alderdice, 'Religious Belief and Behaviour', in P. Stringer and G. Robinson (eds.), *Social Attitudes in Northern Ireland: The Third Report* (Belfast: Blackstaff Press, 1993), 5–20, and C. Mitchell, *Religion, Identity and Politics in Northern Ireland* (Aldershot: Ashgate, 2006).

More telling, the gap between nominal identity and participation is much smaller in Northern Ireland than in Britain. There may be some exaggeration in the claim by two-thirds of Catholics and one-third of mainstream Protestants surveyed in 1998 to have attended church at least once a month, but no allowance for scepticism can bring these figures down close to the less than 10 per cent of British people who attend weekly.

This high degree of church involvement is reflected in responses to questions about beliefs. In a 1991 survey, 57 per cent of Northern Irish respondents but only 10 per cent of British respondents chose 'I know God exists': the most certain of the options. On a wide range of questions about orthodox Christian doctrines (belief in heaven, in miracles, in the status of Jesus as the son of God), Northern Ireland respondents showed themselves far more firmly Christian than their British counterparts. But equally important for our interests is the conservatism of Ulster Protestants. A number of items in the 1991 Life and Times survey make the point. Unfortunately the question 'Would you say that you have been "born again" or have had a "born again" experience—that is, a turning point in your life when you committed yourself to Christ' was not asked of the British sample, but the answers for Northern Ireland are still revealing. Almost all Brethren respondents, 70 per cent of Baptists and two-thirds of Free Presbyterians claimed to have been born again. Given the general ethos of these groups, such figures are no surprise, but 28 per cent of Irish Presbyterians and 19 per cent of Episcopalians claimed a con-version experience and 21 per cent of Methodists—who in Britain are typically very liberal—claimed to be born again.

To get a general sense of conservatism I constructed a scale by merging responses to questions about life after death, the possibility of miracles, the existence of the Devil, and the like. Here the difference between Ulster and British members of the same denomination was striking. Among Episcopalians, 14 per cent of those in Ulster but only 1 per cent of their British counterparts chose the conservative options. For Methodists the respective figures were 15 and 2 per cent; for Presbyterians 20 and 2 per cent; and for Baptists 30 and 18 per cent.

A question about the nature of the Bible produced even larger differences. Respondents could choose between 'the actual word of God . . . to be taken literally word for word', 'the inspired word of God but not everything should be taken literally, word for word', and 'an ancient book of fables, legends, history and moral teachings recorded by man'. The first, literalist, response was chosen by 31 per cent of Ulster Episcopalians but only 2 per cent of their British colleagues and the respective figures for Methodists were 25 to 1; for Presbyterians 35 to 3; and for Baptists 45 to 15.

There have been some signs of secularization in Northern Ireland.[41] For example, in 1968 two-thirds of survey respondents claimed to attend church every week; by 2004 the figure was just 41 per cent. But the decline started later and has been less severe than in England or Scotland, and the explanation is hardly difficult to find. My very compressed account of secularization above took as its hypothetical case a society where religion is not closely tied to other important social divisions (such as national or regional rivalries or structured differences of social status) and it assumed that the society was sufficiently stable politically for elites not to feel the need to use religious affiliation as a ticket for entry to the body politic. In such circumstances most people are happy to accept religion being relegated to a matter of personal taste. Or, to put it another way round, there is nothing inevitable about secularization. If a society is deeply divided between competing ethnic or national groups pursuing irreconcilable political ambitions, then religion may well remain powerful.

Consider intermarriage. There has been some relaxation of the sectarian divide in Ulster. A 1991 survey allows us to compare Catholic–Protestant intermarriage rates for respondents (who typically married in the three previous decades) and for their parents (which would take us back a further two decades). For the survey respondents in Northern Ireland the rate was 9 per cent and for their parents 2 per cent; the corresponding figures for Britain were 13 and 10 per cent (which is extremely high considering the small number of Catholics).[42] In Scotland in 2001 just over half of Catholics under 35 who were married were married to non-Catholics; that is, for young

---

[41] For a detailed description of changes, see Mitchell, *Religion, Identity and Politics*, ch. 2.

[42] V. Morgan, M. Smyth, G. Robinson, and G. Fraser, *Mixed Marriages in Northern Ireland* (Coleraine: Centre for the Study of Conflict, University of Ulster, 1996).

people in Scotland religious identity is not an important consideration in choosing a spouse.[43]

Secondly, consider the politics. In Britain the link between citizenship and religion was slightly revitalized in the 1790s when fears inspired by the French Revolution created new 'Church and King' movements, but it was weak even then and it was broken when the Catholic Emancipation Act of 1829 gave the vote to Catholics and when the Reform Act of 1832 gave the vote to the rising (and often Nonconformist) middle class. Apart from a brief flourishing of anti-Catholic politics in local elections in Scotland in the 1930s, religion has played little or no significant part in British public life since the nineteenth century.[44] As was made clear in Chapter 1, religion has always been deeply implicated in politics in Northern Ireland and nothing that has happened since partition has weakened that association.

All of the above might seem like a very long way to state the obvious, but it is important to spell it out. There are some very general changes that come with modernization that undermine religion but there are also strong retarding factors. The conflict between Catholics and Protestants in Ireland gave each side good reasons to remain committed to their religion and to avoid the sort of social mixing that, in other settings, caused dogmatic and doctrinaire religion to be gradually displaced by liberal and tolerant versions.

HOW DO FREE PRESBYTERIANS DIFFER FROM OTHER ULSTER PROTESTANTS?

It is not difficult to see how the political conflict in Northern Ireland exerts a restraining influence on those general social changes that elsewhere have diminished the importance of religion and encouraged a shift in a liberal direction. Hence it is no surprise that its Protestant churches seem more like their nineteenth-century British

[43] S. Bruce, A. Glendinning, I. Paterson, and M. Rosie, *Sectarianism in Scotland* (Edinburgh: Edinburgh University Press, 2004).
[44] The situation in Scotland was somewhat similar to that of Northern Ireland for a short while (ibid.).

counterparts than their contemporary sister churches. This in turn explains why Paisley could hope to recruit followers. Having dismissed the idea that Paisley's appeal is explained by some personality or intellectual flaw, I want to consider whether there are any shared social characteristics that might distinguish those Protestants who joined Paisley's church from those who did not. I do not want to suggest that we can entirely explain why some people rather than others are attracted to a new set of ideas by identifying background social similarities, but it is often the case that new religious movements flow along particular channels. For example, Pentecostalism often appeals far more to the poor than to the rich. Protestant dissenting movements (such as the Methodists in late-eighteenth- and early nineteenth-century England) often attract skilled artisans, craftsmen, and independent small farmers and have relatively little appeal either to the gentry or to their peasants. The reason for this is simple: people will be more receptive to a reworking of the dominant religious tradition that particularly speaks to their circumstances. If, as the landed gentry did, you see this world as properly hierarchical, with the rulers clearly divided from the ruled, then an egalitarian religion, which stresses the equality of all before the eyes of God, will seem less plausible than one that supposes that a clerical elite has privileged access to the will of God. And if you are a peasant who has absolutely no say in the affairs of this world, you are unlikely to feel qualified to make independent judgements about the next world.

It would be illuminating to have detailed information about the social background of those who were attracted to the FPCU in its early days. Unfortunately we have only the biographies of those prominent enough to be remembered in historical sketches of church formation. Those show that, outside East Belfast, most early Free Presbyterians were small farmers and small businessmen running agriculture-related businesses. Of ten people profiled in an account of the Crossgar split, six were small farmers, one was a gardener, and one a grocer. Only two people did not work on the land—a salesman and an architect—and they both came from farming families. The same could be said for the founders of Cabra and Rasharkin. The Ravenhill and Sandown Road congregations were predominantly working class with a smattering of small shopkeepers and other self-employed business people.

The picture we get from such biographies is confirmed by the 1981 census data (presented in more detail in the Appendix). Compared to Irish Presbyterians, Free Presbyterians were relatively scarce at the top of the occupational scale. Fewer of them were professionals such as doctors and teacher (1.5 per cent compared with 4.5 per cent for Irish Presbyterians) and they were under-represented among professionally qualified engineers (2.0 per cent as compared with 4.4 per cent for Irish Presbyterians). Among those described as managers, Irish Presbyterians were much more likely to run big operations than were Free Presbyterians. Although similar proportions worked in manufacturing or assembling, Free Presbyterians were concentrated in more types of processing work connected with agriculture than with urban hi-tech engineering. Free Presbyterians were more likely than Irish Presbyterians to be self-employed but the self-employed Irish Presbyterians were more likely to employ other people. This suggests that more Free Presbyterians were businessmen in what the Victorians called 'a small way'. The differences in social class and occupation are mirrored in differences in educational qualifications. According to the 1981 census 90.8 per cent of Irish Presbyterians had no post-school qualifications; the figure for Free Presbyterians was 97.5.

We should be cautious of making too much of these differences because the links between them can be extremely complex and the numbers involved are small, but we can be confident of something like the following composite. In its early days, the FPCU tended to attract farmers and people who ran small rural businesses (such as shopkeepers, hauliers, and builders). Even the town churches such as Lisburn and Omagh drew a large part of their congregations from the surrounding farmlands. Very obviously, its people were not cosmopolitan; they were not university-educated mobile professionals who were exposed to a diverse range of social and cultural influences and whose working lives brought them into frequent contact with people from diverse backgrounds. They were firmly rooted local people.

If this gives us some idea of what sort of people were most receptive to Paisley's evangelical preaching, it also identifies a fascinating question that can be illustrated by an event from the early 1980s. The Irish Presbyterian church in Limavady, a strongly Protestant area in the middle of the predominantly Catholic county of Londonderry, called as its minister David Armstrong. Although a committed evangelical as a student, Armstrong had moved in a liberal direction to an extent that set him at odds with his congregants. Armstrong's problems began when he accepted an invitation from the local Catholic priest to attend the opening of the new chapel (the building of which had been slowed down because it had been bombed at an early stage in its construction). Against the expressed wishes of some members of his congregation, he attended and thus initiated a conflict that grew in intensity when the new priest, Kevin Mullen, made the novel gesture of crossing the road on Christmas Day 1983 to wish the Presbyterians a Merry Christmas. Seeing this as precisely the sort of civilized gesture and antidote to sectarian tension that Christians should promote, Armstrong reciprocated. His elders took their objections to the Route Presbytery. Armstrong expected to be supported by his fellow ministers and was greatly disappointed by the Presbytery's failure openly to endorse his stance. In the spring of 1985, he felt he had no alternative but to leave the Presbyterian Church. Although a Presbyterian congregation in Bangor made it known that they would have him, Armstrong had already concluded from the hostile reception to his acts of reconciliation that there was no place for his version of Christianity in Ulster and he went to Oxford to train for the Anglican ministry.[45] The important point about that anecdote is that, although the local Free Presbyterians played some small part in stirring up the controversy by picketing Armstrong's church, it was his own people who drove him out. In that part of the world, there was almost nothing in doctrine, in culture, or in political preferences that separated the typical Irish Presbyterian member of the Orange Order who voted UUP from the Free Presbyterian member of the Independent Orange Order who later voted DUP—except how they felt about Paisley!

To return to the chronological thread, across the province in the 1960s there was a large constituency of conservative Protestants who would have agreed with a great deal of Paisley's positive teaching but did not accept his insistence that they should abandon their churches because they were insufficiently pure.

---

[45] Armstrong's version of the dispute is given in D. Armstrong and H. Saunders, *A Road Too Wide: The Price of Reconciliation in Northern Ireland* (Basingstoke: Marshall, Morgan and Scott, 1985).

COURTING CONTROVERSY

The Free Presbyterian Church did not have a monopoly of conver-
sionist and separatist ascetic Protestantism. The same creed could
have been found in any number of tiny gospel halls and Brethren
meetings. What did make it stand out from the general evangelical
milieu was the willingness of its people publicly to confront those
with whom they disagreed. The Paisleyites were quite unapologetic-
ally objectionable. They saw the 'Protest' in Protestant both as a
necessary requirement of faith and as an extremely useful publicity
device.

Sometimes you've got to—before you can heal, you've got to wound, and,
just to be, like, using an illustration: if a person is in a house sleeping and the
house is on fire, well, who's going to be that person's friend? The one that
goes past and says 'I wouldn't like to disturb them. I'll just let them sleep' or
the person that . . . goes in and breaks the door or breaks the window and
goes in and raises the alarm and tries to get them wakened up?

Paisley and Wylie were active in Protestant rallies, and in the meetings organized by the National Union of Protestants, but their most
public action of the 1950s was, as so many key episodes, thrust upon
them.

Maura Lyons was a young Catholic girl from West Belfast. At work
she started to attend a lunchtime prayer meeting, and one of her
colleagues took her to attend the small Dunmurry Free Presbyterian
Church. Unwilling to court adverse publicity, David Leatham, the
minister, advised her to keep quiet about her conversion until she
was legally of age. One evening she returned home to find her parents
talking to two priests. Thinking that she would be taken away to
some convent for what would now be called 'de-programming',
Lyons left the house and sought the sanctuary of David Leatham.
A lady missionary working for the Sentinel Union took Maura Lyons
to England.

There was a huge outcry in the local press. Paisley and the Free
Presbyterian Church were accused of kidnapping an under-age girl.
Wylie was contacted and asked to assist in moving the girl from her
first hiding place in Dorset to Preston. Paisley decided to take the

initiative and he announced a 'great Protestant rally' in the Ulster Hall and promised some startling revelations. Wylie went to Preston and tape-recorded Maura Lyons 'giving her testimony'. So that Paisley could continue to claim that he did not know where the girl was, Wylie delivered the tape to his doorstep, and Mrs Paisley found it the next morning behind the milk bottles.

The tape was played at a large, well-publicized rally in the Ulster Hall in Belfast and there were immediate calls for Paisley to be arrested and charged with abducting the girl. A few weeks later, when she came of age, Maura Lyons turned up at Paisley's house and asked for his protection. The police took the girl and, in a court case in which Paisley refused to give evidence, Maura Lyons was made a ward of court and returned to her parents. For Lyons that was the end of her dramatic career in evangelical Protestantism. She later renounced her Protestant conversion and married a Catholic.

For Paisley and the Free Presbyterian Church the episode generated a great deal of publicity, all of it hostile, but for some evangelicals it established Paisley's public reputation as a man who would stand up to the Church of Rome. For critics of Paisley's style, the Lyons case was a good demonstration of a weakness that he has shown on many occasions since. While they would not deny him the right to represent his religious beliefs as forcefully as he can and hence to protest against those beliefs that he sees as heretical, they objected to the 'fly dodges' in which he engaged to promote his cause. He maintained throughout the police and media search for Maura Lyons that he had not been responsible for her disappearance (which was strictly speaking true) and that he did not know where she was and so could not tell her parents. This was only minimally true in that Leatham had been involved in her first move, Wylie had been involved in her second move, and Wylie had returned to make the tape recording. Paisley had only to ask Wylie a simple question and he would have known where the girl was.

Although it is not important for understanding the success of Ian Paisley's movement, it is interesting to speculate on aspects of the character of the man. What the Lyons case demonstrated was that he was capable of taking a very legalistic view of morality and ethics when it suited his cause. Like the Jesuits he is so fond of criticizing, Paisley was willing to be less than forthcoming. To his less scrupulous followers, this showed 'that there's no flies on the big man'. His more sensitive and thoughtful followers had to persuade themselves that this sort of activity was justified by the nature of the opposition. The Free Presbyterians were battling not only against secular liberalism and the heretics within the Protestant churches but also against the forces of Rome, and with enemies such as these one must on occasional use tactics that are not as honourable as one might wish them to be.

Now that it is commonplace for people to change religion and most have none, it is difficult to appreciate the public interest that was generated by events such as the disappearance of Maura Lyons and the broadcasting of her taped testimony. In the 1940s and 1950s, an evangelistic rally that had some theatrical element, such as the testimony of an ex-Catholic, was a crowd-puller, as was the staged performance of the blasphemous Mass by ex-priests. Even in the late 1950s, Paisley and Wylie could think it worthwhile to sponsor a tour by an ex-priest who would perform, and then denounce, the Mass. Largely as a result of television and cinema, the market for such performances has disappeared. If we wish a public display of sin to stimulate our sense of righteousness, we do not have to arrange a mimic Mass; the modern world, brought by television into every rural Protestant home, provides enough sin and apostasy to satisfy any curiosity.

The decline of Protestant street theatre has to be seen in the context of several important changes in the general cultural climate and not as a result of a change of attitude by evangelical Protestants. Paisley thinks it is as important now as he did then to save any soul from the clutches of Catholicism. If such souls have ceased to be an important part of his presentations, it is because there are so many of them that they are no longer newsworthy, and because the general climate has shifted to produce so many other challenges to evangelical Protestantism. It is no longer a straight fight between Protestantism and Rome. The Protestants are beset by so many other threats, most of them related to the liberalization of Protestantism. As Paisley put it:

In those days people were Protestants. It was the natural thing. I mean, even the Clerk of the Belfast Presbytery was one of the referees [of the National Union of Protestants]. In all the denominations there was a sprinkling of good strong evangelical men and Protestants. And almost all the clergymen were in the Orange Order. We're living in a different Ulster today.

And it is an Ulster that probably would not care much if a young Catholic girl becomes a Free Presbyterian or if an ex-priest demonstrates the Mass for the entertainment of a Protestant rally.

THE WATERSHED

Paisley began his soul-saving mission in 1945. Over the next two decades, he built the foundations of his Free Presbyterian Church of Ulster, but the growth was slow. Although there were many conservative evangelicals in the main denominations who shared Paisley's basic theological beliefs, few responded to his claim that Protestantism was so threatened by traitors within and by a resurgent Romanism without that a separatist witness was required. And, whatever latent demand there was in Ulster, Paisley was constrained because, although he was extraordinarily energetic, he was not divisible. He could hold a week of meetings here or there and stimulate initial interest, but he needed a cadre of lieutenants to move in and service this interest on a regular basis. From the foundation of the Free Church, he had problems in recruiting competent professionals. As the careers of those ministers already mentioned show, even if he could find people willing to work with him, he had so little choice that he had to take anyone who shared his core objection to modernism. He could not afford to select only those who agreed with him on the whole range of doctrines and practices that gave the Free Church its ethos. Thus the growth of the Free Church was retarded until it could produce enough young men who had been thoroughly socialized within the Free Church and who were competent to give the new organization a solid foundation. And even some of his most loyal lieutenants were reluctant to embrace Paisley's aggressive attitude to competitors. Bert Cooke, who was one of the first men to join the ministry training programme, enrolled only reluctantly and only came to think of himself as a committed protesting Free Presbyterian when, as a student in charge of the Mount Merrion congregation, he was challenged by moderates in his congregation to oppose the

Free Church's pickets of the Irish Presbyterian General Assembly. After serious thought and prayer, he concluded that Paisley was right: that a genuine Christian commitment required a willingness publicly to denounce apostasy.

As the key activists came to a commitment to aggressive evangelism and public protest, there was a weeding-out, as some people who had a tentative commitment found that they did not want to pursue the narrow sectarian ideology of the Free Church. There was a considerable departure of members from Paisley's Ravenhill congregation. People left Mount Merrion when Bert Cooke committed himself to the protesting position. In Ballyhalbert, John Douglas found that many of those who had initially asked the Free Church for preaching offices were not prepared for the preaching they received. To describe the process in general terms, the Free Church was tapping a seam of discontent, but the general unease of individuals and groups with what they were getting in the main churches had yet to be channelled into a coherent shared ideology, and, in the process of refining discontent, some people rejected Paisley's leadership and abandoned the fledgling organization. Those who stayed through this period became convinced Free Presbyterians.

To summarize the story so far, by the start of the 1960s Paisley had moved from being a freelance preacher to being the leader of a small church largely made up of disaffected Irish Presbyterians. To understand the next phase in the history of the Free Church, we must shift our attention from theology and church disputes to the wider sphere of public reputation and political conflict.

3

On the Margins

INTRODUCTION

If we had to compress Ian Paisley's thought into just two propositions, strong candidates would be 'I am doing God's will' and 'You
cannot trust the elite'. At the root of most features of the world that
he finds objectionable is the Vatican, but the immediate source of
danger is the untrustworthiness of those who should know better. Of
course the Devil wants to undermine the true faith and the Catholic
Church wants Christendom reunited under its malign leadership;
that is only to be expected. But it is the Protestant clergy who permit
this baleful state of affairs. The sheep are being led astray by false
shepherds who are negligent, evil, or both. What unifies Paisley's
religious and political visions is the extension of the same principle to
Ulster unionism. It is no surprise that Catholic Irish nationalists wish
to destroy Northern Ireland; it is, after all, one of the last strongholds
of the reformed faith. What surprises and offends Paisley is that the
unionist leadership, which had proved so resolute in 1912, should
now be so weak. This chapter will consider Paisley's early political
career and the impact his political crusade had on his church.

THE AWKWARD SQUAD

From the first elections for the Stormont Parliament in 1921, the
Ulster Unionist Party (UUP) had dominated the politics of Ulster

with a virtual monopoly of Protestant votes.[1] Between 1929 and 1965, the UUP always held 29 of the 48 Stormont constituencies (and often won others) and, of those 29 perpetually UUP seats, 60 per cent were never contested, which tells us a great deal about the sectarian geography of Ulster politics—there was little point in unionists contesting constituencies that had a nationalist majority and vice versa—and about the solidity of Protestant support for the UUP. Almost all Protestants belonged to the Irish Presbyterian Church or the Church of Ireland, very many were in the Orange Order, and the Orange Order had a major say in the composition and policies of the UUP.

However, support for the Ulster Unionist Party was neither total nor uncritical. There was always an independent and irksome unionist fringe that was supported by two sorts of people. There was a working-class element, centred on the Shankill Road, West Belfast, which was suspicious of the party's landed gentry and big business leadership and which campaigned for better wages, housing, and welfare. Although populist, this element was staunchly unionist (often more so than the leadership) and expected the Protestant working class to be rewarded for its loyalty. There was a second marginal element, this time province-wide, which was suspicious of the leadership's lack of evangelical piety.

The two independent unionist members at Stormont during Paisley's early days in Belfast were Tommy Henderson (who sat first for Belfast North and then for Belfast Shankill) and John Nixon (Belfast Woodvale). Henderson had made his reputation as a working-class critic of the economic policies of the Unionist governments of the 1930s. Nixon was a former District Inspector in the Special Constabulary who became notorious in Belfast during the mayhem that surrounded partition. In Belfast over 400 people were killed between 1920 and 1922; a disproportionately large number of them were

---

[1] For a history of the Ulster Unionist Party, see J. F. Harbinson, *The Ulster Unionist Party, 1882–1973* (Belfast: Blackstaff Press, 1973), and G. Walker, *A History of the Ulster Unionist Party: Protest, Pragmatism and Pessimism* (Manchester: Manchester University Press, 2004). Although good on the details of the UUP, Harbinson's short description of Paisley's support is quite misleading. He stresses the urban working-class support for Protestant Unionism and fails to notice that Paisley and Beattie were elected to Stormont in rural constituencies.

Catholic. Although there was never any evidence to charge Nixon, he was widely suspected of leading murder squads of rogue policemen and, in particular, of killing four members of the McMahon family.[2] Nixon was sacked for making an inflammatory speech at an Orange Order function in 1924. In 1929 he won his Woodvale seat, which he held until his death in 1949.

Ian Paisley had been born into the rural Orange tradition of politicized Protestantism in County Armagh. His grandfather and great-grandfather had both been long-serving District Masters and his father had been an Ulster Volunteer. So it is no surprise that Paisley became involved in unionist politics when he moved to Belfast. In 1949 Norman Porter, the general secretary of the National Union of Protestants and then still a close colleague of Paisley, had been asked by a number of conservative clergymen to stand against the Minister for Education in order to protest against amendments to the Education Act that increased and regularized state funding of Catholic schools.[3] However, Éamon de Valera's Republicans decided to defy the spirit of partition and contest seats in the North, which allowed Prime Minister Brooke (later Lord Brookeborough) to present the election as a plebiscite on the border. Unionists pressed Porter to withdraw to avoid splitting the unionist vote and he did so at the last moment when the UUP agreed not to oppose Henderson.[4] Paisley, then a member of the UUP, was asked to stand in the marginal Belfast Dock ward seat. He declined but agreed to campaign for T. L. Cole, and he and Norman Porter worked hard to produce a Unionist victory in a marginal seat. Paisley was given much credit for the win, but his always-thin commitment to the party was eroded and his distrust of the elite reinforced when the Unionist government gave a post in the Ministry of Agriculture to the Labour Party candidate he had worked so hard to defeat.

From 1949 to the late 1950s Paisley remained on the fringes of UUP politics. His sympathies lay with the independents such as

---

[2] J. McDermott, *Northern Divisions: The Old IRA and the Belfast Pogroms, 1920–22* (Belfast: Beyond the Pale Publications, 2002); G. B. Kenna, *The Belfast Pogroms 1920–22* (Dublin: O'Connell Publishing Co., 1922); M. Farrell, *Northern Ireland: The Orange State* (London: Pluto Press, 1980), 39–65. For a rebuttal of the case against Nixon, see D. Trimble, ' "Rebel Heart" Did No Service to the Truth', *Irish News*, 16 Feb. 2001.

[3] D. Harkness, *Northern Ireland since 1920* (Dublin: Helicon, 1985), 116.

[4] *Belfast Telegraph*, 31 Jan. 1949.

Henderson and Nixon (who at one point in the 1930s constituted, in
the absence of the nationalists, the official opposition at Stormont),
but the UUP had not yet shown the degree of liberalism it was to show
under Terence O'Neill in the 1960s, and Paisley confined himself to
promoting various ginger group enterprises. One of these—Ulster
Protestant Action—argued for preferential employment policies to
favour loyal Protestants. It also campaigned for the right to hold
parades and marches.

Much misunderstanding of the conflict in Ulster stems from too
narrow an interpretation of the 'Protestant Ascendancy'. Many critics
of the Orange state suppose that unionists followed the politics they
did in order to maintain and increase their material advantages over
the Catholic nationalist population. It is certainly true that a great
deal of the competition between nationalists and unionists concerned the distribution of resources. Nationalists wanted their fair
share; unionists, especially in the working class, wanted the government to reward its loyal supporters. But jobs and houses were not all
that mattered. Both populations also competed for the prestige of
their culture: flags, banners, and marches. Although most Unionist
politicians were happy to manage the state in a discriminatory fashion
(after all, nationalists had been given three-quarters of the island), the
government also attempted to keep the peace and maintain order. It
frequently banned marches or rerouted them through areas with the
same politics as the marchers. The more militant Protestants saw this
as a weakness and periodically arranged to confront the Stormont
government. Porter and Paisley were frequently to be found leading
such marches and various Ministers for Home Affairs (who were
responsible for law and order) found themselves being denounced
by loyalists at Orange or Protestant Action rallies.

THE ELECT AND THE ELECTED

The first Free Presbyterian involvement in an election was a typically
reactive affair. Paisley had brought an ex-priest, Father J. J. Arrien, to
Northern Ireland, and Wylie booked the Ballymoney town hall for a

meeting. 'I had a poster done out and had it outside the town hall.
I had it in big letters. Father Arrien—the father in inverted commas—
will preach on the blasphemy of the Romish Mass on such and such
an evening—and the priest of the town, he went up to the council
and objected to this and said that Wylie's a trouble maker.' Father
Murphy, the local priest, was joined by the Church of Ireland and
Presbyterian clergymen in his objections, and the council decided to
cancel Wylie's booking. Paisley's rebuttal of Murphy's claims to speak
for the majority of local people was characteristically florid:

Priest Murphy, speak for your own bloodthirsty persecuting intolerant
blaspheming political religious papacy but do not dare to pretend to be
the spokesman of free Ulster men. You are not in the South of Ireland ... Go
back to your priestly intolerance, back to your blasphemous masses, back to
your beads, holy water, holy smoke and stinks and remember we are the sons
of the martyrs whom your church butchered and we know your church to be
the *mother of harlots* and the abominations of the earth.[5]

The meeting went ahead. Under the banner of Ulster Protestant
Action, Paisley brought a busload of supporters and a flute band to
swell the open-air rally. Before Arrien spoke, Paisley, in Lutheran
style, nailed the following 'theses' to the town hall door.

We protest against the iniquitous decision of the Ballymoney Council in
    closing this hall to the message of Protestantism.
We repudiate the lies of Priest Murphy, bachelor agent of a foreign power
    and brand as traitors all those associated with him and those who
    hastened to do his will.
We affirm Article 31 of the church of our Gracious Lady Queen Elizabeth II
    that 'masses are blasphemous fables and dangerous deceits'.

That short text compresses into three sentences almost every element
of Paisley's anti-Catholicism. The false doctrines of Rome are attacked by repeating the judgement of the Mass found in the Articles
of the Church of England, of which the Queen is the head; so correct
religious belief is linked to loyalty to the monarch. The loyalty issue is
again raised in describing the priest as the agent of 'a foreign power'.
Sexual deviance is hinted at in the use of the term 'bachelor', which
manages both to describe, and to cast doubts on, the celibate state of

5 *Revivalist*, 3/11 (May 1958), 1–2.

the priest, and the general honesty of Catholic priests is challenged by branding Murphy as a liar. Finally, there is the criticism of 'those associated with him', presumably the Protestant clergymen who shared his objections to the meeting, and there is the suggestion that they and the Ballymoney Council have been manipulated by Rome.

At the next local council elections, Wylie continued his protest by standing as a Protestant Unionist, and he was elected. The same year, 1958, Albert Duff, a Belfast Alderman and the superintendent of a small mission hall, stood for the Stormont Parliament in the Iveagh constituency. Duff had sat in the Belfast Corporation since 1946 as an official Unionist but he was now backed by Ulster Protestant Action as a protest against Maginess, the Attorney General at the time of the Maura Lyons case. He failed to win. The same year Duff and another candidate won seats in the Belfast Corporation as 'Protestant Unionists'. Three years later, Protestant Action fielded six candidates for the Corporation; two were elected.

REFORMING UNIONISM

Although such fringe successes irritated the UUP, even the victors did not see them as a serious threat. Indeed, on the surface Ulster politics seemed to be moving away from its traditional agenda of the border and loyalty. During the 1960s, under the leadership of Terence O'Neill, the Unionist Parliamentary Party found itself devoting an increasing amount of time to questions of economic and social reform. At the central government level at least, the traditional preoccupation with unionist unity and the constitution seemed to have been superseded by an active concern with modernization and economic development.[6]

Terence O'Neill was the son of a Westminster MP and country squire whose family owned large estates in North Antrim. Educated

---

[6] B. Probert, *Beyond Orange and Green: The Political Economy of the Northern Ireland Crisis* (Dublin: Academy Press, 1978); D. Gordon, *The O'Neill Years: Unionist Politics 1963–69* (Belfast: Athol Books, 1989).

at Eton and then sent to Europe to improve himself, he worked for a short time in various jobs in the City of London before joining the staff of the Governor of Australia. When war broke out he returned to England and was commissioned in the Irish Guards. At the end of the war, he returned to Ulster, hoping to inherit one of the family's traditional seats and a career in politics. He was selected for the Bannside, North Antrim, constituency at Stormont and was returned unopposed to the Northern Ireland Parliament at a by-election in November 1946.

Like most of the Anglo-Irish, the O'Neills were Church of Ireland rather than Presbyterian and moderate in their religion. In his autobiography O'Neill made it clear that he had no sympathy with parochial unionism. The Orange marches during what his cousin Phelim O'Neill (the Westminster MP for North Antrim) called 'the silly season' meant nothing to him. Being a unionist meant being British, or, more exactly, English, rather than being anti-nationalist and anti-Catholic. His values were those of cosmopolitan, highly educated, and cultured London society. In his Stormont career, and especially during his period as Minister of Finance, O'Neill gradually developed a liberal reforming unionism that hoped the pettier aspects of conflict between the two populations would be removed as Protestants and Catholics worked together to modernize the Northern Ireland economy.

With hindsight the reformist tendencies of O'Neill's government seem weak. There was a new more inclusive language, but the B Special Constabulary (a part-time Protestant militia much detested by nationalists) was not disbanded, nothing was done to reverse the gerrymandering of local government boundaries, and the ambitious development plans were sidetracked by traditional Orange interests. For example, the new university was not created in the obvious place: on the site of the long-successful Magee College, Londonderry. Instead it was put in the Protestant town of Coleraine. The new town development was not sited in the Catholic west of the province but between the largely Protestant towns of Lurgan and Portadown.

O'Neill's failure to change Northern Ireland probably owed more to a lack of power than to a lack of desire. Where he could act without the approval of his more conservative colleagues, he did. He became the first Ulster premier to visit a Catholic school. He was photographed with nuns and priests and met a cardinal. He offered the greatest possible affront to traditional unionism by inviting Sean Lemass, the Prime Minister of the Republic, to visit Stormont. Whether O'Neill was committed to the scale of reform that might have won over the Catholic minority is unknown. What is obvious is that he was sufficiently removed from traditional unionism to be quite happy to ignore its symbols and its sacred history in favour of an instrumental and rational view of politics. Critics use the fact that O'Neill joined the Apprentice Boys of Derry and the Royal Black Preceptory (two Protestant fraternal organizations similar to the Orange Order) to portray him as a closet diehard, but in so doing they miss the bigger point: O'Neill had to join these organizations when he set out on his political career because he was not already a member. Any genuinely orthodox unionist would have been a member since adolescence. O'Neill's suspect views were known to many unionists, and the conservatives did not have to wait for the fruits of O'Neillism, however timid they may have been. They already knew that he was a man who could not be trusted to preserve the Union and to safeguard the social superiority of Protestant culture. His subsequent actions in office, however little they may have done to encourage serious Catholic commitment to the Ulster state, were enough to confirm the conservative Protestant suspicion that O'Neill was another Lundy, prepared to follow the original by opening the gates of unionist Ulster's walls to the disloyal Catholics and the Irish Republic.

COURTS AND CONFRONTATIONS

Paisley's commitment to protesting against both religious apostasy and political compromise ensured that he would eventually be confronted by the power of the state. In 1957 Paisley and Wylie were charged with causing a disturbance in Donaghadee by preaching through a loud hailer. The charges were thrown out by the magistrate. Paisley's second court appearance resulted from him, Wylie, and Harold V. Magowan, the short-lived Free Presbyterian minister of Antrim, heckling Donald Soper in Ballymena. Soper was displeasing to the Free Presbyterians for a number of reasons—his commitment to ecumenism, his left-wing politics—but more than anything it was his rationalism that provoked the ire of conservatives. Soper was firmly in the tradition of those liberals who tried to make the Christian gospel more acceptable to 'modern man' by explaining away the supernatural and miraculous elements. He believed, for example, that Christ had been conceived in the normal way and then sanctified by God rather than being born of a virgin. The Free Presbyterian ministers and their supporters heckled Soper's open-air meeting in Ballymena so persistently that the police had to intervene and the meeting was abandoned. They were later charged with disorderly conduct and fined.

The fines created so much public interest that, on the following Sunday, the Ravenhill Church 'was packed half an hour before the service began and throughout the proceedings men climbed onto the windows to listen and people thronged the open doors and queued out in the street at the back and side of the church'.[7] The audience heard Paisley denounce Soper for his blasphemies, the Methodist Church for not opposing them, and the government for misusing the law to punish legal protest. In concluding he promised to go to prison rather than pay his fine. His choice was blocked by the pro-government *Unionist* newspaper, which paid his fine so that the government would not be embarrassed during an impending general election.

Paisley's third court appearance resulted from a protest against Rome rather than against liberal Protestants. In June 1963 Pope John XXIII, the Pope who had called the second Vatican Council, died. O'Neill sent the following message of condolence to Cardinal Conway, the Vicar Capitular of the archdiocese of Armagh: 'Please accept from the Government of Northern Ireland our sympathy on the great loss which your Church sustained on the death of your Spiritual Leader. He had won wide acclaim throughout the world because of his qualities of kindness and humanity.'[8] The Lord Mayor of Belfast had the Union Jack on the City Hall lowered to half-mast. Paisley

[7] *Northern Whig*, 7 Sep. 1959.

[8] T. O'Neill, *The Autobiography of Terence O'Neill: Prime Minister of Northern Ireland 1963–1969* (London: Hart-Davis, 1972), 50.

reacted quickly by calling a rally in the Ulster Hall and then leading a march to the City Hall to protest 'at the lying eulogies now being paid to the Roman antichrist by non-Romanist Church leaders in defiance of their own historic creeds'.[9] Paisley, James McCarroll (a Protestant Unionist Councillor and an elder of the Free Presbyterian Church), and three other Protestant Action activists were summonsed for holding a march without giving the statutory notice to the police and fined £5. For an insight on the complex intertwining of religious, political, and constitutional elements, it is worth quoting at length from a newspaper account, which, despite some odd punctuation and grammar, gives the gist of Paisley's speech:

He referred to the Bible that had been presented to him by the people of Memel St on July 10 at the opening of their march. He said that 'the powers that be' had presented him with a summons and the Protestant people had presented him with that book and he thought a parallel could be drawn between the two. The rank and file of the Ulster people are still loyal to the core, but he declared 'we have been badly led, both politically and religiously.' He then declared that he and those with him on the platform had pledged themselves to pay no fines and refused to be bound over, 'and we have authorised no one to pay these fines for us. Any Protestant who does so will be a Lundy and a traitor. We are ready to take any penalty Mr Mills desires to place upon us.'

He declared by this determination, Ulster is going to see that Protestantism is neither dead nor buried but is on the march. There was a time, let it ever be remembered, only about 400 years ago, when our fathers were ruled over and tyrannised and when men like Calvin, Knox, Cranmer, Ridley and Latimer broke rather than bend for the Gospel and liberty. Mr Paisley declared that Ulster was in terrible jeopardy. We are losing our heritage and he declared 'I tremble what Ulster will be like when the children in our homes reach the years I have reached. Our gospels and their preachers are being assaulted and insulted. Men who have preached for years in the city streets are now under the intimidation of RUC sergeants and police constables'. Continuing a long and impassioned address, Mr Paisley said 'If the Roman Catholic Church flew the Union Jack at their chapel I would have no objection, and when they wished to pull it down was their business and their property, but the City Hall was our property.[10]

Here then was the world as it appeared to Paisley. Disloyal Catholics did not fly the Union flag. Protestants who should have known better

[9] *Revivalist* (July 1963).   [10] *Northern Whig*, 25 July 1963.

paid tribute to the Antichrist, the spiritual leader of the disloyal Catholics. Orthodox Protestants doing no more than exercising their democratic right to protest against the paying of tribute to the Antichrist were taken to court and fined. And the final but crucial element: this scenario was contrasted with the government's failure to punish rebels. In the *Revivalist* that carried the reports, Paisley added that, while loyal Protestants were charged for a peaceful protest, rebels could attach an open-air evangelistic meeting in Dunloy and get off. The end of the story is an anticlimax. The Free Presbyterians' fines were paid by an anonymous donor.

Although Paisley's fight here was ostensibly with the local council, the real target was O'Neill. In his biography, O'Neill mentions his innovation in sending the government's condolences and explains the Lord Mayor's action as 'responding to the general atmosphere'— an atmosphere that O'Neill was helping to create. When the fines were paid and Paisley's martyrdom postponed, he responded by sending a telegram to O'Neill: 'Congratulations to you, the Minister of Home Affairs, the Crown solicitor, the Police and the Unionist Lord Mayor, on not permitting your own law to take its own course, and on arranging for my fine to be paid. NO SURRENDER!'

Despite fielding candidates against Unionists, Paisley was still willing to work with the UUP if the candidate was acceptable. In the 1964 Westminster election in West Belfast, Paisley and Desmond Boal (whose Stormont constituency was encompassed by the Westminster seat) backed the Unionist candidate, James Kilfedder. Gerry Fitt, later one of the founders of the Social Democratic and Labour Party, was contesting the seat under the Republican Labour label, and a tricolour, the flag of the Irish Republic, was flown in the window of the election office in Divis St. Although the Flags and Emblems Act made such displays illegal, the RUC had often ignored them if they were in nationalist areas. On this occasion, Paisley made sure that the display was not ignored. At a meeting in the Ulster Hall, he insisted that, if the RUC did not go in and remove the offensive flag, then he would do it himself. The RUC moved in and triggered what was described as the worst rioting since 1935.[11]

---

[11] M. Farrell, *Northern Ireland: The Orange State* (London: Pluto, 1980), 234.

In the same year, Protestant Action again fielded candidates for the Belfast Corporation. Paisley, with Ivan Foster and William Beattie, two student ministers of the Free Church, was active in campaigning for them. After all, one of them was Mrs Eileen Paisley, who was standing against the outgoing Lord Mayor to protest against his papist flag-lowering. She was roundly defeated by a ratio of two votes to one, and the only Actionists elected were the two sitting members in the St George's ward, which took in the fiercely loyalist area of Sandy Row.

1966: THE BREAKTHROUGH

As the general direction of O'Neill's policies became clear, opposition grew within the party and on the streets. Unionists who opposed his policies, such as Sir Knox Cunningham, the Westminster MP for South Antrim, criticized O'Neill in the media and in private party meetings. Those people who lacked such access took their protests onto the streets, and it was here that Ian Paisley and his followers earned their public reputation. As the examples already given illustrate, most of the protests concerned what the conservatives saw as government weakness. Loyalists feared that any accommodation with nationalists would just encourage them in their campaign to destroy Northern Ireland. If the government would not act, true loyalists would. As often as not, the government would then move against the loyalists. The loyalists would then interpret the government's actions as being proof that there was one law for the nationalists and another for the loyalists.

A classic clash of symbols occurred in April when the government took no action to prevent the 1916 Easter Rising being commemorated in Belfast. This is O'Neill's account:

Considering that Belfast was not involved in that event fifty years previously one might have hoped that those so minded to would have contented themselves with attending the ceremony in Dublin, less than a hundred miles away. But all indications were that there was no prominent Catholic prepared to give a lead in the interests of peace. I decided to form a committee consisting of all former Ministers of Home Affairs under my chairmanship and between us we survived the celebrations.[12]

O'Neill survived but as he goes on to record: 'The Catholic streets in Belfast became and remained a forest of Irish Republic flags for the duration of the celebrations.'[13] Paisley responded with a march of over 6,000 loyalists to the City Hall Cenotaph, where Councillor McCarroll laid a wreath 'in memory of the members of the UVF, RUC and other civilian population [*sic*] who died in defence of the Ulster Constitution at the hands of Rebel Forces during and since the 1916 rising'.[14] Although there was as yet no sign that the Irish Republican Army (IRA) was capable of mounting the sort of offensive that followed four years later, Paisley had no doubt where O'Neill's reforming policy would lead: 'Surely he does not seriously think that appeasement will stop the IRA attacks or the cries of discrimination. Or is he secretly selling us to the South?'[15] Despite the strength of this feeling, Paisley was not unmindful of his public responsibility. After the successful Easter Rising counter-demonstration in Belfast, he cancelled planned demonstrations in Newry and Armagh that would have been considerably more provocative.

Symbols were again at issue in the controversy in 1966 over the name for the new bridge over the Lagan in Belfast. Against the wishes of those who wanted a memorial to Sir Edward Carson, the city council planned to call it the 'Queen Elizabeth Bridge'. So angry was Paisley at the affront to Carson's memory that he persuaded Carson's son to contest the forthcoming Westminster elections and promised three other anti-O'Neill candidates. What would have been a major publicity coup was abandoned when Paisley realised that he did not have the constituency organizations that such a push needed.

As is so often the case in Paisley's career, the crucial step to remedy this weakness was taken by someone else. Noel Doherty, a committed loyalist and a printer to trade, had been a member of Paisley's Raven-hill congregation since 1956. He became a member of Protestant Action and founded Paisley's printing enterprise. In 1966 he suggested the formation of the Ulster Constitution Defence Committee (UCDC)—a body of twelve loyalists chaired by Paisley and quickly

[12] O'Neill, *Autobiography*, 78–9.   [13] Ibid. 79.
[14] *Protestant Telegraph*, 5 May 1966.   [15] Ibid., 18 June 1966.

nicknamed 'the twelve disciples'. Linked to the UCDC would be the Ulster Protestant Volunteers (UPV), which would provide a province-wide structure for rank-and-file supporters. As though anticipating the criticism that it was encouraging vigilante violence, the UPV stressed its commitment to legality. The constitution provided that 'any member associated with, or giving support to, any subversive or lawless activities whatsoever shall he expelled from the body. The chairman of the UCDC has vested in him full authority to act in such cases.'[16] However good the intentions, some Volunteers did not share the chairman's stated views. James Murdoch, a Free Presbyterian and a member of the Loughgall UPV, introduced Noel Doherty to James Marshall, a quarryman who said he could provide explosives, and Doherty arranged a meeting between Marshall and Billy Mitchell, a member of the paramilitary Ulster Volunteer Force, a small organization of Shankill Road loyalists that committed a number of murders in May and June 1966 and was banned by O'Neill.[17]

Although Paisley drove Doherty to his first meeting with Murdoch and Marshall, there is no evidence that he was himself involved in the discussions. The strongest link between the UPV and illegal acts of violence came with a series of bombings in 1969, which, ironically, the *Protestant Telegraph* was quick to blame first on the IRA and then on the Eire government. In fact, they had been organized by members of Paisley's own UPV. The explosions in March and April of 1969 at an electricity substation in Castlereagh and at the Silent Valley reservoir in the Mournes were followed by an explosion at an electricity substation over the border in County Donegal. In this case, the device seems to have exploded early, and Thomas McDowell, a member of the Kilkeel Free Presbyterian Church and the South Down UPV, was fatally wounded.

In the light of what was to follow, the UPV damage to public utilities seems trivial, and Mitchell, who really was a terrorist, was scornful of Doherty's military wing: 'All they had was a few sticks of weeping gelly [gelignite] an auld farmer would use to blow up tree stumps.' But the bombings were profoundly shocking.

[16] D. Boulton, *The UVF 1966–73: An Anatomy of Loyalist Rebellion* (Dublin: Torc Books, 1973), 28.

[17] For a detailed history of the UVF, see S. Bruce, *The Red Hand: Loyalist Paramilitaries in Northern Ireland* (Oxford: Oxford University Press, 1992).

On 6 June, this time wearing his church hat, Paisley clashed with the police when he led members of his church to picket the Irish Presbyterians' General Assembly. In previous years, the Free Presbyterians had gathered outside the Assembly Hall for their picket, which was almost an annual event. This time, Paisley filed notice with the RUC that he intended to lead a march from his church at the bottom of the Ravenhill Road, across the Albert Bridge, and through Cromac Square to the city centre and the Assembly Hall. Accounts of why this route was chosen vary. One marcher thought that it had been deliberately provocative; others said it was simply the most direct route. Most thought nothing of it, and clearly RUC officers did not anticipate any trouble.[18] They did not suggest rerouting the parade. The fact that many of the Free Presbyterian marchers were women and children suggests that they were equally sanguine.

A mob of young Catholics, armed with a good supply of bricks and metal objects to hurl at the marchers, was waiting at Cromac Square. The police called for reinforcements and struggled to keep the rioters back. In view of the subsequent controversy, it is important to note that the Free Presbyterians did not retaliate but maintained their composure under a considerable volley of missiles. As film footage of the riot clearly showed, the rioting was exclusively Catholic against RUC.

When the Free Presbyterians arrived at the Assembly Hall in Fisherwick Place, the police threw a rope across the road and stopped the march. Paisley about-faced and led the parade around the block so that it now came upon Fisherwick Place from the west. In his evidence at the subsequent trial, Paisley maintained that he did this to keep the parade moving and hence diffuse tension. The Paisleyites now flanked both sides of a rope-way stretched between the Assembly Hall and the other Presbyterian building across the street. When the Moderator and the other dignitaries came out of the Assembly to cross the road, they found themselves flanked by Free Presbyterians shouting anti-ecumenical slogans and waving placards. In retrospect,

---

[18] On 22 June the Inspector General of the RUC wrote a lengthy letter, marked 'Secret', to the Minister of Home Affairs (Public Records Office, Northern Ireland, CAB 8A/405/3) in which he detailed the threat to public order of Paisley's campaign. That his officers had not anticipated any trouble with the march through Cromac Square suggests that the later report involved some retrospective exaggeration.

the events of that afternoon seem trivial, but the combination of stone-throwing rioters and Paisleyites abusing the dignitaries of the Irish Presbyterian Church and the Governor of Northern Ireland and his wife triggered a considerable wave of anti-Paisley feeling. There was considerable confusion in the media and Stormont about just who did what. The *Newsletter* ran the story under the headlines:

BATONS IN CITY STREET BATTLE: EIGHT ARRESTED AFTER CLASHES.

PAISLEY MARCH MEETS MOB VIOLENCE.

GOVERNOR FACES STORM OF ABUSE.

Already in this presentation there is ambiguity. We have 'clashes' and 'mob violence' but apart from the Governor we have only one named agent: 'Paisley'. There is no specific mention of Catholics as rioters. By the time Terence O'Neill returned from London to face press questioning on what he intended to do to quell the violence, there was a general notion abroad that it was the Paisleyites who had been violent.[19]

The process of attributing the blame to Paisley continued the next day with a debate in Stormont in which a Labour member said: 'The attack last evening was mainly directed against the Presbyterian Church. The parade was making for the Assembly Hall. I am quite sure that the Moderator and his colleagues will be able to withstand any theological attack directed by the Rev. Ian Paisley, but when it approaches physical violence it is another matter.'[20] Here again the images are being confused. A wide variety of things could be construed as 'approaching' violence, but to use that expression while condemning the events of the previous day and to do so in a critique of Paisley while failing to mention the Cromac Square rioters is to exaggerate. News film of the General Assembly disturbance shows

[19] This fundamental distortion has become part of the historical record. L. De Paor (*Divided Ulster* (Harmondsworth: Penguin, 1971), 154) says that Paisley and his supporters went to the General Assembly 'to attack and insult Lord Erskine...' and that 'a brief but violent riot occurred on the way'. He thus distorts the original purpose of the march and, by failing to mention that the Paisleyites were the passive victims of the riot, he leaves it open for the uninformed reader to suppose that the Paisleyites were involved in the rioting. They were not. The mistaken view is now so firmly entrenched that the anonymous author of a scholarly article submitted to the journal *Irish Political Studies* in 2005 could refer to 'clashes between Paisleyite followers and Catholic residents'.

[20] Stormont, *Hansard*, House of Commons, 7 June 1966, p. 26.

much shouting and placard waving but nothing that comes near the sort of heckling and barracking to which present-day government ministers are regularly subjected.

When O'Neill returned from a meeting with Harold Wilson in London, he reacted in a manner guaranteed to confirm the Free Presbyterian claims that O'Neill's policies were designed to achieve in the political sphere what the ecumenical movement was trying to do in interdenominational cooperation. He delivered a strong attack on Paisley and sent his Minister for Home Affairs to the General Assembly to apologize for the demonstration and to promise that 'the government will take all possible steps to prevent a recurrence of such indignities to the Head of this great church and his distinguished guests'.[21]

On 15 June the House of Commons in Stormont met to debate a motion urging action to preserve law and order. After other speeches condemning Paisley, O'Neill rose and delivered a long statement in which he made it clear that he regarded the defeat of Ian Paisley as a central part of his reformist platform. Paisleyism and republicanism were allies; both movements were bent on destroying Northern Ireland by stirring up community strife. He was able to marshal the support of the Grand Master of the Orange Order, who had previously condemned Paisley's extremism. And he repeated the concern that underpinned his whole political philosophy: the need to placate the sovereign government at Westminster.

Do we want or can we afford to alienate our British friends? Do the mindless individuals who use unspeakable language in the streets and hurl vile insults at Her Majesty's representatives and other dignitaries ever pause to reflect that our standard of living, our Welfare State services...our economic health all depend on our links with Great Britain?[22]

Only one member of the House was at all sympathetic to Paisley. In a brilliant and witty (though unappreciated) speech, Desmond Boal QC did his best to clarify the events of 6 June. He reminded the House that the police had been given forty-eight hours' notification of the proposed route: 'Honourable members on this side of the

---

[21] Northern Ireland Information Service Press release.
[22] Stormont, *Hansard*, House of Commons, 15 June 1966, p. 309.

House who in this respect are charging him [Paisley] with gross civic and social irresponsibility must also charge the police with exactly the same thing.' The critics had argued that the Paisleyites had provoked the Catholic population of the Markets area with the anti-Romanist slogans on their placards. Boal reminded the House that the parade did not pass through any Catholic areas:

If their argument is worth tuppence it means that the people in the Markets area must have been aware of the inscriptions ... before they in fact took the steps they did. It is perfectly clear that long before the procession came into sight, long before the procession had formed, these people in the Markets in their desire to be offended had come down from the side streets and had taken great trouble to be offended, and not only were prepared to be offended but were prepared to throw missiles, stones and other weapons ... There is not a suggestion that one of these missiles were returned; there is not one suggestion which can be made by anybody, no matter how evilly disposed he is to the organiser of the procession or to the purpose of the procession, that any violence was offered by a member of that procession.[23]

For his pains, Boal was fired from his post as counsel to the Attorney-General.

Whether or not the procession from the Ravenhill Church and the barracking of the Presbyterian Church Assembly had been designed to constitute a direct challenge to the government, things were moving rapidly in that direction. Paisley, Wylie, and Ivan Foster, with two others (a Protestant Action councillor and a staunch old loyalist lady from the Shankill Road) were charged with public-order offences. A large crowd marched to the Belfast Magistrates' Court with the accused, who were all found guilty. After some discussion, they decided to go to jail rather than pay their fines. As had happened previously, the fines were paid anonymously, but the magistrates had made it impossible for the situation to be thus defused by also binding them over to keep the peace. They refused to sign the bond, arguing that to do so would prevent them from making *any* public protests. On 20 July the trio entered Crumlin Road prison.

Someone who had worked closely with Paisley in the 1950s claimed that he had once joked that the only way they would get anywhere

---

[23] Stormont, *Hansard*, House of Commons, 7 June 1966, pp. 359–62.

would be if they were sent to prison for the Protestant cause. Whether or not the story is true, there is no doubt that the imprisonment was a major breakthrough for both religious and political Paisleyism. Different sorts of supporters reacted in different ways. Disaffected youth took to the streets:

There was a serious riot with Loyalists fighting the RUC outside the prison on 22 July. The next day the RUC tried to block a 4,000 strong Paisleyite protest march from the centre of Belfast, but the marchers broke through and rampaged through the centre of the city breaking shop windows, stoning the Catholic-owned International Hotel and going on to Sandy Row where they tried to burn down a bookie's shop which employed Catholics. That night there was savage rioting outside the jail with repeated baton-charges by the RUC. Only heavy rain stopped it. The government banned all meetings and parades in Belfast for three months, and gave the RUC power to break up any gathering of three or more people.[24]

Mrs Paisley brought a message from her husband in prison, condemning the rioting and asking for it to stop: 'The people who have been fighting the police have no connection with our church. The vast majority of the rioters are just hooligans.'[25]

The Free Presbyterian ministers remaining at liberty were at first demoralized and confused. Apparently innocent of the opportunity that had been presented to them, they met in the Ravenhill Church and talked about what they should do and even hesitated about talking to the journalists waiting outside. Beattie argued that they should go out and present their case.

Although O'Neill presented the case as a matter of law and order, the Free Presbyterians saw it as the impious state suppressing Bible Protestantism. And, once they started to present their case, they found a receptive audience. Here we can see the value of Paisley's province-wide preaching during his wilderness years. William McCrea's family were Presbyterian farmers from Tyrone who had heard Paisley preach in a tent near Dungannon:

We couldn't get seats in the main tent. It was so crowded they had to unlace the side-flaps of the enormous tent and raise them up so that people could sit outside the tent, down the sides, and though we couldn't see him very

---

[24] Farrell, *Northern Ireland*, 235.   [25] *Sun*, 25 July 1966.

well, we heard him. The word of God was fully preached that afternoon, and many, many souls were saved. It was a wonderful meeting.

When, after that, we used to hear controversy about Dr Paisley and later heard about his imprisonment in 1966, because of that afternoon when we heard the gospel preached with power and conviction, we found ourselves tending to take his side in the controversy.[26]

There was an interesting difference in the political involvement of different generations of Free Presbyterian ministers. Beattie and Foster were fully involved with Paisley and Wylie in their protests and in electioneering. The slightly older students—John Douglas, Alan Cairns, and Bert Cooke—were less often involved in public protests. On this occasion Cooke led a delegation to see O'Neill, who had responded to pressure from a Unionist MP, Austin Ardill, to meet the men. He refused to consider what he regarded as interfering in the judicial process and what they saw as moderating his policy of harassing the Free Church. The campaign was taken to the country. The remaining ministers and elders found themselves being invited to address meetings all over the province to explain the imprisonment. An elder in the Rasharkin church recognized this was a period of unprecedented interest in the Free Church.

At that time that was a sad day for many people, the day he went to prison. I know people who were in tears as a result of Dr Paisley going into jail, but in the long term God answered prayer. If he hadn't been put into the jail, I don't know what would have been the result today but... before he even had his jail sentence served, applications were coming in from town and countryside for churches to be opened up, with the result that in that short space of time about 1966, our church more than doubled in membership and in churches. I think it was very important that he served a term in jail... I look on it as a work of God.

Police harassment did not stop with the imprisonment. John Douglas found himself charged with breach of the peace as a result of remarks he was said to have made at a meeting in Rathfriland; two plain-clothes officers were in the audience with a concealed tape-recorder. Douglas was eventually acquitted, but his initial conviction and the methods of the police—who presented a transcript of his

[26] W. McCrea and D. Porter, *In His Pathway: The Story of Rev. William McCrea* (London: Marshall, Morgan and Scott, 1980), 26.

speech, which was only one-third the length of another tape-recording played to the court—led many Free Presbyterians and sympathizers to believe that the state was determined to crush them.

Paisley was always quick to see publicity opportunities, and every Sunday during his imprisonment the huge congregation gathered in the Ulster Hall heard Mrs Paisley or one of the ministers read out a message from their leader. He was also always sure of divine approval: during his imprisonment he wrote a commentary on Paul's Letter to the Romans, the book that the apostle Paul had himself written in prison.

CHURCH GROWTH

Although initially stunned by Paisley's removal, the young ministers soon found themselves in demand. For the church the main consequences of 1966 was religious revival. In the period from the Church's foundation in 1951 to 1966 only thirteen congregations had been formed and one of those had lapsed. In the eighteen months that followed July 1966, twelve more congregations were added. A growth rate of less than one a year became one every six weeks. On his release, Ivan Foster went to Fermanagh and started meetings in Lisbellaw near Enniskillen. John Wylie held a mission in Londonderry, and a congregation was founded there. Other works were started in Moneyslane, Tandragee, Dungannon, Lurgan, Portadown, Kilkeel, Ballynahinch, Lisburn, and Magherafelt.

In most places, there was considerable opposition to the FPCU from local unionist elites. But such opposition backfired by confirming the very claims that the Free Presbyterians made about the great apostasy and the undemocratic nature of O'Neill's regime. When Beattie tried to hold evangelistic meetings in Hillsborough, the Church of Ireland gentry who controlled the parish council used planning laws to prevent him getting a site. A land developer, who was not an evangelical but who sympathized with claims to freedom of speech and assembly, offered him land in Lisburn. A site was also secured just outside Hillsborough, and thus two more congregations were added to the growing Church by the opposition to one.

This period of growth confirmed the patterns of the earlier period in the support for Paisleyism. Just as Protestant Action had been supported by the almost completely separate constituencies of rural evangelicals and urban loyalists, so the same divisions can be seen in the reaction to the prison sentence. Paisley's standing among the secular urban working class was considerably enhanced, and that support was later to be translated into votes. At the same time, rural conservative Protestants, especially those from the Irish Presbyterian Church, were attracted to the religious movement.

To return to an observation about church growth made at the end of the second chapter, demand is not the only factor in church growth; we must also consider supply, and the Free Church was gradually coming into the position where it could service the new demand. Had the imprisonment come six years earlier, the church would have lacked the personnel to capitalize on the interest it provoked. By 1966 it had a core of Ulstermen who had been converted under Ian Paisley's preaching and who had grown up with his politicized evangelism. They had trained together, they were strongly linked by kinship ties—Beattie, Douglas, and Foster were all in-laws and Menary had married into the large McAuley family, which had founded the Cabra congregation—and they shared a strong sense of solidarity. They were ready to turn the interest that had been generated by the political protests into saved souls.

CONCLUSION

Chronology is important for understanding the religious core of Paisleyism: the movement pre-dated the Civil Rights movement. The FPCU did not grow as a result of Protestants reacting to evidence of increased Catholic nationalist assertiveness. The political crisis that created fertile conditions for the growth of the Church was the earlier struggle between O'Neill's secular and reformist Unionism and Paisley's traditionalist stand.

Paisley's religious appeal was based on the claim that orthodox Protestant beliefs were being downgraded and that liberal Protestants were actively seeking greater harmony with other apostate denominations, in particular the old enemy of Rome. There was a conspiracy to sell out true Bible-believing Protestantism. Even without O'Neill, such claims would have had a better hearing in the 1960s than they had had in the 1920s, when Hunter's schism from the Presbyterian Church failed to attract a following. The ecumenical movement had become better established and, although it would be an exaggeration to say that the major Protestant denominations were heavily committed to a 'Romeward tend', many church leaders were seeking better relations with the Catholic Church. By 1966 it had become common for Protestant church leaders to visit the Pope and to voice ecumenical sentiments. Even though Rome was giving little in return in terms of moderating its claims to be the only true Christian church, faint liberal breezes had been blowing through the Vatican since the Second Vatican Council. Furthermore, some liberals had pushed their rationalizing of the Christian faith to the extreme point where it was fashionable to argue that 'God is dead' and that the true Christian should abandon the churches. Although such heresies were far more common in England than in Ulster, Ulster Protestants knew of these postures and could see that their own denominations were in formal contact with churches that did not move to sack ministers and theologians who had obviously given up the traditional beliefs affirmed at their ordinations. All this meant that Paisley's criticisms of apostasy were being uttered in a considerably more apostate era than the times in which Hunter had failed to promote his schism.

But what really enhanced the receptivity of the market was O'Neillism. It is always possible to compartmentalize one's life; to separate religion and work and politics so that different criteria are used for decision-making in each compartment. The traditional nature of religion in Ulster meant that such compartments were less watertight than they would be in, for example, America, but the deeply divided structure of Ulster society, economy, and polity meant that changes in one sphere would have repercussions in the others. In visiting a Catholic school, O'Neill was doing no more than acknowledging that Catholics formed a sizeable part of the population of Northern Ireland and that Catholic schools were largely supported from public funds, which his government administered. In such a view, 'Catholic' was simply a term that described part of the population. But, for Ulster's evangelical Protestants, Catholic schools were places in which soul-damning heresies were transmitted, and to visit them was to endorse Catholicism as a permitted variant of Christianity. And then all the other elements in the complex that bound religion and politics together would pour down. Catholics were rebels who wanted to destroy Northern Ireland and undermine the Protestant culture of the rest of the United Kingdom and the only thing that maintained civil liberties was adherence to the Protestant faith. Ulster owed its prosperity, such as it was, not to the accident of a good deep-water harbour and its trade links with Glasgow and Liverpool, but to its sabbatarianism, temperance, and evangelical beliefs. If the Romanists did not destroy Ulster by forcing its people into a united papist Ireland, then God would surely destroy it as a punishment for departing from his standards.

What O'Neillism did for Paisley was to raise in a concrete way the possibility of change from being a Protestant society and culture (constantly threatened by the old enemy within and without) to being a secular modern society in which religious affiliation would be of little consequence. Dilution was always a threat to the more ideologically committed evangelicals, but O'Neill's reforms, tepid and half-hearted as they were, raised the spectre to a power and status from which it threatened a far greater number of rural Presbyterians who saw the proposed changes as proof that Paisley had been right all along. In Moneyslane and Tandragee and the farming areas around Hillsborough, the Presbyterians rallied to 'the old paths in perilous times'.

However, the events of 1966 were not entirely positive for the FPCU. From his first battles with the congregation that called him to the Ravenhill Road, Paisley had always been a divisive preacher. His deliberate courting of controversy was intended to force Protestants to choose between the dead conformity of the major denominations and the pure saving word that he offered. The publicity of 1966 brought hundreds into his tent, but it alienated thousands more. And it was not just liberal Protestants who objected to his aggression and rudeness, and who resented his libels against their churches. Joining Paisley's crusade was only one of three options available to the born-again evangelical who shared much of his critique of the state of the world. One alternative was to remain within the Presbyterian Church or the Church of Ireland, continue to represent evangelical beliefs, but reject Paisley's separatism and antagonistic attitude to all who could not agree in every detail with one's own views. Such people tended to stay in the Orange Order (when Paisley left it) and to remain in the Ulster Unionist Party (when Paisley set up his alternative). While Paisley's success strengthened the hand of such people within their own institutions, his character and behaviour ensured that they despised him. The other alternative was the pietistic retreat from the world associated with the Brethren and the gospel halls. It was possible to accept everything Paisley had to say about the apostasy of the churches, the unreliability of the UUP, and the moral degeneration of the world at large, and to conclude that the only option for the saint was to have as little as possible to do with the public world. Over the next two decades, the fastest growing church in Belfast was not Paisley's Martyrs' Memorial but the Church of God Pentecostal congregation on the Whitewell Road led by Pastor James McConnell.

Paisley's success polarized Northern Ireland's Protestants but it did so, not by strengthening liberalism as an alternative, but by forcing those who had much in common with Paisley to decide how they felt about him and his movement.

4

Coming to Power

INTRODUCTION

In 1969 the North Antrim Bannside constituency of the Stormont parliament provided the first rung on Ian Paisley's political ladder. In 2004 it hosted the nearest thing to a Roman 'triumph' that Ulster politics can provide: at a civic reception in the grandest hotel in Bannside, before an audience of his MPs, representatives from councils across the province, clergy colleagues, and his extensive family, Paisley was made a Freeman of the Borough of Ballymena. The following year he was appointed to the Privy Council—the largely ritual but highly select body of politicians that advises the Queen.

This chapter describes the three stages of Paisley's journey from the margins to the centre of Ulster politics: setting out his stall as one voice among a clamour of right-wing dissidents; taking the lead of conservative unionism; and finally triumphing over the Ulster Unionist Party when it gambled on the Belfast Agreement and lost.

THE UNIONIST PARTY IN TROUBLE

By 1966 Prime Minister Terence O'Neill was in an impossible situation. His minor reforms (or, as a perceptive journalist friend described it, his 'government by gesture') served only further to politicize Catholics, without making them any more committed to the Northern Ireland state.[1] He also misjudged the unionist electorate.

---

[1] T. E. Utley, *The Lessons of Ulster* (London: Dent, 1975), 41.

With patrician disdain, O'Neill dismissed Paisley's support as 'a fascist organisation masquerading under the cloak of religion...deluding a lot of sincere people...hell-bent on provoking religious strife in Northern Ireland'[2] and he failed to grasp the extent of hostility within his own party. While attempting to respond to the Civil Rights movement and to moderate the pressure from the Westminster government led by the Labour Prime Minister Harold Wilson, O'Neill was being threatened within the Unionist camp. Although the first revolt was crushed, Desmond Boal could still raise thirteen Unionist backbenchers' signatures for his removal, and only three years after handing over power, the aged patrician Lord Brookeborough was leading a whispering campaign against O'Neill.

There is no need to detail the chaos of the last years of O'Neill's administration. An example will show the precariousness of his position. In November of 1968 he responded to the demands of Derry Catholics by proposing that the Londonderry City Corporation (which since partition had been gerrymandered so that the Protestant minority retained control) be replaced by a nominated body, that housing allocation be removed from political control to be administered on a fair 'points for needs' system, and that the Special Powers Act be re-examined. By then, such gestures were not enough to placate the Civil Rights supporters, who decided to go ahead with a proposed march through Armagh City on 30 November. Predictably Paisley announced a counter-demonstration. William Craig, the Minister for Home Affairs, refused to ban the Paisley demonstration, and, although there was a considerable police presence, nothing was done to stop the Paisleyites blocking the Civil Rights march. Had Craig banned the march, he would have infuriated the Civil Rights people. Had he banned the counter-demonstration, he would have provoked the unionist opposition. And so what credit O'Neill might have acquired for his reform package was instantly lost by what Catholics saw as a refusal to confront the loyalist mobs who really ran Northern Ireland.

O'Neill went on television to defend his programme and concluded with a clever pitch for the supposed moderate centre to make its presence felt:

[2] Stormont, *Hansard,* House of Commons, 15 June 1966, p. 338.

And now a further word to you all. What kind of Ulster do you want? A happy and respected province, in good standing with the rest of the United Kingdom? Or a place continually torn apart by riots and demonstrations, and regarded by the rest of Britain as a political outcast? As always in a democracy, the choice is yours. Please weigh what is at stake and make your voice heard in whatever way you think best, so that we know the views, not of the few, but of the many. For this is truly a time of decision and in your silence all that we have built up could be lost.[3]

For a month or so it looked as if his pleas had succeeded in defusing the tension, but soon Catholic leaders were arguing that nothing was really changing. In January 1968 Michael Farrell and the other militant activists of People's Democracy started a march from Belfast to Londonderry, modelled on the famous American Civil Rights march from Selma to Montgomery. Along the route the marchers were harassed by the RUC and by bands of loyalists, many of whom were off-duty policemen or Special constables. The final bloody confrontation at Burntollet Bridge took place before the eyes of the world's media and united moderate and militant Catholic opinion in a hardening rejection of Unionist rule. To the British government, Burntollet was further evidence of the need to force reform on Stormont. Under Westminster pressure, O'Neill set up the Cameron Commission to investigate the causes of the disturbances.

Unionism was collapsing. Craig had already been sacked for criticizing O'Neill's televised plea to the province. Now Brian Faulkner resigned from the cabinet over O'Neill's capitulation to British pressure. Paisley was back in prison, this time for his part in the Armagh demonstrations, but that did not stop him characterizing the Cameron Commission as a betrayal of the Ulster people to the rebels. Under his direction, the Ulster Constitution Defence Committee maintained its traditional line that O'Neill was not responding to the legitimate demands of a disadvantaged section of the population, but giving in to the demands of the rebels who would never be satisfied with anything less than the destruction of Northern Ireland. Instead of worrying about how to make the RUC acceptable to the minority, O'Neill should have been using the legitimate power of the state to

[3] D. Gordon, *The O'Neill Years: Unionist Politics 1963–1969* (Belfast: Atholl Books, 1989), 135–6.

crush an insurrection. In January 1969 O'Neill took the only course left open to him: he tried to appeal over the heads of his party colleagues to the electorate.

Despite the periodic intervention of maverick candidates, all previous elections had possessed a ritual quality. The outcome was determined in advance by religious demography: almost all Protestants voted for the Ulster Unionist Party and Catholics either voted for nationalists or abstained. The attempts by O'Neill to change the basic grammar of Ulster politics had left both sides in disarray. On the Catholic side, older nationalist members were opposed by a younger generation raised in the Civil Rights movement. Paisley stood against O'Neill in Bannside—the first time O'Neill had been challenged since he inherited the family seat in 1946. Other 'Protestant Unionist' candidates stood against liberal O'Neillites. But there was also a conservative revolt within the UUP, with some branches nominating people who were determined to unseat their leader. When the votes were counted, O'Neill found that his search for a mandate had backfired. He had a minority government and the support of only eleven of his backbenchers. Violence on the streets escalated. Civil Rights marchers continued their demonstrations, and militant loyalists responded with counter-marches and with attacks on nationalist areas. A small group of Paisley's Ulster Protestant Volunteers raised the odds by damaging a public reservoir with a small explosion, which they hoped would be taken as evidence of growing IRA power. The nationalist Bogside in Derry rioted. On 28 April Terence O'Neill resigned and his cousin Major James Chichester-Clark was elected as leader of the Unionist Parliamentary Party and hence Prime Minister.

The by-election opportunity thus created was augmented by a further resignation. The importance of the two contests was well appreciated by the UUP, which sent the Prime Minister and a series of cabinet ministers to Bannside to denounce Paisley. In the event their prestige was not enough to hold the seat. Paisley added another 1,650 votes to his score against O'Neill and achieved the platform he needed. A reporter described the scene at the count:

In the midst of a victory celebration in Ballymena, Mr Paisley said: 'This is the dawn of a new day for Ulster. Goodnight Chichester-Clark.' He was given a rapturous reception by a flag-waving crowed of 5,000 when the result was announced shortly after midnight. Speeches, relayed to the milling crowd outside Ballymena Town Hall, where the count was being held, were drowned by deafening cheers, and as the triumphant Free Presbyterian church leader faced a barrage of questions before TV cameras, an accordion band struck up. 'The Sash'. Wearing his now familiar Russian-style hat and white Ulster Protestant Volunteer sash, Mr Paisley was carried shoulder-high through the town hall's main entrance to 'meet his people'. Despite the late hour the town put on the appearance of a miniature 'Twelfth' as he and his wife Eileen and brother-in-law and election agent, the Rev. James Beggs, were paraded on the back of a Land Rover to the Waveney Road, where Mr Paisley was greeted by his 78-year-old father, the Rev. Kyle Paisley, who was unable to attend the count.[4]

Paisley's victory was indeed a blow to the credibility of Chichester-Clark, who might have saved face by not becoming personally in-volved, but the election of William Beattie in South Antrim was probably more damaging. Beattie was far less well known, was standing in a more cosmopolitan constituency, and was competing against a man who had previously been a cabinet minister. There was no story that could be told about his charisma or name recognition. He had won because unionists did not like the way the country was headed.

Paisley was developing a distinctive political position, which stressed the religious element in the conflict between nationalist and loyalist. While his loyalism gave him urban working-class sup-port, it was the rural Protestants who were most attracted by his evangelical credentials. This rural support was again crucial in June, just two months after the Stormont by-elections, when a Westmin-ster general election allowed Paisley to test his wider appeal. He contested the North Antrim constituency (which took in his Bann-side Stormont area) and defeated Henry Clarke, the sitting MP, who was a liberal and a member of the O'Neill clan.

THE LAST STORMONT

In 1970 and early 1971 the Ulster crisis deepened as the government stumbled on, alternating promises of reform with repression.

[4] *Belfast Telegraph*, 17 Apr. 1970.

Nationalists, having come so far in undermining the Orange state, were not going to be easily satisfied. Urban working-class Protestants were not about to relinquish fifty years of social and political superiority without a fight. Rioting became common and the British army had to be called in to replace the overstretched Royal Ulster Constabulary (RUC). In an attempt to make the RUC more acceptable to the minority, its leadership structure was radically altered, outsiders were brought in to train and lead it, and the B Special Constabulary was disbanded to be replaced by the Ulster Defence Regiment (UDR) under army command. But any popular appeal to Catholics that such moves might have had was undermined by repressive acts such as the introduction of internment—imprisonment without trial—for suspected nationalist terrorists; it was some time before loyalists were interned. Rioting became more severe and began to claims lives. Catholics and Protestants in marginal areas were burnt out of their homes and forced to move into their respective ghettos. In March 1971 Chichester-Clark resigned to be replaced by Brian Faulkner.

For all his previous reputation as a hardliner, Faulkner attempted to broaden his political base with some astute appointments such as that of David Bleakley, ex-Chairman of the Northern Ireland Labour Party (NILP), as Minister for Community Relations. He unveiled plans for involving the minority in administration through the creation of three policy-making committees to review government performance in industrial, social, and environmental services. With the already established public accounts committee, this would have given four such bodies, each with a salaried chairman, and the Catholics were to be given two of the chairs, with the committees being made up to reflect parliamentary seats. This plan was given a cautious welcome by the Social Democratic and Labour Party (SDLP), led by Gerry Fitt, John Hume, and Paddy Devlin, which had taken over the leadership of 'constitutional' nationalist opinion. However, as Harkness puts it:

It was undone immediately by passions once more loosened on the streets of Derry. After sporadic violence there from the beginning of the month full scale rioting erupted on 8 July and in the early hours of 9th two men were shot dead by the army. One died of loss of blood on his way to hospital in Co. Donegal; the other where he stood in the street. Local opinion denied their involvement in terrorism, and John Hume, local SDLP MP, persuaded his party to demand an official enquiry, failing which it would withdraw from Stormont and set up an alternative assembly... No official enquiry could be offered: the SDLP withdrew from Stormont on 16 July; and the IRA campaign increased in ferocity.[5]

Until the middle of 1970, the IRA had played little part in the conflict. It had been largely dormant since the late 1950s, and during the communal violence of the summer of 1969 many embittered nationalists had voiced their anger at its lack of action by saying that IRA stood for 'I Ran Away'. At the annual Sinn Fein conference in Dublin in January 1970 a majority broke away to form the Provisional IRA, and in the following years planned and executed an increasing number of shootings and bombings. Internment, introduced in August, was intended to remove leaders of the IRA from circulation, but the information on which arrests were made was often out of date or just plain mistaken. The republican movement flourished.

Loyalist attitudes were hardened by the new IRA campaign and by rumblings from the South. Three leading Fianna Fail politicians who were open and vocal in their support for the IRA were charged with illegally importing arms and ammunition for use in the North and dismissed from the cabinet. That one of the three was Charles Haughey explains why unionists found his later involvement in northern affairs, when he became Prime Minister, particularly hard to stomach. At the height of the Troubles in 1970, the Irish Army brought field hospitals to the border ready for refugees from Ulster. Although the open civil war that so many feared did not then break out, something more important happened.

The Civil Rights movement had apparently begun as the vehicle for Catholic claims to full and equal participation in the Northern Ireland state. In its early phase it reflected broad Catholic opinion, which wanted acceptance as full citizens of the North and had some liberal unionist support. The inability of O'Neill and Chichester-Clark to satisfy those demands without destabilizing the state had created the very condition that people such as Paisley had argued had obtained from the first: the return of 1916 'physical force' republicanism. The aim was now not equality within the Northern Ireland state but its

---

[5] D. Harkness, *Northern Ireland since 1920* (Dublin: Helicon Books, 1983), 168.

destruction. As the minority population became more vociferous in its demands and more openly nationalist and republican, the stature of Paisley in the loyalist camp proportionately increased because Protestants looked back at what he had been saying in the early days of O'Neill's reign and saw that 'he had been right all along'.

Increased polarization boosted Paisley's standing, but he was still a marginal figure. Most conservative unionists looked for leadership not to the Protestant Unionists but to right-wingers within the Ulster Unionist Party. One such was Harry West, who led the West Ulster Unionist Council (UUC)—a grouping of conservatives west of the Bann. Another was Bill Craig, who, despite his sacking, had remained in the party. With considerable support from the paramilitary Ulster Defence Association (UDA) Craig toured the province building support for what, when it was launched in 1972, was called the Vanguard Movement. He was supported by Martin Smyth, a Presbyterian minister who was the leader of the Belfast Orangemen and about to become Grand Master of the Order, and Billy Hull, the founder of the large Loyalist Association of Workers.[6]

Many Paisleyites insist they would never have become involved in politics if the Ulster Unionist Party had remained sound. This would certainly be the case for someone like Gordon Cooke, the Free Presbyterian minister of Rasharkin, who found himself chairman of the 'parent' branch of the officially constituted Protestant Unionist Party largely because he was a strong supporter of Paisley's political line and a leading evangelical in the Bannside area at the time when Paisley decided to stand against O'Neill. He didn't want a new party; he wanted the existing one to return to its correct position. But, as conservatives across the province weighed the chances of a restoration, they also talked about an alternative. Throughout the summer of 1971 Paisley and Boal talked to dissident Unionists about the formation of a new inclusive party. The dissidents were reluctant participants in such talks. Pride was an obstacle: why should a party that had embodied the unionist cause for over eighty years dissolve itself to accommodate some mad preachers? Another obstacle was the growing belief—encouraged by the selection of some anti-O'Neill

  [6] Steve Bruce, *The Red Hand: Loyalist Paramilitaries in Northern Ireland* (Oxford: Oxford University Press, 1992), 80–7.

candidates in elections of 1970—that the Ulster Unionist Party could
be restored to orthodoxy. Boal sought and received assurances from
a number of leading Unionists that they would join it, but, when
the Ulster Democratic Unionist Party (DUP) was launched on 30
October 1971, most of those who had expressed interest were absent.

Many Protestant Unionists also had doubts about the new party.
Their party was doing well. It now had members in Stormont and
increasingly popular support and, more importantly, it had a clear
Protestant identity. In many areas, it took the full weight of Paisley's
authority, exercised either directly or through loyal supporters such
as Gordon Cooke, to persuade the Protestant Unionists to dissolve in
favour of the new organization. In the event, the lack of Unionist
defectors meant that the new party was a good deal less new than
they had feared. Protestant Unionists made up about two-thirds of
the DUP. The two new Stormont MPs to join Paisley and Beattie were
Desmond Boal and Johnny McQuade. Boal was a successful barrister
who combined staunch unionism with a left-of-centre position on
social and economic issues. McQuade was a working-class Protestant, ex-soldier, docker, and professional boxer who sat for North
Belfast and continued the independent unionist tradition of men
such as Henderson and Nixon.

On 23 February 1972 the DUP took a major step towards establishing its political identity when the four MPs crossed the floor at
Stormont to take up the position as Her Majesty's Loyal Opposition
that had been vacated by the SDLP. The period of opposition was
almost comically short and its brevity showed how far events in
Northern Ireland had passed out of Stormont's control. A month
after the DUP had crossed the floor the British government in
London suspended Stormont. The politics of the street, which had
played such a large part in putting Paisley into Stormont, had now
returned him and his supporters to the streets.

SUNNINGDALE

The DUP's first eighteen months were not especially auspicious. As
the party's official history of the period concedes, recruitment was

slow.[7] Craig's Vanguard was making the running on the right wing of unionist politics and the DUP seemed to lack a clear policy direction. Paisley had strengthened his reputation for prophecy by accurately predicting the introduction of direct rule, but his lack of tears for the end of Stormont (which, after all, was dominated by Faulknerites) left the DUP's attitude to devolution unclear. Fortunately, Craig's position was no clearer, and he was weakened when leading Unionists declined to follow him in turning his ginger group into a political party.

For most of 1972 and early 1973 the eyes of political observers were focused as much on London as on Ulster. Introducing direct rule had been easy; ending it was a problem. A conference of the British and Irish governments and Northern Ireland parties (minus the DUP and Vanguard) at the Civil Service college at Sunningdale, Berkshire, produced a scheme for a power-sharing government in which ministries would be divided between liberal Unionists and the SDLP. It was also suggested that some sort of 'Irish dimension' be institutionalized by the creation of a Council of Ireland made up of representatives of the Westminster and Dublin parliaments and members from whatever assembly was created in Belfast. Although the Council of Ireland proposal was by no means an open door to a united Ireland, it would be enough to concentrate loyalist voters in opposition to the new proposals.

The DUP's view of the Ulster crisis, its solution, and the proposed assembly were presented to the Ulster electorate in a manifesto that, with very little editing, would be reproduced at every election for the next thirty years:

The DUP says that Republican violence paid off in the disarming of the RUC, the disbanding of the B Specials, the banning of Orange, Black and Apprentice Boys' parades resulting in the imprisonment of Loyalists, the overthrow of Ulster's parliament, the plan for talks with Dublin to change the status of Northern Ireland within the United Kingdom, the abolishing of the Oath of Allegiance to the Queen in the new Assembly and Executive, the making of such oaths illegal for appointment to government boards, the removal of the Governor, the obliteration of 'On Her Majesty's Service' from official paid envelopes, the attempt to destroy democracy by power-sharing

---

[7] D. Calvert, *A Decade of the DUP* (Belfast: Crown Publications, 1981), 6.

which was a blow at the secrecy of the ballot box and an insult to British citizenship and standards, the proposal to set up machinery for the transfer of Northern Ireland's powers to a body or bodies in or with the Irish Republic, and the continued existence of areas in Northern Ireland where the Queen's writ did not effectually run.[8]

Seventy-two per cent of the electorate decided to voice an opinion. The DUP won eight seats, Vanguard took seven, and Faulkner had twenty-two. But some branches of the UUP he nominally led had nominated candidates opposed to his agenda, and ten of them were elected. This meant that, with the nineteen SDLP members, Faulkner could form a government, but he represented only a minority of the unionist voters.

From Paisley's position, the elections were an important point on the road to political legitimacy. He was no longer a marginal figure in the tradition of Henderson or Nixon: he was part of a coalition with people who had held cabinet office in Stormont, and, more than that, his party had polled *better* than one led by an ex-minister. Craig had fielded twice as many candidates and won fewer seats—a result that partly reflected a lack of enthusiasm for particular Vanguard candidates. It was generally the case that working-class loyalists, especially those connected with the paramilitary organizations, fared less well in the election than more 'respectable' conservatives, and Vanguard had a larger number of such candidates than the DUP.[9]

The DUP also had a major advantage in cohesion. Unlike Vanguard (and even more so the bloc of conservatives still within the UUP), the DUP spoke with a single clear voice. Even before Desmond Boal had stepped down from the chairmanship of the party, the DUP was very much what a DUP activist of the time called 'Paisley's fan club'. There was hardly any organized party structure. Peter Robinson, who was later to create one, said 'there was no party'. Hence Paisley was free to create policy and to articulate it in his headline-grabbing manner without having to convince a large membership. Furthermore, other activists such as William Beattie and Ivan Foster were very obviously

---

[8] *Irish Times*, 8 June 1973.

[9] For a detailed account of the UDA and its links with Vanguard, see S. Nelson, *Ulster's Uncertain Defenders: Loyalists and the Northern Ireland Conflict* (Belfast: Appletree Press, 1984), and Bruce, *Red Hand*.

his juniors. In the two other loyalist groupings a number of senior figures competed.

The absence of a viable organization was not something in which the DUP rejoiced. Beattie as deputy leader devoted a lot of energy to trying to build up branches, and Robinson, on becoming party secretary, hired the party's first full-time worker before himself becoming a paid official. Thereafter all press statements were produced from the party office, but the cohesion advantage remained because the leadership of the party was still very clearly in the hands of one man. This is not to say that Paisley was dictatorial and simply imposed his will on other activists. Rather, he was able to use his considerable personal appeal and powers of persuasion to convince others to take his line. As Robinson put it: 'even with a less persuasive argument he has been able to get a democratic decision in his favour but the democratic process is used throughout the party.'

According to one survey, over two-thirds of the people of Northern Ireland thought that the power-sharing executive should be given a chance to govern, but opinion polls routinely exaggerate moderation.[10] Quite what the Faulkner/SDLP cabinet might have achieved must remain a matter of speculation, because it was crippled at birth by the Conservative government at Westminster and loyalist workers at home.

In February 1974, just a month after the executive had taken office, Edward Heath called a general election on the theme of 'who rules Britain?': the elected government or striking miners. Being entirely free of miners, striking or otherwise, Northern Ireland treated the election as a referendum on the power-sharing system. The DUP and Vanguard were joined in a 'United Ulster Unionist Coalition' by the anti-Faulkner section of the UUP, and the coalition won every seat except the West Belfast constituency of the SDLP's Gerry Fitt, Deputy Chief Executive. The loyalists now had the grounds they needed to argue that the executive was undemocratic: the people of Ulster had finally been given a chance to vote on the issue and 51 per cent of them (and hence a much larger proportion of unionists) were opposed to power-sharing.

[10] R. Deutsch and V. Magowan, *Northern Ireland, 1968–74: A Chronology of Events* (Belfast: Blackstaff, 1974), ii. 43.

The second blow to the power-sharing experiment came from the streets. Since the start of the Troubles, a number of trade unionists had tried to create a province-wide organization of unionist workers, and by late 1973 their plans were sufficiently advanced to propose to politicians that the province could be brought to a halt by a strike. Largely because a strike the previous year, led by many of the same people, had been a dismal failure, the politicians were initially opposed. The executive of the Ulster Workers Council (UWC) decided to force their hand.

The strike began on the morning of Wednesday 15 May, and within a week Ulster was close to a standstill.[11] Public support for the strike was hardly necessary when the electricity workers could reduce the supply so much that basic economic activity had to stop. With the UDA and the UVF setting up road blocks and, in some areas, intimidating people from their workplaces, the government was seriously challenged, and it hardly responded. The army refused to become involved in what it maintained was an industrial dispute, and anyway its engineers could not run the electricity generators. But, most importantly, once the strike had lasted out its first week, a large number of businessmen and middle-class professionals began tacitly to cooperate with the strikers in return for being able to pursue some of their normal business. All round there was a lack of shared will to break the strike and maintain Faulkner's executive. On 28 May, with the electricity supply all but cut and threats of sewage rising in the streets of Belfast, Faulkner resigned. The Sunningdale accord was put back in the drawer, where it remained for twenty-four years.

Of right-wing unionists, Craig was the most involved in the strike: Vanguard's offices in Hawthornden Road, East Belfast, provided the base for the UWC, and Craig's people were closer to the paramilitaries than the Paisleyites. Even in the country, where Paisley was stronger, his supporters were much less active than those of the UUP in blockading roads with tractors. Indeed Paisley was so distanced

---

[11] For an excellent contemporary journalistic account of the strike, see R. Fisk, *The Point of No Return: The Strike which Broke the British in Ulster* (London: André Deutsch, 1975). See also D. Anderson, *14 May Days* (Dublin: Gill and Macmillan, 1994).

that he felt able to fly to Canada to attend a funeral. On his return he tried to take a greater role but was ill received. Members of the strike committee tell with relish the story of Paisley being put in his place. At the start of a planning meeting, whether accidentally or deliberately, Paisley sat himself at the head of the table, in the seat usually occupied by Glen Barr, the political spokesman for the UDA. He was immediately told by one hard man 'to get out of Glennie's chair'. Relations between Paisley and the paramilitaries were never cordial or trusting. They feared that the politicians were using their muscle because they needed it but would spurn them once the threat of anarchy had achieved the desired end of bringing down Brian Faulkner. They were, of course, right.

The autumn of 1974 saw the DUP's position further consolidated when Harold Wilson decided to call a general election only seven months after forming a minority government. Once again the three main anti-power-sharing groups—the DUP, Vanguard, and the conservative Unionists—fought the election as a coalition. Brian Faulkner, having lost control of the UUP, formed a new party, but it could field only two candidates and won less than 3 per cent of the poll. The non-sectarian Alliance Party won only 6.3 per cent of the votes cast. The majority of Ulster voters supported the SDLP, if they were Catholics, or the unionist coalition, if they were Protestant. Ian Paisley held his North Antrim seat with a massive personal majority of 34,497 voters. Almost half of the eligible voters had chosen Paisley as their representative.

The collapse of the strike council and the failure of the paramilitaries to pursue a consistent and popular policy left three competitors for the support of Ulster loyalists: Paisley, Craig, and West. There were soon just two. Craig was an intriguing character. A Lurgan solicitor who could speak menacing words in a slow quiet voice, he had come close to winning the leadership of the Ulster Unionist Party, had held cabinet office, and had retained good links with the paramilitaries and the UWC leaders after the strike. Vanguard had performed well in the elections for the Convention, the constitutional debating chamber established in May 1975 to find an agreed political structure for Ulster. With the political atmosphere charged by violence—in 1974 and 1975 512 people were killed—and with London pressing unionist politicians to accommodate the SDLP, the unionist electorate was unforgiving of deviation. Having done nothing to prepare his core supporters for this about-turn, Craig proposed an emergency voluntary coalition with the SDLP, which he saw as the only way to restore some sort of devolved government. His initiative was repudiated by a majority of his elected Convention members, and Paisley had him expelled from the unionist coalition.

The kaleidoscopic world of unionist politics gradually simplified into the shape it was to retain until 2004. Voters could choose between the Ulster Unionist Party, which was once again mostly orthodox but still retained a small and potentially accommodating liberal wing, and the DUP. The DUP was much the smaller party. In the local elections of 1977, for example, the UUP took 30 per cent of the vote to the DUP's 13 per cent. In 1979 it gained two Westminster seats to add to Paisley's North Antrim one (which he was now winning by the sorts of majorities found in the communist states of eastern Europe). The three MPs between them represented the full spectrum of DUP support. Paisley was the evangelical preacher, embracing the religious and the political in his two careers, and he was backed by rural Protestants. Johnny McQuade, elected for West Belfast, represented the old working-class independent unionist combination of militant loyalism and a populist critique of the ruling elite. The MP for East Belfast, Peter Robinson, represented the new generation of Paisleyites. As a teenager he had been attracted to hear Paisley because he shared his evangelical religion. He quickly became convinced of the need for political action and founded a branch of the Ulster Protestant Volunteers. Better educated, brighter, and more articulate than many of the older men who had supported Paisley since the 1950s, Robinson gave the party managerial and organizational skills it had previously lacked.

THE 1980s: GROWTH AND CONSOLIDATION

Winning three Westminster seats gave the DUP an important edge in the first elections to the European Parliament. When the UK had entered the EEC, it had asked the major parties to nominate representatives to the Parliament. In 1979 British voters were given their first opportunity to elect representatives. To ensure that the Catholic population won at least one of the three seats allocated to Northern Ireland, the whole of the province was treated as one constituency with three members. The election could hardly have been better designed to promote the DUP. Although Robinson and others were achieving success in building province-wide organization, the DUP's greatest asset was its leader. Treating the whole province as a single constituency gave Paisley a chance to cash in on his considerable personal support. Paisley was the sole DUP candidate, and John Hume (who had displaced Gerry Fitt as the real power) was the candidate for the SDLP, but the UUP made the tactical mistake of fielding two candidates. Paisley's view of Europe was eccentric but that hardly mattered in an election that, like every other, was treated as a constitutional referendum. Hume easily won the Catholic vote. With 30 per cent of the first preference votes, Paisley won the unionist battle. The UUP did not win its seat until Harry West had been eliminated and his votes transferred to John Taylor. In a 1967 opinion poll, 84 per cent of unionists said they preferred Terence O'Neill to Ian Paisley. Twelve years later, in the first province-wide beauty contest, the majority of unionist voters chose Paisley as their spokesman.

The details of the continuing terrorist violence, political initiatives, and elections of the twenty-five years after Paisley's election to the European Parliament could easily fill a large book, but they seem quite easy to summarize. The reorganized RUC and the British army achieved a degree of control over security, which reduced the killings to what one British Secretary of State called 'an acceptable level of violence'. In the peak year of 1972, 496 people had been killed. From 1977 to 1992 the average annual figure was 94. Terrorism became more focused. The steady trickle of assassinations created a great deal of anguish, and few families were left untouched, but the people of Northern Ireland found a way of sustaining a degree of normality. From their peak in the 1974 strike, the UDA and UVF lost public support and members. In contrast, the IRA grew in power and popularity, and its political wing Sinn Fein entered electoral politics.

The opening for what is arguably the greatest change in Ulster politics was fortuitous. In 1981 a number of republican prisoners started a hunger strike that was at first seen as just another phase in the long battle over the status and conditions of terrorist prisoners. In March, Frank Maguire, the MP for Fermanagh and South Tyrone, died. Bobby Sands, the first of the prisoners to begin his fast, was nominated for the by-election. The SDLP candidate withdrew, as did Maguire's brother, and the election became republican hunger-strike hero versus leading Unionist Harry West. Sands was MP for less than a month before he died, on the sixty-sixth day of refusing food. When the British government changed the law to prevent another hunger-striker following Sands, Owen Carron was elected. At Sinn Fein's October 1981 conference, its press officer Danny Morrison confirmed the party's intention to fight elections by saying: 'who here really believes we can win the war through the ballot box? But will anyone here object if, with a ballot paper in one hand and the Armalite in the other, we take power in Ireland?'[12] In the general election of 1983 Sinn Fein took 13.4 per cent of the vote; a creditable performance against the SDLP's 17.9 per cent. It was fear of this threat to the SDLP that persuaded Westminster to allow Dublin to become increasingly involved and led to the Anglo-Irish accord of 1985.

The details of that accord (which did little more than give Dublin the right to voice the grievances of northern nationalists) are much less important than what each side made of it. Politicians in the Irish Republic claimed 'in effect we have been given a major and substantial role in the day-to-day running of Northern Ireland'.[13] Peter Robinson for the DUP thought it was worse: 'The Prime Minister signed away the Union at Hillsborough Castle yesterday. We are on the window ledge of the Union.' But he added: 'But I can tell you that this does not mean we will jump off.'[14] The previous summer had already shown a marked escalation of civil disturbance, with a Twelfth of July parade in Portadown staging a full dress rehearsal of the role it was to play in 1995 as the home of the contested Drumcree march. On 25 November at least 100,000 unionists (and there may have been twice that number) attended a massive demonstration at the City Hall in Belfast. Unionists started an 'Ulster Says No'

---

[12] P. Bew and G. Gillespie, *Northern Ireland: A Chronology of the Troubles 1968–1993* (Dublin: Gill and Macmillan, 1993), 157.

[13] Irish Justice Minister Michael Noonan, in ibid. 190.

[14] Ibid.

campaign that included a boycott of local council business, illegal parades, and a mass resignation of Westminster seats.

None of these shifted British government resolve. The council boycott proved difficult to sustain after the courts had made it clear that councillors who failed to set budgets and carry out their statutory duties would be surcharged. Refusing to deal with British ministers might have given some satisfaction, but it very obviously damaged the interests of constituents. The staged by-elections of January 1986 provided a rather hollow victory. Unionist voters told the world what it already knew—that they hated the Anglo-Irish accord—but the SDLP took the seat of Newry and Armagh and did so well in South Down that it won the seat at the general election a year later. A 'Day of Action' on 3 March shut down most industry and commerce in Northern Ireland. In rioting that evening forty-seven RUC officers were injured. Over the next few months loyalists attacked over 500 police homes, and 150 police officers had to be relocated from the Protestant areas that they had previously thought to be safe. In July Paisley and Robinson led some 4,000 supporters to blockade Hillsborough and in November they addressed a packed Ulster Hall for the inauguration of the newest 'third force': Ulster Resistance.

James Molyneaux, who led the UUP from 1979 to 1995, could hardly have been less like Paisley. He was quiet to the point of reticence and uncomfortable with mass meetings and rabble-rousing rhetoric. In a party divided between devolutionists who shared the DUP's desire for a return to Stormont and others, such as former Conservative MP Enoch Powell, who wanted closer integration with Britain, Molyneaux leant to integration, though he kept the peace by promoting a limited form of administrative devolution: Northern Ireland as a large English county council. Both party leaders were disturbed by the violence that attended the Day of Action and ran through the summer, and they issued frequent joint calls for calm, but there was a real difference between the parties. Most Ulster Unionists wanted nothing to do with street protests; most Democratic Unionists saw regular confrontation with British politicians as a useful demonstration of sentiment and power.

Within six months it was clear that the campaign of abstention was going nowhere. The two parties appointed Peter Robinson, Harold

McCusker, and Frank Millar to consider new options. In terms that sound remarkably like a liberal critique of Paisleyism, the Task Force said: 'Those who counsel against negotiation must make plain the alternative means by which they propose to determine the future of the people of Northern Ireland...Reliance on other people to undertake a campaign of violence which can be disowned but from which can be extracted political advantage would be disreputable.'[15] When Paisley and Molyneaux declined to show any great interest in the Task Force report, Robinson resigned his position as deputy leader. He returned three months later.

Paisley is so widely seen as a self-interested megalomaniac that it is worth noting how often in this period he tried to maintain a united front with the UUP. On at least three occasions it cost him close allies. Jim Allister was a lawyer who had worked for Paisley as his European Parliament assistant and a senior party activist in Newtownabbey. It was obviously damaging for two unionist parties to compete where splitting the vote would permit a nationalist victory, and, as the junior party, the DUP repeatedly gave way to the UUP. This frustrated party activists, and tensions rose after the UUP had distanced itself from some of the DUP's tactics in opposing the Anglo-Irish Accord. Roy Beggs was particularly unpopular with the DUP. He had defected from the UUP to the DUP shortly after its formation. In 1980 as Mayor of Larne he accepted an invitation to attend a civic function in the Republic. His party executive suspended him, and he resigned and rejoined the UUP. In the 1983 Westminster general election, when the two unionist parties competed against each other in fourteen seats, he only narrowly beat Allister in East Antrim. Allister wanted a re-match in 1987 and was first promised it, but in the interests of unionist unity Paisley accepted that there should be no such contests and Allister quit.[16] Two years later, Ivan Foster quietly left the party because he felt Paisley's

[15] *Guardian*, 2 July 1987.

[16] Allister remained a family friend and acted as Paisley's legal agent. When the Belfast Agreement of 1998 again clearly divided the UUP and DUP, he returned to the party and in 2004 he replaced Paisley as the DUP's candidate for the European Parliament. Kane retired entirely from politics. Foster remained a prominent commentator through his editorship of the *Burning Bush*.

closeness to Molyneaux was compromising the DUP's witness, and in 1991 prominent Omagh councillor Alan Kane (like Allister, a lawyer who had worked as Paisley's assistant) resigned for similar reasons.

THE WORLD POST-CEASEFIRE

There were four major developments in the early 1990s: three public and one secret. One of the public developments was the announcement in November 1990 by Secretary of State Peter Brooke that Britain had no 'selfish strategic or economic interest' in Northern Ireland. Although it was taken by unionists as a snub, it was intended as an invitation to all the protagonists to engage in realistic discussions about the future. By presenting itself as a disinterested facilitator, the British government hoped to encourage a new political openness, and to an extent it succeeded. There then followed the second major development: eighteen months of round table talks that eventually failed to reach agreement but were highly significant in that, for the first time in seventy years, Dublin politicians came to a negotiating table in the North, and Ulster unionists travelled south to Dublin, and loyalist paramilitaries called a ceasefire to make the atmosphere more conducive to finding a negotiated settlement.

The third major development was a series of meetings between John Hume of the SDLP and Gerry Adams of Sinn Fein. At the time the talks were denounced as Hume abandoning his pacifist principles to form a pan-nationalist front with terrorists, but with hindsight we can see that the commitment Adams made in those discussions to the principle of self-determination—though ambiguous enough—was a major step on the road from 1981's 'Armalite and ballot-box' strategy to 1998's Belfast Agreement.

What was then known only to a handful of people was the fourth development: tentative arm's-length exchanges between leaders of the IRA and the British government. In the spring of 1993 the veteran journalist Eamonn Mallie got word of these contacts and began to pester Secretary of State Sir Patrick Mayhew, who repeatedly denied them. In November an anonymous source provided Willie McCrea, the DUP MP and Free Presbyterian minister, with a copy of instructions from Mayhew to an intermediary in talks with the IRA. On 15 November Prime Minister John Major declared he would 'never talk to organizations which did not renounce violence'.[17] Less than a fortnight later, Mayhew admitted that the government had long been in secret contact with the IRA.

The outcome of these developments was the Downing Street Declaration of September 1993—a lengthy statement of positions agreed between London and Dublin that were intended to capitalize on a growing expectation of serious IRA commitment to talks.[18] In order to pre-empt the obvious unionist response that the IRA was being bought off with the promise that it would get its way, the Northern Ireland Office felt obliged to add an annex called *What the Joint Declaration Does Not Do*. Apparently, it did not assert the value of achieving a united Ireland nor assert the legitimacy of a united Ireland in the absence of majority consent; it did not commit the British government to joining the ranks of 'persuaders for a united Ireland' (as Gerry Adams insisted it must); it did not set any time-scale for a united Ireland to come about nor indicate that this was probable; it did not commit the people of Northern Ireland to joining a united Ireland against their democratic wishes; it did not establish arrangements for the exercise of joint authority between the British and Irish governments over Northern Ireland; it did not derogate in any way from UK sovereignty over Northern Ireland; it did not contain any reference or implicit commitment to the withdrawal of British troops from Northern Ireland; and it did not give Sinn Fein any immediate place at the Talks table. Unionists were not reassured. The UUP announced that it would not take part in 'three-stranded' talks (the three strands being concerned with devolved government for Northern Ireland; Belfast–Dublin links, and London–Dublin links). Molyneaux wanted a devolved assembly that would negotiate any new relations with the Irish Republic. The DUP described the Declaration as a 'rotten sinking vessel which is going down in confusion'.[19] At a meeting in the Cabinet room in Downing Street Paisley

---

[17] E. Mallie and D. McKittrick, *The Fight for Peace: The Secret Story behind the Irish Peace Process* (London: Heinemann, 1996), 234.

[18] For a detailed discussion of the Downing Street Declaration, see P. Bew and G. Gillespie, *The Northern Ireland Peace Process 1993–1996* (London: Serif, 1996).

[19] *Herald*, 22 Mar. 1994.

enraged John Major by describing him as a back-seat passenger in a car being driven by the Irish Prime Minister.

On 31 August 1994, after eleven months of posturing and haggling (and only after it had tidied up some unfinished business by murdering three prominent loyalists), the IRA called an indefinite ceasefire. The loyalist UVF painted a wall with the slogan: 'On behalf of the loyalist people on the Shankill Road we accept the unconditional surrender of the IRA.' The UDA was less immediately persuaded. Over a hectic four weeks, the leaders of the political parties that fronted for the loyalist paramilitaries—the Ulster Democratic Party (UDP) for the UDA and the Progressive Unionist Party for the UVF—held a series of talks with their rank-and-file members to persuade them to reciprocate. On 13 October, on behalf of the Combined Loyalist Military Command (CLMC), Gusty Spence announced:

After a widespread consultative process initiated by representations from the Ulster Democratic and Progressive Unionist parties, and after having received confirmation and guarantees in relation to Northern Ireland's constitutional position within the United Kingdom...and in the belief that the democratically expressed wishes of the greater number of people in Northern Ireland will be respected and upheld, the CLMC will universally cease all operational hostilities as from 12 midnight on Thursday...

In an unusual act of political sensitivity, the CLMC also did what the IRA signally failed to do: it apologized. 'In all sincerity, we offer to the loved ones of all innocent victims of the past 25 years, abject and true remorse. No words of ours will compensate for the intolerable suffering they have undergone during this conflict.'[20] With a typically black-humoured reference to the Malvern Street killings of 1966, one of the CLMC told me that Spence had been chosen to read the statement because 'He bloody well started it. He might as well finish it'.

There were many hesitations and reversals on the road from the first IRA ceasefire to all-inclusive negotiations. Although Sinn Fein was quickly rewarded with various marks of acceptance (such as a visa that allowed Adams to fund-raise in the USA, permission for Adams

---

[20] Bew and Gillespie, *The Northern Ireland Peace Process*, 71–2.

and McGuinness to use the facilities of the House of Commons even though they would not take their seats, and frequent meetings with London and Dublin ministers), republicans objected to the slow pace of change; unionists objected to any change at all when all the republicans were doing was promising not to kill anyone for a while, and even that promise was narrower than it seemed. The IRA continued to murder its own people. Decommissioning became a major concern and for much of 1995 seemed an obstacle to progress. Eventually the issue was sidelined with the creation of an International Monitoring Commission, which was given the task of liaising with representatives of the paramilitary organizations and managing disarmament while politicians got on with the movement to talks.

Whether it was an expression of frustration at the slow progress towards its goal or a cynical attempt to remind people why it should be placated is not clear, but on 9 February 1996 the IRA dramatically ended its ceasefire with a bomb at Canary Wharf in East London that killed two people and caused over £80 million worth of damage to office buildings. Despite this, London and Dublin, encouraged by President Clinton's direct involvement, managed to construct an agreed way forward. A compromise between unionist and nationalist timetables (elected body first, then talks; and vice versa) was found with proposals for an elected Forum from which negotiating teams for the serious talks would be drawn. To ensure that all the small parties (in particular the fronts for the loyalist paramilitaries) were on board, the Forum was to be elected by a conventional proportional representation system with an additional two-member top-up for any party that passed a certain province-wide threshold.

In August 1995 James Molyneaux resigned as leader of the UUP. His long tenure had been an unhappy one, and he had the distinction of having been betrayed not once but twice by Conservative leaders in whom he had placed his trust: when Thatcher signed the Anglo-Irish accord in 1993, and when John Major produced the Downing Street Declaration. Almost every UUP Westminster MP considered himself a plausible successor, but the victor was the youngest: David Trimble.

Trimble was widely regarded as a hardliner. Twenty years earlier he had been involved with Bill Craig's Vanguard and the organization of the 1974 strike. Those who knew only recent events had seen him hand in hand with Ian Paisley at the end of what retrospectively came to known as 'Drumcree I'. Portadown had long been the scene of vicious sectarian confrontations. In the summer of 1986 it had witnessed a series of violent confrontations over banned marches. In 1995, on the Sunday before the traditional Twelfth of July celebrations, Orangemen planned to march along the Garvaghy Road on their return to Portadown town centre from their annual church service at Drumcree parish church. Local nationalist residents were determined to stop them. The RUC banned the march and initially blocked the road. Loyalists blockading the port of Larne and rioting elsewhere in the province inclined the RUC to accept a compromise. As the local MP (and an Orangeman), Trimble probably had no choice but to become involved in the wrangling. The Orange Order agreed to walk without their bands. The local residents cleared the road to allow them through. Paisley and Trimble led the march, and, when they reached the town centre, they celebrated by raising their joined hands in triumph. Trimble insists that his main role was to broker a compromise; what television viewers saw was Trimble and Paisley celebrating an Orange victory.[21]

That Trimble was a considerably more complex politician than was widely recognized ensured that the Drumcree march was the last time he and Paisley held hands. Trimble was persuaded that the best long-term interests of unionism would be served by entering the talks. Freed from its obligation to maintain a united unionist front, the DUP could strike its most comfortable posture: outright opposition to whatever the London and Dublin governments proposed and condemnation of the UUP for being drawn into the process. The differences between the parties and the extent of animosity are clear from the rival manifestos for the May 1996 elections to the Forum. The UUP's *Building your Future within the Union* offered a pragmatic vision for the future and simply expressed its view of the DUP: 'The UUP exists to serve the people by advancing and promoting the

[21] Trimble's version is given in F. Millar, *David Trimble: The Price of Peace* (Dublin: Liffey Press, 2004), 46–7. For a very detailed account of the various Drumcree disturbances, see C. Ryder and V. Kearney, *Drumcree: The Orange Order's Last Stand* (London: Methuen, 2001), and G. Lucy, *Stand-Off at Drumcree: July 1995 and 1996* (Lurgan: Ulster Society Publications, 1996).

UNION. It has never been the party of extravagant talk and improvised stunts.'[22] The party of extravagant stunts preferred to describe itself as *The Unionist Team You Can Trust* and was equally blunt about the UUP:

The Forum and its negotiations are not places for faint-hearted or white-flag unionists. What Ulster needs [are] men and women who will not be bribed, bought or intimidated into the surrender of any more ground to republicanism. The DUP's judgement of the bogus IRA ceasefire, the Downing Street Declaration sell-out and the treacherous Framework Document, has been totally vindicated. You can have no trust in those other unionists who got it completely wrong.[23]

If it was an accident, it was telling, but it is more likely a snide reminder of previous Paisley victories that the stirring call to vote DUP ended with the phrase 'Ulster is at the crossroad'—an echo of Terence O'Neill's famous declaration of 1969 before the election that began Paisley's electoral career.

The Forum election was the first opportunity for Northern Ireland to vote on the 'peace process', and the results were disappointing for the centre parties and encouraging for the extremes. The DUP took 19 per cent to the UUP's 24 and Sinn Fein gained 15 per cent compared to the SDLP's 21. The DUP further took heart from the 4 per cent of votes that went to maverick unionist Robert McCartney's United Kingdom Unionist Party (UKUP)[24] and from the knowledge that among the UUP members elected were several who were at best lukewarm about the prospects of negotiating with the SDLP and Dublin.

A brief personal anecdote will remind us of the nature of the DUP. In June 1996 I happened to be in Belfast shortly before the formal talks were due to start and in conversation with Paisley casually said that I would love to be a fly on the wall during the negotiations.

[22] F. Cochrane, *Unionist Politics and the Politics of Unionism since the Anglo-Irish Agreement* (Cork: Cork University Press, 1997), 355.

[23] Ibid. 355–6.

[24] Robert McCartney QC is a curious figure. Initially a very liberal and secular unionist, he first came to public notice for very publicly challenging Paisley, but his opposition to government policy (on the grounds that it represented and encouraged the worst kind of religio-ethnic bloc politics) was so vehement that he became a firm ally of the DUP.

Paisley turned to his son and asked him to check the rules. It turned out that the structure did allow for the teams of talks representatives who had been elected to the Forum to be augmented by a limited number of 'specialist advisers' and I was duly so accredited. And so on the first day of the talks I walked into the nondescript office building on the Stormont estate that was to be their venue carrying Ian Paisley Jnr's bag. The start of the talks was delayed while Paisley and McCartney tried to persuade Senator George Mitchell that he was not a suitable candidate for the job. When Paisley returned to the DUP base room to report progress, his son asked me to leave, so the party talks team could be briefed in private. As I rose to make for the door, Paisley pushed me back into my chair, and said: 'The Professor can stay for the prayers!' He took from his pocket a small and well-thumbed Bible, quickly found an apposite passage from the Old Testament about treachery in high places, read it and then delivered a long extempore prayer calling for divine guidance to help resist yet another in a long line of assaults on the Protestant people of Ulster. If not the exact words, the sentiments were sufficiently familiar for my attention to wander, and, as I looked at the faces in the room, two things struck me. With possibly two exceptions, all of the thirty or so people in the room were born-again Christians and almost all of them had been active in the DUP since its foundation and three who had not were children of founder members. The party that prays together stays together. After the prayer I tactfully left for the canteen.

Later at lunch in the canteen, Paisley sat down next to me and boomed: 'And what does my special adviser advise I do now?' I replied: 'As you heed only the advice of God, I suggest you enjoy your lunch.' Paisley paused for a moment, as if considering whether the line of permissible banter had been crossed, and then guffawed: 'Now this man understands me!'

The talks were extremely slow to get off the ground, and it is a mark of the DUP's astuteness that it managed to record its objections to most of what was on offer without actually subverting the process: the party wanted to make its own positions clear while allowing others to commit themselves to contentious positions that could later be used against them. With a fine mixing of metaphors, one DUP strategist said: 'We're going to keep our powder dry and give Trimble enough rope to hang himself.' The first days of the talks

provided a nice example of Peter Robinson's eye for tactical detail.
When endless haggling over procedural rules seemed likely to prevent serious negotiations even starting, Robinson approached Senator Mitchell and suggested that he allow a separate vote on each rule
item and then a single vote on the whole package. That way the DUP
could vote for procedures it favoured but oppose the whole package:
thus maintaining its protesting posture but ensuring (because the
other parties would vote for the rules) that the talks did not end
before they began.[25] When the IRA's resumption of its ceasefire
allowed Sinn Fein to join the talks, the DUP packed its bags: 'We
have now left this process for there is nothing in it for the Union or
for the unionist people, or for any law-abiding citizen in Northern
Ireland.'[26]

The agreement that was eventually produced was described by
Seamus Mallon, increasingly the effective leader of the SDLP as
John Hume's health failed and his interest waned, as 'Sunningdale
for Slow Learners'. There is something in that. The devolved government for Northern Ireland would be based on proportional power-
sharing principles. There would be formal contact between Belfast
and Dublin in a North/South Ministerial Council—the 'Irish dimension' required by nationalists. There would also be formal contact
between Dublin and London—the 'east–west' links required by
unionists to balance the deal.[27]

In many respects it was a settlement that could have pleased
unionists. The hated Anglo-Irish Accord (with its model of London
and Dublin deciding the fate of Northern Ireland while consulting
nationalists and ignoring unionists) was set aside. The Irish Republic
renounced its territorial claims to the North and agreed to a referendum of its people that would end its romantic attachment to the goal
of reunification. Sinn Fein accepted the continuation of the Union,
at least for the time being. And at the heart of a series of complex

[25] G. Mitchell, *Making Peace: The Inside Story of the Good Friday Agreement*
(London: Heinemann, 1999), 63.
[26] *Irish News*, 24 July 1997.
[27] There is a good summary of the Belfast Agreement and responses to it in
J. Tonge, *The New Northern Ireland Politics* (London: Palgrave, 2005). Mitchell,
Making Peace, records the chairman's views of proceedings. David Trimble's justification can be found in Millar, *David Trimble*.

procedural rules was the principle of 'dual consent'. All representatives had to register as unionist or nationalist or 'other', and important decisions (such as the choice of First Minister and Deputy) required a majority of votes of each bloc. Unionists might not like it that they were constrained by nationalists, but they enjoyed a matching veto on any nationalist schemes to increase the power of the North–South dimension. If they had wanted to be bullish about it, unionists could have favourably cited the response of bitter hardline republicans: the long war had been fought to destroy the Orange state and end partition and instead Sinn Fein had settled for a role in managing Northern Ireland as part of the UK.

However, the Agreement also contained much that was abhorrent to unionists. It promised reform of the RUC, it recognized the legitimacy of Irish nationalist aspirations, it gave Sinn Fein leaders the respectability of government office, and it provided for the phased early release of terrorist prisoners. It was very easy for critics to present it as a bad deal that, in order to draw republicans into the process, conceded too much to Irish nationalism and offered no assurance that nationalists would not use this settlement as a new baseline from which to argue for new concessions. And, because it did not insist that terrorist groups decommission their weapons before their political representatives took office, it allowed the DUP and the UKUP to portray it as a victory for the IRA.

Opinion polls showed unionist opinion finely balanced and divided on lines that did not entirely match party allegiance. Some DUP identifiers hoped it would work, while some UUP activists were sceptical. Martin Smyth, UUP MP for South Belfast and Grand Master of the Orange Order, urged a 'No' vote.[28] Although he denies this interpretation, Trimble seemed somewhat lukewarm himself: asking that unionist voters vote for this deal because the next one would be worse. The only unionist party that campaigned enthusiastically for the Agreement was the Progressive Unionist Party (PUP), the front for the paramilitary UVF. The former gunmen argued that its core principle of power-sharing (they preferred the term 'sharing

[28] In a rather bizarre echo of the distant past, Smyth was joined in this dissent by Austin Ardill, who, in 1974, had been one of the leading UUP men who flirted with joining the DUP but then pulled out. *Belfast Telegraph*, 11 May 1998.

responsibility') was exactly what they had promoted for many years, but their target audience gave them a hard time. At one meeting in South Belfast, Hughie Smyth, endlessly heckled by Paisleyites, finally lost his temper with their refusal to accept that nationalists deserved a place in government and challenged them: 'If youse just hate Taigs, then tell me that!'

It is worth adding an important aside here. The support of loyalist paramilitary organizations was vital to the peace process because it forced unionists to be honest. As I will argue in Chapter 7, the vast majority of Ulster unionists have always been law-abiding, but some have periodically flirted with the idea of armed resistance. The pivotal role of the UVF especially can be illustrated with what happened at a public meeting on the Shankill Road in the gap between the ceasefires and the start of negotiations. During a heated debate, a DUP supporter fell into the traditional militant rhetoric and somewhat unwisely, given the number of former prisoners in the audience, used the phrase 'Ulster will fight'. This was greeted with raucous guffawing. A well-known UVF man, only recently released from prison, replied with an offer: 'Come round to my house now and I'll give youse a gun and I'll show you where a Provie lives and you can kill him! Come on!' Others added such sentiments as 'We've done our fighting for youse. We're not doing it again' and 'How many years [in prison] have you done?'

David Ervine, Billy Hutchinson, and other former terrorists repeatedly challenged conservative unionists to put up or shut up. That they could speak with the authority of men who had inflicted great damage on others and served long sentences 'for God and Ulster', and could do so in the deliberately coarse language of people who were on the front line of the Ulster conflict, played a considerable part in protecting the back of Trimble and the liberal unionists. The PUP leaders could also respond authoritatively to those right-wing unionists who objected to the inclusion of Sinn Fein in the talks process on the grounds that one should not 'talk to terrorists' by reminding the DUP that it had worked with loyalist paramilitaries in the strikes of 1974 and 1977. Liberal critics were quick to remind Paisley of his Third Force and Ulster Resistance, but the point had much greater force when made by former terrorists. Ervine and Hutchinson became the darlings of the media and of the liberal middle classes, who understood that they were preventing the alliance that had defeated Sunningdale in 1974 being re-created. By making it clear that they would resume 'operational hostilities' only if the IRA mounted a major campaign, the gunmen of the UVF and UDA reminded those who should have known better what it was they should have known. Unionists politicians ceased the martial rhetoric, and it is a mark of how completely that option was closed off that, when, in August 1998, twenty-nine men, women, and children were killed by a car bomb in Omagh, no one talked about 'killing the killers'.

Although the UDA and UVF peaceniks could bait DUP politicians, one of whom spat back that they were just 'the Alliance party with guns', they gave the DUP a handy weapon to use against the UUP. While David Trimble negotiated the early release of murderers, the DUP called for the return of the death penalty and claimed the moral high ground. As a newspaper advert signed by all the Free Presbyterian clergy and some 100 other evangelical ministers put it: the Agreement 'flies in the face of Holy Scripture and punishes those that do well and praises those that are evil-doers'.

In the week before the referendum on the agreement I accompanied Paisley on some of his engagements. One in particular was memorable because anyone who witnessed it could see why Paisley would eventually win and Trimble would lose. Despite being an elected member of the Westminster and European parliaments, a full-time minister, and the leader of a large church and party, Paisley had accepted an invitation from the Drumderg Loyalist Volunteers Flute Band to dedicate new uniforms. The tiny Orange Hall was set in beautiful rolling hills of Armagh. The crowd of some 150 unionists was too large for the hall, so Paisley and his son Ian Jr joined the local DUP councillor Brian Hutchinson and the Revd Thomas Murray on a farm cart that had been pressed into use as a podium. Hutchinson was the second generation of his family to be active in the DUP. His father had been a founding member and a local councillor. Thomas Murray was minister of the nearby Markethill Free Presbyterian congregation. Paisley began by delivering an extempore prayer that used the theme of deliverance neatly to elide personal sin and political treachery. Ulster needed firm leadership to deliver it from treacherous politicians. His audience needed salvation to deliver them from sin. He did not hesitate to tell his listeners that being political Protestants would not win them salvation. He then led the crowd in singing 'Abide with Me'—a theologically sound hymn that is well known even to those who rarely attend church because of its popularity with football crowds and with funeral parties. Thomas Murray read a passage of scripture and then led in the singing of 'Oh God our Help in Ages Past'. Paisley then delivered a long speech that wove together family reminiscence, political critique, humour, and revival-meeting badgering in a style that treated the audience as if they were equals in a common enterprise. Again he was quite clear that they needed to get saved: nothing else would do. But while he was on the subject, he would tell them a few good reasons why the Belfast Agreement was a very bad thing. Political opponents were mentioned as if they were well known to the audience: Trimble was supported only by Ken Maginnis and John Taylor, 'and he has said he will not touch it with a barge pole!', and Cecil Walker, 'and he only supports it because the UVF has told him to'. Despite the fact that some of these young bandsmen would themselves have been on the fringes of loyalist paramilitary organizations, Paisley reserved some of his strongest fire for decommissioning and the early release of prisoners, and the crowd responded with particular enthusiasm to Paisley's point that the early prisoner release scheme was negotiated by David Ervine of the UVF and Gerry Kelly of the IRA: 'fine bed-fellows!' Reference to the money the government was spending trying to 'hoodwink you' allowed a scornful mention of the fact that a video being sent to all first-time voters was being produced by Mark Chichester-Clark, a relative of the second Ulster Unionist prime minister that Paisley saw off: 'Yes, they're bringing them out of the deep freeze now!' Having pointedly reminded the crowd (as if they needed it) of his own long political record, he added a few personal touches by telling them that this area had a special place in his affections because his father had held his first mission nearby. He also mentioned the local preaching of Albert Duff, who was active in the Protestant Unionist Party in the early 1960s (and after whom one of the FPC's small Belfast halls is named). Despite his age, frailty, and hearing problems, he sparkled when he teased the young band members: one about his girlfriend; another about his haircut.

The small crowd listened intently to every word of the long rambling address and applauded rapturously at the end. On the way home, visibly tired, Paisley said: 'The outliers. You have to take care of the outliers. This is the true Ulster Protestantism.'

A tiny crowd of people in a remote place, most of whom would never have met a very important person, had been given the afternoon of Ulster's most senior politician. True, he had nagged them about their souls, and in other company some of the young men might have objected to his criticisms of the UVF, but the great man had taken the effort to visit their tiny hall, had spoken to them as friends and equals, had reminded them of their glorious past and of the part that revival religion had played in it, had stirred them by listing all the threats to their precarious position within the Union, and had then reassured them with the promise that he would not rest till he had seen off these threats, just as he had seen off all the others before: a majestic performance from a man who understood his people.

The referendum vote was close. As the government intended it to be, it was hard to disaggregate by religion, but opinion polls give us some good idea. While some 90 per cent of Catholics voted in favour, Protestants only marginally approved: probably about 45–55 per cent.[29] In the elections for the Assembly the DUP polled slightly better than it had in the local council elections the year before and slightly less well than for the 1996 Forum. But the UUP fared worse: in 1993 its council vote was 29 per cent; in 1997 it was 28; and in the Assembly elections it won only 21 per cent of the vote.

While the DUP vote might have seemed static, the first phase of a significant shift was under way: a number of anti-agreement independent unionists were elected. Trimble commanded a thin majority of unionist assembly men and women: enough for the devolved government to begin its work but not enough to prevent it remaining precarious. It met, elected Trimble First Minister and Seamus Mallon his deputy, and was then suspended because the UUP was not happy with the progress on decommissioning. A year later, in November

[29] For full details of various polls, see Colin Irwin, *The People's Peace Process in Northern Ireland* (London: Palgrave, 2002). Also available at www.peacepolls.org. It is worth noting that 20 % of DUP identifiers voted for the Belfast Agreement.

1999, Trimble was persuaded enough had been done for him to allow Sinn Fein to join the executive and for it to function. Mallon described the first day of operations as 'the birth of a new era in our lives'.[30] After just three months, devolution was suspended again. After the IRA promised to 'completely and verifiably put its weapons beyond use' the Assembly opened again in June 2000. A year later Trimble resigned because there had still not been enough movement on decommissioning. After a further IRA gesture, the Assembly opened again for business in October, and this time managed a year of work before the discovery that Sinn Fein officials had been using their access to the Stormont Parliament to spy on unionists again caused Trimble to pull the plug.[31]

Many commentators thought that the successful functioning of the Assembly would embarrass the DUP. Paisley and his lieutenants could help the Assembly work, in which case their opposition to the Belfast Agreement would seem dishonest. Or they could subvert it, in which case they would seem like spoilers who had nothing to offer the people of Northern Ireland but who liked the salaries enough to take their seats. In the event, the DUP performed its balancing act very effectively. Dodds and Robinson accepted office and won the admiration of civil servants and journalists as they proved themselves highly competent ministers.[32] But they refused to attend meetings of the executive with Sinn Fein and never missed a chance to criticize the agreement or the specific changes (such as reform of the RUC) that followed from it. The case they put to unionist voters in the following quote from a 2003 manifesto was that they could be effective managers and remain principled, and, if they could win a mandate to do so, they would force London and Dublin to renegotiate the deal.

[30] *BBC News*, http://news.bbc.co.uk/1/m/uk/1170629.stm.

[31] In December 2005 Denis Donaldson, a close confidant of Gerry Adams and one of those charged with the spy ring, admitted that he had been working for the RUC and British intelligence for twenty years. It may be some time before the truth of who was actually working for whom is known. He was murdered in April 2006, presumably by dissident republicans.

[32] For a detailed account of the operations of the first Assembly, see M. Purdy, *Room 21: Stormont—behind Closed Doors* (Belfast: Brehon Press, 2005).

For almost 30 years the DUP has been a devolutionist party, believing it is right that the decisions affecting Northern Ireland are best taken by the people of Northern Ireland. We can never, however, accept a form of devolution which, if left unchanged, will undermine democracy and the union itself. Despite our fundamental and unequivocal opposition to the Belfast agreement we have proved in the assembly that we have been able to work with other parties and get things done. Our members have demonstrated how to deliver for their constituents and our ministers for us all. However, we will never accept the presence of terrorists in government and oppose them at every opportunity.

Gradually unionist opinion shifted towards the DUP. Polls between 2000 and 2003 show Protestant positive answers to the question 'Would you still vote for the Belfast Agreement?' falling steadily from 55 to 36 per cent.[33] In a by-election in South Antrim in September 2000, the UUP lost a 16,000-vote majority and the seat to the DUP's gospel-singing cleric William McCrea. That election was instructive because it exposed the UUP's fundamental problem. Its candidate was David Burnside, an opponent of the Belfast Agreement who frequently criticized the party leader. Had South Antrim UUP fielded a liberal, it would at least have given the electorate a choice. By putting forward Burnside, it was inviting unionists to choose between an unreliably anti-Agreement candidate and one with a lifetime track record of opposition.

The causes of growing unionist disaffection were predictable. Murderers had been released from prison, in some cases having served only a few years.[34] The RUC had been radically changed and quotas introduced for the recruitment of Catholics. Catholics had been appointed to high-profile public posts. The army had been withdrawn. Security bases had been dismantled. Sinn Fein ministers were chauffeured to meetings with Dublin officials. And still the IRA maintained its weapons, killed its opponents, intimidated the

[33] www.peacepolls.org.
[34] It is hard to overestimate the importance of this. J. Tonge and J. Evans, 'Eating the Oranges: The DUP and the Orange Order vote in Northern Ireland' (unpublished paper, PSA Elections, Public Opinions and Parties annual conference, Nuffield College, 2004), shows the prisoner-release scheme as the most frequently stated reason for opposing the Belfast Agreement in a survey of some 400 Orange Order members.

residents of nationalist areas, robbed businesses, and made a fortune from rackets. And still nationalists did not seem to be trying to make a go of Northern Ireland. Instead of behaving like members of the government, nationalists sounded like the perennial opposition. The sentiment could be articulated in many different ways, but it was clear and widespread: the British government keeps making concessions to win over nationalists and they always want more. A DUP councillor said of his target voters: 'They... see everything Gaelic, Republican and Irish promoted while everything British, Unionist or Orange is derided or reviled.'[35] Surveys supported his baleful view: in one, no Protestant respondents thought unionists had benefited from the Agreement, 18 per cent thought unionists and nationalists had benefited equally, and 53 per cent thought nationalists had 'benefited a lot'.[36]

The IRA's foot-dragging on weapons had left Trimble in a difficult position. He shared the DUP reservations about Sinn Fein's commitment to exclusively democratic politics and he felt he had been cheated by Tony Blair's clear promise to make the presence of the Sinn Fein in government conditional on IRA disarmament. When he allowed the Assembly to operate without decommissioning, he was seen as weak. When he closed it down, he just proved that the DUP had been right all along.[37]

The 2003 elections for the second Assembly gave voters a chance to pass judgement, and for unionists that judgement was 'Ulster Says No!' As they were designed to do, the Forum elections had seen a number of independents and smaller parties (such as the UKUP, Women's Coalition, the PUP, and the UDP) take almost a fifth of the unionist vote—very little of that at the expense of the DUP. The first Assembly elections in 1998 had maintained the same pattern. But the next five years had helped many unionists make up their

[35] *Mourne Observer*, 6 June 2001.

[36] Northern Ireland Life and Times survey reported in C. Mitchell, *Religion, Identity and Politics in Northern Ireland* (Aldershot: Ashgate, 2006), ch. 2. Surveys supported his analysis: the proportion of unionists who thought that the Agreement disproportionately benefited nationalists rose from 58 % in 1998 to nearly 80 % in 2003.

[37] Trimble gives a very clear account of his actions and expectations in Millar, *David Trimble*.

minds about the peace process. The Women's Coalition, Alliance Party, and PUP lost half their votes. The anti-agreement UKUP lost four of its five seats. The UUP actually gained votes but lost one seat. And Paisley's party increased its vote from 18 per cent in 1998 to 26 per cent and gained ten extra seats. The shift in unionist preferences had been a macabre game of musical chairs. When the music started, the UUP lost support to a variety of fringe groups; when it stopped, a significant chunk of those voters were sitting in the DUP seats, and the net transfer continued after the election when three UUP members of the Assembly abandoned their party.

The electoral judgement on the first Assembly was a clear victory for the extremes in both communities. In a series of elections before the ceasefires of 1994, Sinn Fein averaged 11 per cent of the vote. In 2003 it took 24 per cent and displaced the SDLP as the major nationalist party. The change on the unionist side had been as great. At the start of the Troubles, the party of Carson, Craigavon, and Brookeborough took 69 per cent of the vote. In 1982 it still managed 30 per cent. In 2003 it was reduced to 23 per cent before the three MLAs defected. The DUP now had an effective veto, because, as of January 2004, the 'No' unionists outnumbered the Trimbalistas by 34 to 25.

If anyone doubted the DUP's ascendancy, the fifth round of elections for the European Parliament settled the matter. Despite Paisley's enormous stamina, old age was taking its toll and the travel was particularly wearing. He stood down and was replaced by his former assistant Jim Allister, who had been encouraged back into the party by Robinson and Dodds. Allister not only held but increased what some had thought of as Paisley's personal vote and he polled twice as well as the UUP candidate.

A tipping point in unionist politics had been reached. After the South Antrim by-election the DUP had started to receive a steady trickle of councillors from the UUP and the small UKUP. In March 2002 a member of the UUP executive had defected to the DUP. A month later, Peter Weir, a well-known North Down barrister who had once been a Trimble confidant, followed suit. But the clearest public marker was the defection of Jeffrey Donaldson. Donaldson was the Ulster Unionist MP for Lagan Valley. Although relatively young, he had been a member of the UUP negotiations team. His frequent expressions of first reservation and then open dissent as he wrestled with his conscience (rather too publicly for decorum) had made him a standard bearer for the right within the UUP and a persistent thorn in Trimble's side.[38] In January 2004 he announced that he was joining the DUP. Although DUP leaders had spent the previous five years being extremely rude about Donaldson's unwillingness to quit the UUP, when he did they made space for him in the negotiating team: past differences would be put aside in the interests of unionist unity. The magnanimity worked. In the twin elections of 2005, the Ulster Unionist Party collapsed.[39] In the local government elections, the DUP took almost twice as many votes as the UUP. It did even better in the Westminster elections. With 34 per cent, the DUP gained the largest share of the vote and won nine of the ten seats previously held by unionists. Trimble lost his Upper Bann seat to a little-known local councillor, and Paisley was returned with over 50 per cent of the votes in North Antrim. The only Ulster Unionist MP left was Lady Sylvia Hermon, wife of a former Chief Constable and representative from North Down—the richest constituency in Northern Ireland. It is significant for understanding a social-class element in the divisions within unionism that no Paisleyite could have won 'the Gold Coast', but more significant that Lady Sylvia could not get elected anywhere else in Northern Ireland.

A DEMOCRAT AFTER ALL?

In November 2003 Paisley's judgement of his place in Ulster politics and his influence over future negotiations was succinct and accurate: 'I may be in the driving seat now but I don't necessarily have to drive.

---

[38] J. Donaldson, *Not by Might: A Journey in Faith and Politics* (Belfast: Ambassador, 2004).

[39] Analysis of turnout suggests that the DUP victory owes something to abstention by previous UUP voters. T. Tonge and J. Evans, 'The Onward March of Paisleyism or a Triumph for Unionist Apathy? Turnout and Voting for the Democratic Unionist Party in the 2005 Westminster Election in Northern Ireland' (unpublished paper, PSA Elections, Public Opinions and Parties annual conference, University of Essex, 2005). For a party official's insider view of the UUP in this period, see M. Kerr, *Transforming Unionism: David Trimble in the 2005 Election* (Dublin: Irish Academic Press, 2005).

I can sit in that seat and give Tony Blair a poke in the ribs, but I don't need to come up with any formula or solutions.'[40]

But actually he did. The DUP responded to its new status by being positively upbeat. As Paisley put it: 'The people we represent have voted for constructive change.' In essence the DUP was prepared to accept devolved government, provided it did not include Sinn Fein until the IRA had been stood down and decommissioned its weapons in a way that was 'complete, time-tabled, verifiable, transparent, witnessed and photographed'.[41] David Simpson, the affable gospel-singing businessman who had displaced Trimble, said: 'Business people were saying to us on the door that the decontamination period has to be extended. They [Sinn Fein] know what they have to do and, if they do it, then come back and talk to us.'[42] If Sinn Fein could not make a clean break with its terrorist past then:

The DUP believes Sinn Fein should be left behind and those wedded to exclusively peaceful and democratic politics should move forward together. Indeed, to those who hold to the seemingly forlorn hope that Sinn Fein can eventually be sanitised, we argue that it is more likely that Sinn Fein would be forced to fall into line if the process moved on without them. It is the belief held by republicans that they can dictate the pace of progress and as a consequence gain concessions, which ensures they will not confront and deal decisively with their unacceptable activities.[43]

Rather than try to form a devolved administration using the complex formulae of the first assembly, the DUP would lead a voluntary coalition of all parties 'who want to have a future free from violence, criminality and guns'.

This was a significant shift for the party that had spent twenty-five years saying 'No'. When Bill Craig had suggested a voluntary coalition in 1974, the DUP had denounced him as a traitor. When I asked one DUP leader what was the difference between 1974 and 2004, he replied 'Thirty years!' The party was realistic enough to appreciate that, while some elements of the Agreement could be renegotiated, much of it was what military strategists call 'realities on the ground'.

---

[40] *Sunday Telegraph*, 30 Nov. 2003.

[41] For a detailed journalistic account of the negotiations of this period, see B. Rowan, *Paisley and the Provos* (Belfast: Brehon Press, 2005).

[42] *Times Online*, 24 Apr. 2005.

[43] www.dup.org.uk/movingon.asp. 2005.

Power would have to be shared; the nationalist mandate would have to be accepted; the equality agenda was in place; the Irish Republic could not be ignored. But the DUP had the philosophical resources for this realism. After all, it had never taken the view of many Islamic fundamentalists that only those with the right religion should have a vote or be able to stand for office.[44] Without having to wriggle too much, it could argue that it had never been against Catholics getting their political due: it had opposed schemes that gave Catholics more than their due. Of course, we can point to an element of self-deception in such claims for consistency of principle. At the start of the Troubles, Paisleyites did not oppose boundary gerrymandering when electoral structures very obviously undervalued nationalist votes. We can also note that it is easy to be in favour of a principle when it serves your interests. But such cynicism should not blind us to the role that ideas can play in helping people accept a necessary change. As the DUP moved from the margins to the centre of power, it was able to call on Protestantism's claim to be in favour of democracy to justify its new position.

For two decades from 1981, the DUP had asserted its commitment to liberal democracy and refused to accept Sinn Fein, and had reconciled the two by asserting that Sinn Fein was contaminated by its organic links to the IRA. The sticking point was Sinn Fein's ballot box and Armalite strategy. 'Democracy never approves of the ruthless killing of people. If Catholics want to disenfranchise themselves by voting for murderers that is their business.' For the DUP 'the key is the need for repentance. We can forgive those who have sincerely repented.' What is needed is 'a turning away, a change of heart, not just a tactical shift'.

For most of 2004 the DUP was pressed by London, Dublin, Washington, and the majority voice of the British press to relax its

---

[44] In the view of most Islamic fundamentalist groups (and a good part of mainstream Islamic opinion), democracy must be constrained by right religion. The demos may be confined to Muslims; or constrained by religious principles (for example, denying women the vote); the will of the demos may be vetted by the pious (as in Iran, where all laws have to be approved by a body of the clergy), and only the suitably pious may be allowed to stand for office. For discussions of these issues, see N. Ayubi, *Political Islam: Religion and Politics in the Arab World* (London: Routledge, 1991), G. E. Fuller, *The Future of Political Islam* (London, Palgrave, 2003), and S. Bruce, *Politics and Religion* (Cambridge: Polity, 2003).

criteria for the rehabilitation of Sinn Fein. The pressure became particularly intense in early December when the Leeds Castle renegotiation of the Agreement[45] very nearly triggered the restoration of devolved government, only for the DUP to announce that the proposals for putting the remaining IRA weapons beyond use were not sufficiently transparent. That pressure was relieved by two events: a bank robbery and a murder. On 20 December, £26.5 million was stolen from the Northern Bank headquarters in Belfast: Britain's largest bank robbery. Although the IRA denied involvement and Sinn Fein leaders supported the denial, the body set up to manage decommissioning—the Independent Monitoring Commission— reported that the IRA was responsible for that and other robberies and stated that 'Sinn Fein must bear its share of responsibility for the incidents. Some of its senior members, who are also members of PIRA, were involved in sanctioning the series of robberies.'[46] The Irish Prime Minister made the obvious point: 'An operation of this magnitude...has obviously been planned at a stage when I was in negotiations with those who would know the leadership of the Provisional movement.'[47] Further evidence of the arrogance of the republican movement was inadvertently provided just over a month after the bank job. On 30 January 2005 a Belfast republican, Robert McCartney, was stabbed to death by a group of IRA men outside a Belfast pub. That itself was not an unusual occurrence in Belfast, but McCartney's five sisters made the murder a cause célèbre by very publicly and repeatedly criticizing the IRA for intimidating the very many witnesses to the killing into silence. To compound Sinn Fein's political problems, the IRA offered to execute those who were responsible—an offer that the McCartney sisters scornfully declined. Gerry Adams condemned the killing and asked that those who had information present it to him so that he could arrange for a solicitor to give it to the Police Ombudsman for Northern Ireland. Taken together, the IRA's corrupt notion of justice and Adams's convoluted way of avoiding telling republicans that it was time they supported

---

[45] The details of what was agreed and the 'choreography' of statements and actions that should have occurred is given in *Irish News*, 9 Dec. 2004. See also Rowan, *Paisley and the Provos*.

[46] *BBC News*, 10 Feb. 2005.   [47] Ibid. 7 Jan. 2005.

the police, combined with the sheer effrontery of the bank robbery, let the DUP off the hook. Ivan Foster certainly took the view that the Lord had sent a great deliverance:

It was the providential mercy of God that prevented Sinn Fein entering government a few weeks ago. That must now surely be seen and acknowledged by every Christian who seeks the welfare of all the citizens of this land. Once again, God has made the pride of man to serve His purpose and advance the good of His people. Were it not for the pride of Sinn Fein/IRA, we would now have this murky and murderous organization restored to the governmental posts that Ulster Unionist leader David Trimble negotiated for them. May God be pleased to over-rule and frustrate every attempt by London and Dublin to put Adams and his fellow gangsters in power in Ulster.[48]

But providence remained inscrutable. In 2006 the IRA completed the process of putting its weapons beyond use and the 10th report of the International Monitoring Committee announced that, in its view, the IRA had lived up to the commitments made the previous year to give up recruitment, victim targeting, intelligence gathering, rioting and other violence, criminality, and illegal fund-raising. The DUP, as ever, snorted at the upbeat conclusions but privately accepted that Sinn Fein was moving in the right direction. The final sticking point was policing. Sinn Fein had to prove its good faith by joining the police boards and telling nationalists to accept the reformed Police Service of Northern Ireland.

The Paisleyite political vision remains profoundly paradoxical. On the one hand, there is a comforting almost restful consistency in many of Paisley's sermons and speeches, in Foster's editorials in the *Burning Bush*, and in addresses made by other Free Presbyterian clerics and DUP activists: the Protestant people of Ulster are still threatened by a Vatican-inspired physical-force republicanism aided by a treacherous British government. On the other hand, party officials make it clear that, if the IRA really does go out of business, and if Sinn Fein can persuade the unionist electorate that it really accepts the democratic principles laid down by Senator George Mitchell at the start of the talks process, then the DUP will work with Sinn Fein in operating the institutions laid down by the Belfast Agreement.

---

[48] *Burning Bush*, 35 (Jan. 2005), 1.

5

Church Established

INTRODUCTION

In March 2001 the Free Presbyterian Church of Ulster celebrated its fiftieth anniversary with a day of special services in the Odyssey Arena in Belfast. A crowd of almost 10,000 people gathered in one of Northern Ireland's largest arenas to celebrate its survival and success. John Douglas and Alan Cairns led Bible readings, Bert Cooke, James Beggs, and Frank McClelland prayed, Willie McCrea sang 'How Great Thou Art', and Ian Paisley preached on 'the pre-eminence of Christ'. Fifty years earlier, at the Crossgar foundation, Paisley had said: 'Just as the Free Church of Scotland grew in strength till it was almost as big as the church it left, so I believe that this church, with the blessing of God, will go forward till all Ulster rings with its teaching.'[1]

This chapter will detail the growth of the FPCU and examine the various ways in which it has changed since the volatile 1960s. Particular attention will be given to the ways in which the Church has diversified and professionalized its activities. Over the intervening forty years, the FPCU has largely become accepted. Its long-serving ministers are awarded civic honours; its church services are broadcast on the BBC's Radio Ulster; and its periodic protests against lap-dancing clubs and sex shops are reported as quaint eccentricities. For an organization that always stressed the first two syllables of the word 'Protestant', this success raises the possibility of corruption: as it has become accepted, has the FPCU lost its soul?

[1] FPCU, *50th Anniversary Souvenir Programme* (Belfast: FPCU, 2001).

NUMBERS

Although Northern Ireland remains markedly more churchgoing than other parts of the United Kingdom, the last quarter of the twentieth century saw a decline in the numbers who described themselves as Christian, attended church, and were church members. To get a proper sense of how the FPCU has fared, it is useful to describe the general populations from which it might recruit and the performance of its competitors.

Between the 1971 and 2001 censuses, the non-Catholic population of Northern Ireland fell 3 per cent: from 1.04 million to 1.01 million. The decline in the major Protestant churches was steeper. The number of those who described themselves as Irish Presbyterian, for example, fell from 405,717 in 1971 to 348,742 in 2001: a drop of 14 per cent. Over the same thirty years, the Church of Ireland lost 22 per cent of its population.[2]

This decline in identification has been matched by a decline in church attendance. Detailed social surveys show that claimed weekly church attendance for Protestants fell from 46 per cent in 1968 to 34 per cent in 2003.[3] Between 1989 and 2002, the proportion of Church of Ireland survey respondents who said they attended every week fell from 35 to 30 per cent.[4] Not surprisingly, the same surveys show a decline in the numbers who describe themselves as religious, and in the frequency of prayer, with the largest changes apparently coming from a decline in the commitment and interest of the previously lukewarm.[5] The Protestant population seems to be separating out, with some giving up their religion and a smaller number becoming more religious (often with a move from a mainstream denomination to a conservative alternative).

[2] These figures are calculated from data provided by the NI Census Office in its published reports (e.g. Department of Health and Social Services/Registrar General Northern Ireland, *The Northern Ireland Census 1981 Religion Report* (Belfast: Her Majesty's Stationary Office, 1984)) and website.

[3] C. Mitchell, *Religion, Identity and Politics in Northern Ireland* (Aldershot: Ashgate, 2006), 25.

[4] J. Mehaffey, 'The Church of Ireland in Northern Ireland: A Decade of Change?', *Research Update*, 23 (Jan. 2004); www.ark.ac.uk.

[5] J. Brewer, 'Are there any Christians in Northern Ireland?', in A. M. Gray, K. Lloyd, P. Devine, G. Robinson, and D. Heenan (eds.), *Social Attitudes in Northern Ireland: The Eighth Report* (London: Pluto Press, 2002), ch. 2.

The history of the FPCU is part of that broader pattern of conservative growth within overall decline. The trajectory is very clearly characterized by three phases. From 1951 to 1966 growth was slow.[6] There was then a period of rapid expansion, which had ended by the time of the 1971 census. Since then the FPCU has grown slowly and then plateaued. According to the 1971 census, 7,349 people identified themselves as Free Presbyterians. In 1981 it was 9,621, and by 1991 a further 28 per cent had been added to take the total to 12,314. Over the next ten years, the total fell by 1 per cent: to 11,989. Some of this fall-off is almost certainly a result of a general decline in family size, but a good deal of it is due to migration. Since the early 1970s large numbers of young Protestants have gone to university and college in Britain; in 2005 there were 14,000 such education migrants. Many have not returned. That background makes the following small advert in the Free Presbyterian *Truth for Youth* rather poignant: 'Female student commencing studies at Stirling University would like to contact other young Christians in the area.'[7] Her parents may wish that she will return, but the chances are she will not. And after higher education, there is the draw of wider career opportunities: almost every Free Presbyterian family I interviewed had at least one child who had left Northern Ireland for work.

The growth of Free Presbyterians—from 0.7 per cent of non-Catholics in 1971 to 1.2 per cent in 2001—will disappoint those who in 1970 saw the possibility of a great revival, but it does represent a significant achievement. It took the FPCU past other evangelical bodies (such as the Evangelical Presbyterian Church and the Reformed Presbyterian Church) that could be considered similar in being conservative in doctrine but not Pentecostal and it under-represents the Church's strength. Censuses flatter the larger and better-established organizations because they encourage nominalism. People with only a nostalgic church connection may call themselves Church of Ireland or Irish Presbyterian; only people who really are Free Presbyterians would describe themselves as such, and we see the difference in the proportions who attend church

---

[6] Details are provided in the Appendix. I am grateful to the Northern Ireland Statistics and Research Agency for providing me with these data.

[7] *Truth for Youth* (Aug.–Sept. 2000), 3.

regularly. As we can see from Table 5.1,[8] over two-thirds of those who identify themselves in surveys as Free Presbyterians attend church almost every week; for Irish Presbyterians the comparable figure is less than half. One reason for having confidence in these numbers is that they are similar to those we can arrive at using a very different source. The FPCU's official history[9] contains a potted history of every congregation with an estimate of the numbers who normally attend (see the Appendix) and they add up to 8,835, which is 74 per cent of those who reported themselves as Free Presbyterians in the 2001 census.

FPCU CHURCH PLANTING AND CHURCH LIFE

As can be seen from the details in the Appendix, the growth of the FPCU has come in distinct phases. In the first period, over the fifteen years from 1946 to 1964, ten congregations were created. There then

TABLE 5.1. *Church attendance of Irish Presbyterians and Free Presbyterians, 1989–2003* (%)

Attendance	Irish Presbyterian	Free Presbyterian
Weekly or more	32.3	60.0
2–3 times a month	11.1	7.8
Monthly	9.7	8.2
Several times a year	13.3	6.9
Less often	15.0	7.8
Varies	17.3	8.2
Never	1.2	1.2
	100	100

Sources: Northern Ireland Social Attitudes Survey, 1989–96; Northern Ireland Life and Times Survey, 1998–2003.

[8] I am grateful to my Aberdeen University colleague Bernadette Hayes for providing these data. It is difficult to infer much about Free Presbyterians because, when even large-scale surveys use samples of only 1,000, there may, depending on the sampling pattern, be as few as 50 FP respondents. In order to create a sample large enough to produce these comparisons, Hayes 'pooled' the data from all the NIAS and NILT surveys between 1989 and 2003.

[9] P. Kyle, *Our Own Heritage: Not to be Thrown away* (Tavistock: Tavistock Free Presbyterian Church, 2002).

followed the boom associated with the conflicts of the O'Neill era. Between 1964 and 1969 nineteen congregations were planted. In the next decade twenty-one churches were added. Since 1982 a further eleven have been added to what was by then pretty well province-wide coverage. By and large these third-generation congregations have been planted in between the first- and second-wave churches and most have come about in a similar way. Free Presbyterians who were travelling some distance to attend church found this a consid-erable handicap to their own personal outreach work. As one of the founding elders of the Bangor congregation put it, one can hardly invite relative strangers to 'come to hear a certain preacher or come to a special meeting' when that involves a fifty-mile round trip. In many cases, a tentative start would be made with the hiring or erection of a temporary hall and the holding of Sunday afternoon services. In others a fortnight of mission services would be held in a tent or a hired hall, and if sufficient interest was shown a nucleus would organize services. When the local promoters felt confident enough, they would take on a student minister, purchase land, or perhaps buy a vacant building. The local Free Presbyterians who had previously travelled to their old church would then constitute the core of a new congregation. For example, the Mulvin congregation was formed as a result of the coincidence of an old Reformed Presbyterian building coming on the market at the same time as two elders of the Castlederg congregation who lived locally were considering starting a 'work' in their own area.

Thus, in addition to slow but steady growth in membership, there has also been a shift from Free Presbyterianism being concentrated on a small number of major centres to a structure closer to parishes of the major denominations, with a meeting house within easy travelling distance of most people in the province. As well as making it easier to attract potential new members, the church building programme has been an important morale booster.

Building is not just about bricks and wood; there are important sociological consequences of a major building programme. My at-tention was first drawn to these by ministers themselves, who were well aware of the value that church-building has for creating and sustaining members' commitment. If a building is purchased from another denomination or some secular structure is acquired (in two cases, disused cinemas were bought), there will be an official opening ceremony and some initial pleasure at entering a newly refurbished building, but there the process ends. But if the initial pioneers buy land, erect a portable building, and then, when numbers justify it, build a small church and every decade expand it, then a strong sense of progress can be maintained through a series of morale-boosting special services to which Dr Paisley and other ministers are invited and that can be reported in the local press. To take the example of Magherafelt, the church began in August 1969 in a small corrugated iron hut. Four months later it had to be extended. Within another four months it was too small, and in August 1970 Paisley opened a second extension. In June 1973 about 1,000 people gathered to watch Paisley cut the sod for a permanent church building. Two years later the foundation stones were laid. Volunteers, supervised by a professional builder, gradually constructed the church, and in August 1978 over 3,000 people attended the official opening.

This model of incremental expansion has the great benefit of avoiding the empty church problem that has blighted British Christianity since the mid-nineteenth century. Robin Gill made an important contribution to our understanding of church decline when he detailed the way that the Victorian enthusiasm for church-building combined with aggressive competition between sects to provide far more places of worship (and seats within them) than were required. 'The Free Churches in all major urban areas built so vigorously that their chapels were always physically emptier by the 1880s than they had been in 1851, even when their church-going rates were still rising.'[10] The result was that even growing congregations often found themselves depressed by worshipping in buildings that were far too big. That meant not just unnecessarily high heating and maintenance costs (on top of the problem of servicing the loan that funded the building in the first place). There was also the demoralizing effect of being surrounded by empty pews. The seats were empty because recruitment targets had been overly ambitious and not because the number of the faithful had declined, but it still felt like decline, and potential recruits were hardly attracted by an echoing half-empty building. It is worth noting that many of the FPCU congregations that began in acquired premises later

---

[10] Robin Gill, *The Myth of the Empty Church* (London: SPCK, 1993), 10.

moved to new buildings and prospered after the move. The former Irish Presbyterian Church in Clifton Park Avenue, North Belfast, which was bought in 1972 and opened as the John Knox Memorial, was always cold and uninviting, and republicans probably did the congregation a favour by burning out the church in 1986. After meeting in the West Belfast Orange Hall for a number of years, the congregation bought a site in Northumberland Street and built a small adaptable building that they could fill and in which they could worship in comfort. John Wyllie bought a disused Covenanter church in Garvagh in 1970, but the congregation remained small until 2001, when it built a new church on a prominent green field site.

WORSHIP

In the nineteenth century most Protestant churches held two (and sometimes three) services on a Sunday, and zealous clergy chided their people for the sin of 'half day hearing'. The FPCU churches have two sabbath services. The morning service tends to be the conventional Presbyterian worship service with hymns, a psalm, scripture reading, a sermon, and more hymns. It differs from the services of the Irish Presbyterian Church only in the length and nature of the sermon—normally over thirty minutes long and heavy on Bible exposition, with congregants carefully following the text in the King James version of the Bible. Communion, on those Sundays on which it is taken, would follow or be part of the morning worship. As the history of the Crossgar congregation says: 'In the main, the morning services have focussed on building up and edifying those already on the Christian journey while the evening services, by convention, have been most directly used for presenting the Gospel message to those not yet saved.'[11] Starting with community singing and sometimes involving an invited soloist, the evening service is intended to be more relaxed than the morning one. In Dr Paisley's congregation, the evening meeting is usually also the more topical and controversial in that he will deal with contemporary political

---

[11] G. Moore and S. Dick, *The History of the Crossgar Free Presbyterian Church of Ulster* (Crossgar: Crossgar FPCU, 2001), 82.

issues. In most of the major denominations attendance at evening meetings has declined so much since the Second World War that they have either been abandoned or are now shared by a number of churches in a neighbourhood. Many Free Presbyterians attend both Sunday services, and committed core members will often arrive an hour or thirty minutes before the services for Bible study or intensive prayer.

The hymns are a mixture of the popular Victorian hymns that were the mainstay of British Nonconformity for the first half of the twentieth century and some more recent upbeat gospel music. The selection is careful to avoid the doctrinally suspect songs that became popular in charismatic circles in the last two decades of the twentieth century, and the accompaniment is only ever piano or organ. The Free Church has very deliberately not followed the lead of churches such as the Belfast Metropolitan Tabernacle that, like many American evangelical congregations, have married the secular form of the rock group to the large choirs common in black churches to produce loud and intense music.

As well as the Sabbath services, Free Presbyterian congregations have a variety of mid-week events. Crossgar, for example, has a Youth Fellowship, a children's meeting, and an adult Bible class and prayer meeting. Attendance at such meetings is expected of a sincerely converted Christian, who should display hunger for gospel teaching:

The worldly Church says 'What nonsense to have a prayer meeting. Let us organise. Let us get money in. Let us have discos in the Church Hall. And ping pong and pool and everything else in the Church Hall and get all the young people in and have a jollification'. Utter nonsense. It is not the policy of the church to entertain the goats. It is the policy of the Church to feed the sheep.[12]

If a minister decides to have a week or a fortnight of special evangelistic meetings, the core of his congregation will turn out night after night to support his efforts.

It is clear from the total income and memberships of the organizations that Free Presbyterians give far more money to church work than do Irish Presbyterians. Perhaps more important, to Free Presbyterians at least, is the manner in which they give it. Free Presbyterians will not organize raffles, tombolas, dinner dances, jumble sales, or fêtes to raise money. To do so would be to fall into the sin of 'worldliness'. Paisley has a well-practised and much-loved line in denouncing such methods:

[12] *Revivalist* (Feb. 1982).

Like these descendants of Tetzel, the notorious peddler of the Pope's indul-
gences, many men who have vowed to preach the whole counsel of God have
become organisers of dances, parties, stewardship dinners, etc in a vain attempt
to bolster up the crumbling structure of their Church finances...No Free
Presbyterian minister will stoop to such miserable tactics. When we need
money we pray and God's people give as unto him.[13]

And give they certainly do. In 2004 the members of the Armagh
congregation gave an average of £12 per week to the church and most
will have more than doubled that with donations to special causes
such as the radio ministry, support for a missionary family, or the
costs of the many new church buildings that the FPCU has erected.
Free Presbyterians take obvious pride in their missionary support
and their new church building, but, as Paisley's judgement on those
who raise money by secular means make clear, it is not so much the
amounts of money as the manner in which it is raised that produces
their sense of satisfaction. Unlike the followers of Antichrist who
hold raffles and the 'ecumeniacs' who have dances, Free Presbyterians
need no motive other than the belief that they are engaged in the
work of the Lord to persuade them to support the Church.

One aspect of a Free Presbyterian service that is unusual these days
is the dress of the congregants. Women wear hats and men wear suits
and ties. In liberal congregations and in those evangelical groups that
have been influenced by the charismatic movement and by American
evangelicalism, casual dress is commonplace: Free Presbyterians dress
for church in the style of their grandparents: 'For me it's a mark of
respect. After all, you'd put on your best suit for a job interview. Is
the Lord's house not more important than a job interview? Casual
clothes—casual attitude, I say.' The dress code is just one small element
of a generally conservative 'walk with the Lord' that Free Presbyterians
expect of the saved Christian.

MORES AND MORALS

The dress styles, the hymns, and the long exegetical sermons firmly
place the FPCU somewhere between 1940 and 1963, and its moral
and behavioural requirements would be familiar to any conservative

[13] Ibid. (Jan. 1978).

Christian from the same era. The Church is opposed to homosexuality, premarital sex, and divorce, and to mothers working full-time outside the home. It condemns drinking, smoking, and recreational drug use. Dancing is prohibited, watching television for entertainment is regarded with suspicion, and even dining out is frowned upon. It is suspicious of all forms of sensual pleasure and prefers self-control to self-expression. Modesty is expected in all matters of appearance: exotic and revealing clothing is forbidden and only the lightest make-up is tolerated.

The clergy have a sufficiently good grasp of history to appreciate that fashions change (Victorian evangelical men often had beards; by the 1960s facial hair was deeply suspect) and that it is unwise to assemble too many taboos, but they are quite clear about the need for discipline. Underlying all the FPCU's moral thinking is the classic ascetic principle that the human self in its natural form is bad and that we become good only by subjecting ourselves to Godly discipline. Free Presbyterians are expected to be diligent, temperant, responsible, self-reliant, and hard-working and to have more of a mind on the next life than on this. Though quite what counts as worldliness changes, 'worldliness' is always a term of condemnation.

TRAINING THE CLERGY

An earlier chapter noted that the early years of the church were characterized by considerable turnover in the ministry, particularly among those men who were recruited from outside Northern Ireland or who had previous experience of full-time Christian work and hence clear expectations that were likely to jar with their new roles. Crucial to the FPCU's later expansion was its ability to recruit an increasing proportion of candidates for the ministry from a membership that has been saved or raised in the Free Church. There were also important changes in the organization of ministerial training.

When the FPCU was founded, theological training for the ministry was provided by Ian Paisley, his father, and Dr H. H. Aitchison, an ex-Presbyterian and ex-Congregational Union minister whose doctorate had been awarded by a rather dubious American mail-order college for a series of lectures on the psychology of religion (published by

Pitman as *Psychology without Sighs*). Although, as an evangelical, Paisley would have put personal piety before theological qualifications as a mark of the man of God, he had great respect for formal education.[14] Candidates who did not possess basic credentials in English and arithmetic, for example, were sent to evening classes. At least two ministerial candidates dropped out because they found the scholarly elements of the training too difficult. Although Paisley was personally quite capable of providing theological training of a standard that would be accepted in many Protestant denominations, he simply did not have the time to devote to the creation of a theological college. Like many of the other factors that hampered the growth of the Church, this problem was gradually resolved by initial growth creating the right conditions for more rapid growth. Once the first generation of John Douglas, S. B. Cooke, and Alan Cairns had finished their training, they were able to devote part of their energies to training the next generation. As the total number of ministers increased, these three were able to devote more time and effort to teaching, as the others shouldered the burden of evangelistic meetings. The enlarged pool also included some men, such as Gordon Ferguson, who had a good degree in Classics from London University, with particular skills to contribute.

A sign of the increased attention to training is the increase in the number of years the students were expected to spend in college. At first the training period was three years, but in 1976 a fourth year was added. Perhaps more significant was the increased delay in putting a student in charge of a congregation. Until the 1970s, candidates were

---

[14] Paisley's fondness for initials after his name has given his critics ample opportunity for ridicule. The basic facts are these. In 1946 he successfully completed a three-year course with the Reformed Presbyterians. In April and November 1954 he joined the Geographical Society, the Royal Society of Literature, and the Philosophical Society—all organizations that one joins by paying a fee. In March and October 1954 he was given a BD and a Ph.D. by Pioneer Theological Seminary, Rockford, Illinois. In March 1958 he acquired an MA from Burton College and Seminary, Manitou Springs. Both Pioneer and Burton were degree 'mills': phoney postal colleges that offered no tuition. Qualifications were supposedly awarded for written work but were in fact awarded for the payment of fees irrespective of the quality of work submitted. The *Revivalist* (Sept.–Oct. 1959) described him as working for a Ph.D. from Burton with his history of the 1859 Ulster revivals. However, his book on the subject, which might well have been awarded a higher degree at some institutions, was first published the previous year. In 1966 Bob Jones University, an educationally respectable, though thoroughly fundamentalist institution in Greenville, South Carolina, gave Paisley an honorary degree in recognition of his services to fundamentalism. It is this qualification that entitles him to be styled 'Doctor'.

usually placed in congregations as soon as they had been accepted for the ministry. By the 1980s students usually studied full-time for two years before being given ministerial duties. In addition to improving the teaching, the Church has insisted that its students pass their examinations. One man who was pastoring a growth congregation in Armagh was reluctant to complete his courses, which, after a sixteen-year absence from formal education, he found difficult, arguing that the success of his ministry demonstrated his competence. He was cautioned by the Presbytery and later removed when he continued to refuse to complete his college work.

A major step forward came in 1981 with the purchase of a large house near Banbridge, which became the Whitefield College of the Bible. Although its main business was training men for the FPCU ministry, its two-year- and four-year-long courses (the former intended for those with varied reasons for wanting to deepen their Christian knowledge; the latter being the ministerial course) were open to all who shared the FPCU's evangelical principles.

Free Presbyterianism is not, as some detractors suppose, anti-intellectual. It violently disagrees with many of the specific beliefs offered by modern liberal education institutions, but it retains the respect for an educated and learned ministry, which was so characteristic of Scottish and Ulster Presbyterianism and which separates it from many other varieties of conservative Protestantism. In some respect its intellectual demands are actually more severe than those of more mainstream Reformed churches: it requires its ministerial candidates to learn the Bible languages of Hebrew and Greek. The reasons for this are fairly obvious and are related to the question of authority. Conservative Protestants differ from other Christians in the stress they place on the authority of the Bible. For them the Bible is the centre of Christianity because it and it alone contains the accounts of the life and teaching of Christ and the information needed for salvation. Free Presbyterians constantly return to the Bible and the study of it, and the preaching of its message is the core of Free Presbyterianism. The problem is that the Bible is not self-interpreting. Or, to be more precise, even within those variants of Christianity that claim no source of authority other than the Bible, there are considerable differences of opinion about what the Bible actually teaches. The practical solution is to accept as 'standards subordinate to the Scriptures' documents that clearly express particular interpretations of the Bible. Hence, the role played by the Westminster Confession of Faith and the Longer and Shorter Catechisms—the classic statements of traditional Presbyterianism. Free Presbyterians insist that the church traditions that they use to guide their interpretation of the Bible are quite different from those used by the Roman Catholic Church for the same purpose. In the first place, they claim their traditions represent the essence of Bible Christianity and Rome's traditions do not. Secondly, their traditions are subordinate to the Bible. However, leaving aside the truth or falsity of such claims, it is clear that, from an organizational point of view, Protestant creeds perform a task similar to that performed by the bureaucracy of the Roman Catholic Church in codifying the faith and in setting the limits to the valid interpretation of the faith. The mastery of the doctrine expressed in such creeds requires considerable study.

Charismatic religious groups, which believe that the Holy Spirit leads believers, can have leaders with little formal training. A religious culture that lays great stress on doctrinal orthodoxy has to ensure that its leaders acquire the correct doctrine. Ritual plays so little part in Free Presbyterianism that learning what a minister does takes little time but learning what a minister thinks and says is time consuming. Furthermore, the widespread acceptance in educated circles of liberal interpretations of the Scriptures has meant that conservatives are under considerable pressure to defend their ideology and, in order to do this, they must become reasonably familiar with Greek and Hebrew so that they can justify to their flocks their refusal to accept modern interpretations of the Bible. From the point of view of the individual who feels called to preach the word, the lengthy and difficult training may seem like an uncalled-for encumbrance, but, from the point of view of the organization, it is justified by the greater cohesion produced and by the increased likelihood that the Church will survive as a homogenous unit after its founder ceases to be active and his personal leadership ceases to be a source of unity.

SCHOOLING THE CHILDREN

In any society that is not culturally homogeneous, education will be an arena for social conflict because it plays a major part in the socialization of the next generation. A culture reproduces itself through education. In common with many basically Protestant societies, Northern Ireland has a system of state schools that was formed by the government acquisition of schools that had previously been run by the various denominations.[15] The Roman Catholic Church insisted on maintaining its own schools, initially at some cost because Catholics were supporting both a state system through their taxes and a Catholic system through donations. The logic of Catholic education is that it is not enough to add a few hours of 'Catholic' teaching on to the end of a secular curriculum: all subjects have to be taught within the context of Catholicism. Gradually the state increased its contribution to the voluntary schools, so that now all teachers' salaries and almost all costs are paid for by the state.

At the outset of the Northern Ireland state, the government's intention had been to create a national system of non-sectarian schools. This was sabotaged first by the Catholic Church refusing even to enter negotiations, and then by a number of Protestant clerics, in alliance with the Orange Order, successfully agitating to improve the terms under which church schools would be transferred to state control. Despite the puzzlement of one Minister of Education who could not see 'why an exhaustive knowledge of the Apocalypse should necessarily qualify any man to decide the amount of money to be expended on lavatory accommodation in any given primary school', the 1923 Education Act was amended so as to increase the influence of the clergy in the management of the schools.[16] Whatever the merits of their case, the Protestant churches won the right to ensure that only Protestant teachers were appointed, enshrined one hour of 'simple Bible teaching' in each school week, and forced teachers to give such instruction as part of their normal teaching duties. One might have thought that these provisions would have ensured that the ex-Protestant schools remained more than non-Catholic, but they became fairly thoroughly secularized. The 1944 Education Act had moderated the success of the 1920s campaign for greater church control. For example, teachers could no longer be

---

[15] A good account of the organization and funding of Northern Ireland's schools can be found in P. Buckland, *The Factory of Grievances: Devolved Government in Northern Ireland, 1921–39* (Dublin: Gill and Macmillan, 1979), ch. 11.

[16] Ibid. 257.

required to teach Bible study. By the 1960s most religious education classes had moved away from Bible exposition. In part this drift was inevitable. Clerical representation on management committees could not prevent what religion there was in schools being 'diluted' because the clergy were themselves not united in doctrine. With considerable doctrinal deviation both within and between the Protestant denominations, it was impossible to maintain any strong religious influence, and religion in schools now generally means what one critic called 'vacuous piety of the lowest common denominator type'. The present Northern Ireland school system thus consists of a Roman Catholic sector and a non-Catholic sector that has become largely secularized.

For conservative evangelicals, state schools have become worrisome for a variety of reasons. First, there is non-religious teaching that offends their beliefs. In biology classes, for example, children may be taught evolutionary theories of the origins of the species. Even if children are not directly confronted with evolution, they will certainly not be taught the Genesis creation story. More generally, children may be presented with views on sex education and related moral issues, or on current affairs, that are at odds with what their parents teach them at home.

Secondly, when the state schools are not actually short of religion, they offer the wrong kind. Even when Protestant clerics were at their most influential in educational policy, the Bible instruction that they had insisted upon was 'to be Protestant in nature but not distinctive of a Protestant denomination', which effectively meant that, as the main denominations became more liberal in their theology, religious education ceased to be dogmatic. This alone would be anathema to evangelicals, but the problem is often compounded by religious instruction being directed by teachers who see an opportunity for broadening children's horizons by making them acquainted with a variety of religious cultures. Throughout the United Kingdom, religious education has become education about religion rather than schooling in any particular variety, and widely used teaching materials present the major world religions as equally plausible alternatives. The Oxford Reading Tree, which is widely used in UK primary schools, has a series of books that present the religious cultures of Muslim, Sikh, Hindu, Jewish, and Christian families in an entirely even-handed manner. The implication is clear: all are equally valid.

Conservative Protestants in Northern Ireland had a particular grievance. In 1989 the government introduced Education for Mutual Understanding (EMU), and the related theme of Cultural Heritage, as part of the curriculum for all grant-aided schools in Northern Ireland. The purpose was to improve relationships between people of 'differing cultural traditions' (that is, Catholics and Protestants), and one way to achieve that was to present each to the other in a positive light. While no Free Presbyterian would argue with one of the stated aims of EMU—to help people manage conflict in a non-violent way— none would wish to see Catholicism presented as a viable alternative to his or her own faith and very few would wish the political aspirations of nationalists similarly presented. As Paisley put it: 'we have teachers in our primary schools engaged in a great ecumenical operation to take the children and condition them to Roman Catholicism and to apostasy. I tell you, we'd better wake up and know what is happening in Northern Ireland.'[17]

Finally, evangelicals have vague, but nonetheless strongly felt, fears about discipline. People who believe in original sin have little reason to encourage children to express themselves. Free Presbyterians believe that children need to be taught manners and respect for authority. Liberal educationalists with their belief in child-centred learning and distaste for corporal punishment are blamed for vandalism, bad language, adolescent sexual activity, and all the other things that evangelicals believe characterize modern youth.

It is worth adding an aside at this point. The above has been presented in largely negative terms, and some critics of the Free Church would go further. One critic believes that unionist objections to government plans to promote mutual understanding are a result of 'the inherent insecurity and fear within some sections of the unionist community'.[18] There is nothing grammatically or logically wrong with talking of evangelical attitudes to state schooling in terms of what evangelicals are trying to avoid, but it creates a misleading impression. True, parents often focus on what they wish to avoid, but their attitudes could equally well be expressed in a series of positive

[17] N. Southern, 'God's People and Fundamentalist Ideology in the Classroom: An Examination of Free Presbyterian Schooling in Northern Ireland', *Religion and Education*, 31 (2004), 52.

[18] F. Cochrane, *Unionist Politics* (Cork: Cork University Press, 2001), 53.

statements. Evangelicals have a culture that they believe is better than the alternatives and they wish to maximize the opportunities to pass it intact to their children. Talk of 'insecurity' and 'fear' is further misleading because it suggests that those who reject secular liberal and ecumenical education have some sort of psychological problem. By such terms liberals cheat in the arguments. Instead of recognizing that conservatives are merely trying to exercise the right to raise their children as they wish, liberals imply that those who wish to maintain a distinctive religion are feeble-minded and psychologically deficient. By his choice of words, the liberal presents himself as a confident humanitarian and the conservative as a fearful bigot!

To return to the main thread: most evangelicals find ways of living with the problem of unhelpful state schooling. They work hard at home to counter the malign influence of the school. Or they try to intervene whenever possible. One Free Presbyterian minister recalled the occasion when his children brought home a BBC carol book that contained 'a carol in it that was pure Mary worship'. He went to see the senior teachers, expressed his concern, and found the staff willing to accommodate him by passing over that particular carol. In general, he found that he could maintain a working relationship with the staff of the particular school that his children attended, although he did recognize that other schools were less cooperative. There are also some evangelicals who accept the separatist critique but do not consider removing their children because, they argue, young evangelicals will come face to face with sin and apostasy sometime and it is better to let them get used to being surrounded by unbelief gradually rather than have them cocooned until 18 and then thrown straight in at the deep end.

It is against this sort of background that the Free Presbyterian Church's establishment of seven independent Christian schools has to be seen. The first was founded by the Fosters in Kilskeery. Mrs Foster was a well-qualified and experienced teacher in a state school who became so disillusioned with the education being given to her children that she withdrew them and began to teach them at home. It seemed sensible to offer the service to other Free Presbyterians, and in September 1979 the Kilskeery Independent Christian School opened its doors. Kilskeery was followed in 1983 by Ballymoney, where the minister was a qualified teacher, and Newtownabbey, where the minister had been deeply impressed by a lecture on Christian education delivered at the 1978 World Fundamentalist Congress in Edinburgh. In researching the possibilities, Reggie Cranston visited fundamentalist schools in Ohio and at Bob Jones University in South Carolina, where he took a short course in school management. In 1985 a fourth school opened in Bangor. Clogher Valley opened in 1987, and Portadown and Mourne started their schools the following year.

The schools are, as the name boasts, entirely independent. They receive no state funding and, within the constraints set by the University of London examination papers, are free to teach what they like. They are subject to government inspection, and the inspectors' reports have been generally favourable. They have, however, expressed concern about what the Free Presbyterians see as a major advantage of their schools: the well-mannered and disciplined behaviour of the pupils. Such behaviour is fundamental to what the schools are trying to do, and until 2003 all parents signed an agreement with the school in which they accepted the following:

I fully realise that the Bible sets forth plain standards for any institution which claims to be Christian. On the question of modesty (1 Tim. 2: 9–10) and of tidiness and length of hair (1 Cor. 11: 13) plain instructions are given. I undertake to see that my child(ren) at all times uphold(s) the standards of appearance set by the Scripture. I understand that learning can only take place in an atmosphere of disciplined obedience to the teacher. In order to maintain discipline a teacher must exercise authority in a fair, firm and kindly manner. Where punitive measures are necessary to maintain authority, I hereby give permission for appropriate corporal punishment to be administered to my child(ren).

The 2003 extension of the ban on corporal punishment from state schools to private schools meant the last sentence had to be dropped:

We still believe that scripture teaches that corporal punishment is right when it is administered in love . . . This new document means that the parents will be informed if the child misbehaves and it is the parents' responsibility to correct in whatever form they see fit. You can't tell them they must do it according to the Word of God. The child now faces suspension and expulsion which is a lot more severe in one sense, but that's where the law has sent us.[19]

[19] N. Southern, 'God's People and Fundamentalist Ideology in the Classroom: An Examination of Free Presbyterian Schooling in Northern Ireland', *Religion and Education*, 31 (2004), 49.

In its publicity literature, the Newtownabbey school lists the fundamentalist Christian beliefs of the Free Presbyterian Church, stresses
the importance of discipline and authority, and states that 'All members of staff in a Christian school must be born again'. Apart from the
children being sufficiently quiet and well behaved for the inspectors
to fret about it, the other defining characteristic of the schools is their
frequent recourse to religious activities. The week begins with the
reciting of the school creed:

I believe the Bible to be the Word of God. I believe that Jesus Christ is God's
only begotten Son. I believe that by faith in his atoning death alone I can be
saved from sin and everlasting punishment. I believe that all those who fully
trust in Him should live holy lives and avoid lying and all things that would
dishonour the Lord's great name. I will not dishonour the name of the Lord
Jesus or the name of our school by improper behaviour of any kind at home,
in church, in class, or in any other place. I will not be ashamed of or deny this
statement of my faith.

One of the Kilskeery teachers described the place of the Bible in the
work of the schools:

Each school day starts with half an hour's devotion in which the Bible is read
and taught. After lunch there is another time set aside for Bible reading. Each
pupil learns at least one Bible verse every week, while those in Form 1 learn
four. We have two periods of Scripture lesson every week. The Bible obviously
is *the* textbook here, and while we must use other textbooks for our many
subjects, anything contrary to the word of God is utterly rejected.[20]

There is frequent prayer. When the children in one primary school
class returned from playing outside during break, the teacher asked
which children want to pray. Almost all clamoured to be chosen. The
chosen ones prayed for Dr Paisley and all the Christian schools. Two
ministers who had recently visited the school were also mentioned.

The schools rely heavily on the willingness of teachers to accept
lower salaries than they would command in the state sector. In 2005
the Kilskeery fees were £485 per child per year (with reductions for
second and third children) if the family were not Free Presbyterians
and £400 if they were; a private school in Aberdeen costs about
£9,000 a year. The dual pricing is explained by the feature that

[20] *Truth for Youth* (Mar.–Apr. 1981), 7.

makes the endeavour possible: the FPCU provides the plant. Many of
the new churches are built with specially designed Sunday school
complexes of halls and classrooms. Apart from the additional heating
and lighting costs, the buildings come free to the schools.

Although separate schools seem an obvious weapon in the ar-
moury of an avowedly separatist church, Free Presbyterians have
not united behind the schools. In 2002 Newtownabbey had 38 pupils
and Portadown had 70 across its nursery, primary, and secondary
division. In 2005 the flagship Kilskeery school had 56. Paisley strongly
supports the initiative, and I have never heard any minister criticize it,
but most parents send their children to state schools. As the fees are
less than a motorist will pay to insure and tax a car, cost is unlikely to
be the major barrier. More likely obstacles are the distances that most
children would need to be transported and concerns about possible
constraints on children's future academic careers. Although the FPCU
schools have excellent academic records, their size inevitably means
narrower ranges of subject choice than are available in large state
schools. 'If we'd introduced it twenty years earlier, it might have
caught on but now the wealthier parents, and there's more of them
now, would be worried about academic success and what will employers think. Actually I've never heard of our children having any
such problems. We've one boy who's doing law at Queens. But people
might fear it.'

FREE PRESBYTERIAN GROWTH OUTSIDE ULSTER

In 2005 there were two symbolically potent events in the life of the
FPCU. On 17 May in Toronto the Ulster Presbytery wound up the
Standing Commission that had supervised its work in Canada and
the USA and inaugurated the Free Presbyterian Church of North
America: an autonomous organization with twenty-nine congregations. The same month the missionary outreach work in Spain took a
significant step forward with the ordination of Dr Jorge Ruiz. Remarkably for an organization so closely associated with the political
conflict in Northern Ireland, there are now almost as many Free

Presbyterian congregations outside than within its original home: fifty-three abroad and sixty-two at home.

Growth abroad is now possible because the FPCU has ministers to spare. The slight decline in overall Free Presbyterian numbers between 1991 and 2001, the very few congregations established since 1994, and the smallness of many of the newer congregations together suggest that the opportunities for expansion within Ulster are few. We can go further and say that, barring a great revival, there is little possibility of growth in Ulster. Somewhat ironically, the rise of Free Presbyterianism undermined the conditions for recruiting adult shifters by rallying the conservatives within the Irish Presbyterian Church. The obvious popularity of Paisley's critique of ecumenism allowed those evangelicals who remained in the IPC to force it to the right. One mark of their success was quitting the World Council of Churches (WCC). Founded on the base of an evangelical missionary conference in 1910, the international organization had gradually expanded by bringing in the Anglican communion and liberal Protestant denominations, and the Orthodox churches of the East, and finally the Catholic Church. For a strict evangelical the WCC was doctrinally unacceptable; for an Ulster evangelical it was particularly undesirable because in the later 1960s and early 1970s it supported a number of African national liberation movements. Ulster critics frequently linked those political postures to support for the IRA. The Irish Presbyterian withdrawal began with a resolution from the kirk session of Ahoghill (a village in Paisley's North Antrim heartland). In 1971 the General Assembly resolved by 219 to 168 votes to stay in the WCC. In 1976 the vote was 481 to 381. In 1979 the Assembly voted to suspend membership, and a year later it voted by 448 to 388 to withdraw. As the IPC shifted to the right, the pressure on conservatives within it to depart for the Free Presbyterian Church was reduced.

A wave of major church unions might have triggered further defections from the mainstream churches, but to date all the talk of ecumenism has produced only one significant British church union. In 1972 the majority of Presbyterians and Congregationalists in England formed the United Reformed Church. The more extravagant schemes for uniting Methodists and Anglicans, or Anglicans and Roman Catholics, have all led to nothing; hardly surprising when

we note that the sort of changes in the Anglican Church that would
make it more acceptable to Rome or to the Orthodox churches are
precisely the same things that would make it less acceptable to the
Reformed churches.

Relationships between individual congregations of different churches
improved over the twentieth century, and in unusual circumstances
(university chaplaincies and new housing estates, for example) churches
have created joint facilities and cross-denominational ministries, but
such local initiatives need not force other members of the same denomination to re-evaluate their affiliation. If your own minister is too liberal,
you can move to another congregation.

Although there have been long-term shifts within Ulster Protestantism, these have not fitted neatly into the neat conservative–liberal
divide that might have precipitated further defections to the FPCU.
Or, to put it more precisely, although Free Presbyterians see such
trends in those terms, others do not. One such trend is the growth of a
modern Pentecostalism that is strong on references to Jesus and
salvation but light on doctrine, encourages informality in dress and
in worship, stresses the therapeutic value of religion over the need to
glorify God, and borrows the very much musically based styles of
church service from the US and African Black church tradition: Pastor
James McConnell's Belfast Metropolitan Tabernacle is an example,
as are those bodies that call themselves Christian Fellowships. Another trend that muddies the waters is the combination of a personal
evangelical faith with an ecumenical attitude to other Christians and
fairly liberal socio-moral and political attitudes. Ken Newell, an Irish
Presbyterian with a popular ministry in the University area of Belfast,
is a good example. Paisleyites regard Newell as the old liberal wolf
in evangelical sheep disguise, but his continued use of evangelical
language is enough to allow young people to feel that they are both
modern and orthodox.

Finally it is worth noting the effect of fifty years of Paisleyite
condemnation of the mainstream churches. Although an infection
analogy may seem a little cruel, it makes the point. Paisleyism has
affected Ulster Protestantism in much the same way as a virus works
through a population. Some people have succumbed to it while the
rest have developed immunity. Actually, loathing might be a better
term. Those who did not jump ship the first few times that Paisley

and his ministers told them they were going to hell are not going to do so now. Whatever sympathy they have for the evangelical core of FPCU preaching, they long ago decided that they do not like Free Presbyterians.

In brief, the Northern Ireland market for a separatist conservative evangelicalism is probably now saturated, and this leaves the FPCU with the capacity to respond positively to approaches from evangelicals elsewhere. Foreign congregations have generally come about in one of three ways: adoption, migration, and, more common now, native creation.

The Liverpool congregation is a good example of the FPCU adopting an orphan. With its large Irish population, in the nineteenth and early twentieth centuries Liverpool often displayed the same sectarian conflict as Belfast. George Wise founded the Protestant Reformers Church in 1903 and created a following of thousands for his aggressive anti-Catholic preaching. He was elected to the council for Kirkdale as a 'Protestant' but did not re-contest his seat in 1906 because, as a paid official of a dissenting denomination, he was barred from election. After his death, his combination of evangelistic preaching and political activity was continued by H. D. Longbottom, who increased the congregation so that at one time it boasted over a thousand attenders at its Men's Bible Class. Though not as severely as Belfast, Liverpool was residentially segregated on sectarian lines, and Longbottom's Liverpool Protestant Party maintained a presence in the council for the areas of St Domingo and Netherfields. The movement flagged in 1956, with Longbottom failing to get re-elected, but he returned to the council in 1960 'after the Education Act aided new Catholic schools and [Cardinal] Heenan advanced the Cathedral'. [21]

After Longbottom's death in 1962, the party, under his son-in-law, Ron Henderson, struggled. In the late 1960s, the Ulster crisis gave it a new relevance, and Henderson joined Ian Paisley in the British Constitution Defence Committee. But the religious base of the movement had been eroded by secularization and by population shifts that had removed the Protestants who had supported the church and the party. What the German bombing blitz of the Second

---

[21] P. J. Waller, *Democracy and Sectarianism: A Political and Social History of Liverpool, 1868–1939* (Liverpool: Liverpool University Press, 1981).

World War had started, council rebuilding schemes finished: the traditionally Orange areas of St Domingo and Netherfields were transformed.[22] By the late 1970s, it was clear to Henderson that the Protestant Reformers could no longer continue as an independent church, and, in 1982, the Free Presbyterian Church of Ulster was asked to take the remnant congregation under its wing.

Although the political dimension was missing, the Toronto congregation has a somewhat similar history. As young boys, Frank and James McClelland had attended Paisley's Ravenhill church. James joined the Free Presbyterian ministry and Frank became an aircraft design draftsman. After working for Shorts in Belfast, he went to Seattle and later Toronto. In Seattle, he became active in a new Bible Presbyterian congregation, where he had the unnerving experience of almost being killed by a disgruntled member of the congregation. As the only elder, he was with the pastor when he was shot dead by a man who had been suspended from membership. Had the man remembered to re-cock the gun, McClelland would also have been shot. Seeing the experience as a major turning-point in his life, Frank McClelland returned to Ulster to train for the Free Presbyterian ministry and became the pastor of the Tandragee congregation. In 1974 he returned to Toronto for a holiday, and while there he was invited to a very small Bible Presbyterian group whose pastor was about to retire. McClelland was asked to take over the ministry and agreed on the condition that the work was conducted under the auspices of the Free Presbyterian Church.

Apart from loyalty, there were a number of good reasons for this decision. Evangelicals believe in the power of prayer and are loath to engage in any work for which there will not be 'prayer support'. Frank McClelland had few friends in Canada, but he knew that he would be supported by the prayers of the Free Church. There is, of course, a mundane side to prayer support: people who pray for work will also be willing to support it financially. Such support was not needed for long. Although there was considerable early opposition to a 'Paisley' church in Toronto (for example, the local authorities prevented the

[22] Apart from Waller, *Democracy*, my main sources for this information are interviews with former members of the Liverpool Protestant Party (LPP) and various pamphlets written by Ron Henderson such as *George Wise: Protestant Stalwart Twice Imprisoned for the Gospel's Sake* and *Seventy Five Years of Protestant Witness*.

congregation using the hall they had previously rented), the congregation grew rapidly and was soon able both to support itself and to assist new enterprises in Calgary and Vancouver.

The fishing villages on the north coast of Aberdeenshire have a long tradition of evangelicalism. Jacob Primmer, Scotland's last prominent anti-Romanist preacher, worked as an assistant minister in Gardenstown in the 1870s.[23] The Brethren were strong in the coastal villages, and in 1921 there was a major revival that affected the Aberdeenshire fishing communities and the East Anglian ports to which the Scottish fleets sailed in summer.[24] In the 1960s, before he became notorious, Paisley had preached in Cairnbulg. In 1995 a small number of people in Gardenstown left the Church of Scotland in protest against its liberal ethos and met as an independent group in the village hall.

In the providence of God, Mr Ian McVeigh, an elder from the Sandown Road congregation [of the FPCU] had close connections with a number of people in the new congregation. This friendship paved the way for an opportunity for both him and Rev David McIlveen to come and preach at the June conference in 1996. During those meetings, the bond of friendship was strengthened and the brethren were invited back the following year.[25]

The Gardenstown people asked for a trainee minister to preach to them for three months. Noel Hughes was so popular that his invitation was extended, and, after Paisley had led a series of gospel services, the congregation asked to be admitted to the FPCU. Despite some opposition from unsympathetic locals (who bizarrely objected to planning permission for a new church building on the grounds that Dr Paisley's occasional visits might encourage terrorist attacks on Gardenstown), a fine new church was erected, and under Hughes's ministry the congregation grew to some sixty regular attenders.

These adoption examples show a general problem that explains the appeal of the Free Presbyterian Church for declining conservative congregations. Independency has the great weakness that it produces

[23] See J. B. Primmer, *The Life of Jacob Primmer: Minister of the Church of Scotland* (Edinburgh: William Bishop, 1916), and S. Bruce, *No Pope of Rome: Militant Protestantism in Modern Scotland* (Edinburgh: Mainstream, 1985), 39–41.
[24] S. C. Griffin, *A Forgotten Revival: Recollections of the Great Revivals of East Anglia and North-East Scotland of 1921* (Epsom: Day One Publications, 1992).
[25] Kyle, *Our Own Heritage*, 127.

short-lived congregations. Dynamic pastors such as Wise and Long-bottom were able to create huge personal followings, but, when they died or retired, the work declined. Liverpool was unusual in being able to repeat the process, but there was a collapse in between the pastorates of Wise and Longbottom, and neither of the men who followed 'Longie' was able to command similar loyalty. In his explanation for the survival of the Free Church, Paisley stresses the continuity that the Presbyterian structure provides. Each congregation is under the super-vision of all the congregations. The Presbytery regularly visits its congregations to inspect premises, check the accounts, question the minister and elders on their beliefs and practices, and ensure good order. If a congregation falls vacant, the Presbytery appoints a senior minister to take charge until the vacancy is filled. The Presbytery can ensure that all people who are licensed as Free Presbyterian ministers will believe and will preach the same things. Small groups of believers can rest assured that they will be supported by the resources of the Church and that any minister who comes to them will continue where the previous one left off. As one minister put it: 'People like to know where they are. Congregations do not like change. They want the same preaching. Familiar services. Familiar hymns. They want the home and hospital visiting to continue. Continuity. You can't ensure that if you're just a lone congregation.'

A second source of overseas congregations is migration. One of the first families involved in the Vancouver church had come from Northern Ireland, and much of the impetus for the foundation of the first two Australian churches came from people who had been members of the Free Church in Ulster before emigrating.

As congregations formed by the first two routes have prospered, so they have opened up the third: members of the new congregations have felt called to the ministry and have pioneered works in new towns and cities that have been encouraged and supported by the Ulster base but have largely been self-generating. In 1976 Alan Cairns, an Ulsterman who was among the first generation of Paisley's converts and trained ministers, was invited to take over a Presbyter-ian congregation in Greenville, South Carolina. Although located in one of the centres of Baptist fundamentalism—Bob Jones University is in Greenville—Faith Free Presbyterian Church prospered and Cairns remained on very good terms with the Jones family. In the

1980s Cairns recruited a number of young Americans to the Free Presbyterian ministry and, with help from Bob Jones staff, was able to provide ministerial training.

The expansion overseas has not been without its problems. Although almost all the congregations have resulted from a core of believers approaching the FPCU for support, the lesson that a large, cold, crumbling building demoralizes the faithful and discourages potential newcomers has sometimes been forgotten. The town of Lewes in East Sussex has a long history of Reformed Protestantism that is now known mainly through its spectacular fire celebrations of the failure of the Gunpowder Plot. In 1805 a chapel that could seat a thousand people was built for the ministry of Revd Jenkin Jenkins. Jireh Chapel was given listed-building status because of its age, but by the 1980s its size bore a profoundly ironic relationship to its popularity. Pastor Jim North found himself ministering to fewer than ten people, and, possibly impressed by Jireh's glorious past, the FPCU accepted his invitation to adopt the work. Under FPCU auspices the congregation grew, but by 2002 it had only twenty regular attenders— enough to fill one row of pews!

It is worth adding that Britain has become so secular that, in seeking some shelter, conservative believers often have to abandon some of the distinctive beliefs that, in better times, were the cause of major schisms. The final custodians of Jireh Chapel approached the FPCU because it was Calvinist and used the King James version of the Bible; the rest of Jireh's traditionally distinctive culture could not be preserved. The Bristol congregation were Anglicans (albeit very Protestant ones), but they gave up their Anglicanism in order to preserve their evangelical mission.

The FPCU involvement in Britain has not been a great success. The average attendance for the British congregation is about twenty people; only the Gardenstown congregation claims more than fifty. It is tempting to conclude that Free Presbyterianism is so closely associated with Northern Ireland that it does not travel well to places where the main threat to believers is not Rome but indifference. However, a brief survey of recent changes in British Protestantism suggests another explanation. Within the general pattern of church decline, there has been a shift from doctrine-heavy, theologically conservative Protestantism to 'doctrine-lite' charismatic fellowships.

It is this shift that has undermined the congregations that now call for FPCU help and that explains why that help is not producing congregations to match their Ulster counterparts.

FOREIGN MISSIONS AND BROADCASTING

Although its primary purpose was to oppose modernism and ecumenism within Ulster Protestantism, the Free Church has always been mindful of the wider Christian mission. In addition to the Spanish work already mentioned, Free Presbyterians support a school and a group of churches in Kenya. In 1997 Ian Harris, the minister of Carrickfergus, moved to Kitale, where, as well as pastoring a church, he trains Kenyan students for the ministry. His wife oversees two Christian bookshops and her sister and another lady from Ballymoney run a Christian school with over 400 pupils. Whitefield College students have worked in Spain, West Germany, and India. As well as preaching (with the help of a local pastor translating) in Romania, Stanley Barnes and others of the Hillsborough congregation gave a great deal of financial and practical support to Romanian orphanages. A number of young Free Presbyterians have served abroad with the New Tribes Mission.

Another branch of the missionary endeavour is the radio ministry now called 'Let the Bible Speak' (or LTBS). The old Free Presbyterian church in Cabra, spare since the congregation moved to a new building in Rasharkin, was converted into a studio for the preparation of tapes, which, since 1973, have been broadcast on such stations as Manx Radio, Radio Star Country (which broadcasts to most of Ireland from County Monaghan), and Premier Radio (which serves London and the southeast). LTBS also reaches large parts of Africa, India, and Asia. In 1999 it raised over £81,000 from Free Presbyterian congregations, enough to support a full-time worker and to fund a considerable amount of bought air time. LTBS produces an attractive glossy magazine, which goes to Free Presbyterians to remind them of the need to support the radio ministry and to enquirers worldwide who respond to the radio broadcasts. It is significant that the magazine has quite a different tone from other Free Presbyterian publications. It is less antagonistic and argumentative and concentrates on a positive presentation of key evangelical beliefs.

HAS SUCCESS SPOILED THE FPCU?

The Free Church has always existed in a state of tension with its wider society. Indeed, it has from the first gone out of its way to heighten that tension by protesting both against signs of public ungodliness (such as the Sunday opening of leisure facilities and shops) and against the errors of the main Protestant churches. Not surprisingly, this provoked a hostile reaction. As Paisley put it:

> If you are going to be Godly men in a Godless age, you will be persecuted. When this Church *ceases* to be hated, and when this Church *ceases* to be reviled, and when this preacher *ceases* to be [tape inaudible] in this country, he's finished. He can pack it up and go home forever. But as long as men hate us and as long as men revile us and as long as the newspaper editorials write against us, praise God, we'll be doing something.[26]

Doubtless many people still hate and revile the FPCU, but, as the church has grown and as the party with which it is closely associated has prospered, there has been a growing acceptance that Free Presbyterian-ism is a legitimate part of Ulster's religious landscape. The religion department of BBC Northern Ireland now treats the Free Presbyterian Church as a legitimate minor denomination and broadcasts its Sunday morning services in rotation with those of other churches (although it is noticeable that it is those congregations with 'reasonable' ministers that are invited to broadcast). This degree of acceptance by an important medium has a slightly moderating influence in that Free Presbyterian ministers know that their allocation will be withdrawn if they infringe the norms of good taste and openly attack other denominations during a live transmission. In practice, few ministers would have trouble with this restriction, as they are capable of delivering sound gospel messages without criticizing the 'great apostasy', and, because they know it is temporary, they do not find the constraint onerous.

[26] I. R. K. Paisley, *The Is My Life* (cassette series) (Belfast: Martyrs Memorial Publications, 1980), tape 3, side 1.

Another minor element of the tension between Free Presbyterianism
and the surrounding culture has gradually disappeared. Since the
DUP became a major force in a number of district councils and Ian
Paisley established himself as the single most popular unionist leader in
Ulster, there have been fewer problems with the local authorities being
obstructive about planning permission for Free Presbyterian churches
or the hire of public halls. In the late 1970s, the Housing Executive
offered sites to two other denominations for new churches in the
growing Newtownabbey area, but denied the FPCU a site for a decade.
In 1966 John Douglas found himself arrested for breach of the peace
after he had addressed a meeting in Rathfriland. Thirty years later his
retirement was marked with a dinner in Craigavon Civic Centre, and
the Mayor of Craigavon presented him with a borough plaque in
recognition of his long Christian ministry. David Creane was similarly
rewarded for twenty-five years in the ministry in Lurgan.

Where the mass media in the 1970s would routinely disparage
Free Presbyterian ministers, since the 1990s it has treated them
much like it treats other clergy. The Church's protests are no longer
described as major threats to public order, and, if they are reported
in any manner other than with a straight face, it is with the mild
smile of cosmopolitan condescension towards quaint moralists.
David McIlveen of Sandown Road, Belfast, who became familiar
for his protests against a sex shop in East Belfast, was treated to a
very positive profile in the *Newsletter* when it was still a very firmly
UUP-supporting paper.[27]

There has also been a small but noticeable improvement in relations
between the FPCU and other evangelical clergy. Its petition against the
Belfast Agreement was signed by Elim, Baptist, Brethren, Independent
Methodist, and gospel-hall pastors. It was also signed by Irish Presbyterian and Church of Ireland clergy. In 2005 Dr Paisley was invited
to give the keynote speech at the annual conference of the Evangelical Protestant Society (EPS) in the Knock Evangelical Presbyterian
Church.

A good reason for thinking that success might have moderated the
Free Church is that the history of radical religion shows countless
examples of once-radical sects gradually moderating as they grow

---

[27] L. Trainor, 'Life and Times of a Moral Crusader', *Newsletter*, 4 Nov. 1999.

and become established.[28] Two powerful examples from British church history are the Quakers and the Methodists. The founders of a radical movement often made great sacrifices for their faith, and their commitment was correspondingly great: George Fox, the English Quaker pioneer, was ostracized, attacked, and imprisoned. But the second generation did not choose to make sacrifices. They inherited their faith, and, despite the best efforts of their parents, few developed the commitment of the founders. The pressure on subsequent generations to become more moderate is often increased by growing prosperity. In part this is just the by-product of the overall increase in prosperity that industrial societies have enjoyed. Give or take some short-lived recessions, the West has gradually and steadily become richer. The asceticism characteristic of many sects is relatively easy for the poor; they have little to give up anyway. By stressing the threat to salvation that wealth always offers, they can make something positive of their privations. They can console themselves that it is easier for a camel to pass through the eye of a needle than for a rich man to enter the kingdom of God. Those who will inherit little or nothing in this life can take comfort in the assurance that their piety will ensure they inherit everything in the next. Increased prosperity makes it ever harder to be a Puritan.

Ascetic religion itself compounds the problem by increasing the standard of living of the sectarian faster than the national average. If people refrain from smoking, drinking, gambling, womanizing, and other sins of the flesh, work diligently, and acquire a reputation for trustworthiness, then, like the Quakers, they may start out doing good and end up doing rather well. In class terms, subsequent generations become 'upwardly mobile'. Quaker families such as the Barclays, Gurneys, Trittons, and Backhouses prospered mightily in banking. They bought large houses. They sent their children to good schools. They could, if they wished, mix as equals with the gentry. All that kept them apart was their religion. The desire for social acceptance was a powerful stimulus to compromise and this is exactly what we find. Over a number of generations these families shifted from being

---

[28] The process is so common that its explanation has a name—the Niebuhr thesis—after H. R. Niebuhr, *The Social Sources of Denominationalism* (New York: Meridian, 1962).

evangelical Quakers, to being evangelicals within the Church of England, and finally to being mainstream Anglicans.

The seductive appeal of upward mobility bore especially heavily on the ministry. As the size, wealth, and social standing of Baptist and Methodist congregations rose in the early nineteenth century, so they began to expect more of their clergy, and the clergy started to think better of themselves. Sects built theological training colleges and extended the periods of formal training. When Oxford and Cambridge were opened to dissenters, some sects moved their training facilities into what had previously been seen as the Lion's den. As the sects became more accepted, their clergy started to mix as social equals with Anglican clergy. Relations with, and comparisons with, other clergy gradually weakened commitment to the original radical dissenting creed.

It is perhaps a little premature to ask how the Free Presbyterian experience fits this model. After all, the church is only in its second generation, and some of the founding generation is still active. But it is the case that the majority of Free Presbyterians now know the struggles of the 1960s and 1970s only from the accounts of their elders. A majority of ministers were born after Paisley's 1966 imprisonment. And the Free Church has enjoyed a general increase in prosperity and a marked improvement in its social position.

With the exception of the Belfast congregations, the early FPCU was overwhelmingly rural. Most members were farmers or worked in related agricultural industries (such as market gardening, haulage, and meat processing). As the figures given in the Appendix show, the Free Presbyterians in the 1981 census had a markedly lower social-class profile than Irish Presbyterians and were less likely to have any formal education beyond school level. Twenty years later the 2001 census showed that Northern Ireland had been influenced by the same trends as the rest of the UK: the manual working class had shrunk, the white-collar middle class had grown, and farming had declined relative to other spheres of work. There is still a noticeable difference between the typical Free Presbyterian and the typical Irish Presbyterian, but both differ from the previous generation. If social advance and prosperity encourage moderation in religion, then the FPCU might well have changed.

CHANGING MORES

The Free Presbyterian ordination oath requires ministers to promise to preach and contend against the pleasure crazes of the age, and the promises are being kept. Browsing through issues of *Truth for Youth* (as its name suggests, a magazine directed at the church's young people) from the 1990s and subsequently, we find the following. J. K. Rowling's Harry Potter stories were denounced: 'No good can come from encouraging young people to read material that promotes and glorifies sin.'[29] Anathema was pronounced on the National Lottery.[30] Prohibitions on alcohol were repeated.[31] Rock music, especially 'Christian rock music' (the first adjective would be contested), was denounced.[32] The Pokemon game was described as dangerous because (and few parents would disagree with this claim) it encouraged obsessive behaviour and avarice. It also involved the occult.[33] Line dancing was judged to be 'as sinful as any other type of dancing with its sexual gestures and touching'.[34] Television watching was still regarded with suspicion: 'There is nothing wrong or sinful with the *concept* of television ... but very often the *content* of television is wrong and sinful.'[35] Of particular concern were social facilities for young Christians that aped the mores of the secular world. A young Free Presbyterian reported on 'Exodus', a Christian nightclub in Portrush:

Within moments we saw a young couple behaving in a grossly immodest and indecent fashion just inside the main door and heard two people swearing, using the foulest of language. Inside, to the left there was a large bar where soft drinks were sold, but in a fashion which copied the world's drinking places. ... The music that was being played can only be described as 'pop music'. There was nothing in the place which remotely resembled a Christian meeting place.[36]

Truth for Youth subsequently carried a lengthy critique of Exodus and of The Cleft, a similar function in Craigavon.[37] In successive issues of the

[29] *Truth for Youth* (Nov.–Dec. 2000), 11.
[30] Ibid. (Nov.–Dec. 1994), 4.
[31] Ibid. (Sept.–Oct. 1992), 10.
[32] Ibid. (Mar.–Apr. 1993).
[33] Ibid. (Jan.–Feb. 2001), 4.   [34] *Guardian*, 19 May 2001.
[35] *Truth for Youth* (Mar.–Apr. 2005), 9.   [36] *Burning Bush* (May 1997), 2.
[37] *Truth for Youth* (Nov. 1991–Feb. 1992; May–June 1998).

Burning Bush, two ministers warned against the dangers of 'formal dinners'. Such social functions were dangerous because they broke down the barriers between the godly and the ungodly and they encouraged young Christians to ape the behaviour of 'worldlings'.[38]

If there is no obvious evidence of relaxation in its behavioural requirements, there is little sign that the FPCU clergy have lost the enthusiasm for protesting. We would not expect Paisley to have changed his spots, and his protests against the apostasy of the Irish Presbyterian Church are as much an annual event as the General Assembly at which he makes them. He has also continued to use his public positions to demonstrate his anti-Romanism. When the Pope visited the European Parliament in 1988, Paisley shouted from his seat: 'I renounce you as the Antichrist.' In case anyone doubted him, he informed the press: 'My protest against Rome will never be over. I shall carry on until I'm dead!'[39] The key question is the attitude of younger ministers. Certainly some of the first generation are concerned. One man said: 'Respectability and acceptance do not help us. We don't have the same fire in our hearts for protesting.' Another worried that 'young men are coming up who were not part of the conflict in the early days. They may have a blunted ministry.'

The hostile response of an Irish Presbyterian congregation in Limavady to the ecumenical gestures of its minister, David Armstrong, has already been mentioned. The involvement of the local Free Presbyterian minister Wesley McDowell is interesting because he had been a childhood friend of Armstrong. While McDowell had become a convinced conservative, Armstrong had shifted sufficiently far for McDowell to refuse an invitation to his ordination. But he did not just decline. He very publicly repudiated his former friend by sending to the local newspapers a copy of his letter to Armstrong's elders explaining why he could not attend the service. I asked McDowell if he did not feel sad that he should end up denouncing a former close friend.

No. I relished the opportunity to protest against him, you know, because the original Free Presbyterians, they had to take a lot of stick. It meant sacrifice. I relished the opportunity because as a relatively young chap . . . I missed all that and I wanted to make my stand. Not that I did it for any ulterior motive.

---

[38] *Burning Bush* (Mar. 2000; Apr. 2000).
[39] *Newsletter*, 12 Oct. 1998.

My motive in the whole thing was the Lord's honour and I think the Lord worked the whole thing out because in the end the man was removed.

Here is a second-generation Free Presbyterian making the sort of public protest that made the first generation so unpopular and recognizing the part that his protests played in allowing him to share in some way in the unpopularity of the founders.

The following is a selection of protests made by younger men since the mid-1990s. In 1996 McDowell protested against his local council sponsoring an ecumenical gathering. In 1999 a large Free Presbyterian crowd picketed a performance of *Jesus Christ: Superstar* at the Grand Opera House in Belfast. In 1998 Ian Brown protested at a meeting of the World Council of Churches in Zimbabwe; the same year six ministers picketed a WCC meeting in Amsterdam. In 1996 three ministers picketed an ecumenical service in St Anne's Cathedral in Belfast. Gary Goodes picketed meetings led by the promoter of the 'Toronto Blessing', a charismatic movement, in Perth, Western Australia, in 1996. In 2000 Ron Johnstone, the Armagh minister, led a picket outside a Church of Ireland conference in Armagh. And, as Sunday opening became common, Free Presbyterian ministers were to be found making their protest. In 2003 young minister Colin Mercer protested outside the Safeway supermarket in Kilkeel. In 1995 four ministers picketed a gay festival in Londonderry, and David Park publicly protested against the granting of a liquor licence in Portavogie, one of the last dry villages in Ulster.[40]

For all that they have not relaxed their standards, many ministers express concern that the Church is having increasing difficulty enforcing them: 'Prosperity is a problem. People have so much more. When I was a child I had one pair of "serviceable", that was the word, grey trousers because that was all we could afford and I didn't resent it. Children now want everything and resent not getting it.' In 1986 Alan Cairns told me that he had recently cautioned a congregation about declining standards; among his concerns was unsupervised television watching. The theme was repeated in 2005 by Ivan Foster:

TV is another big thing. I don't think there is anything that some of our young people wouldn't watch now. This technology is the greatest threat to spirituality within the home now because you cannot control it. With

[40] *Irish News*, 14 June 1994.

computers and videos and DVDs, parents cannot stop their children having access to all the imagery of the world and it leaves an impression. It must do.

The worldly practice of going to the pictures has also become increasingly common among Free Presbyterians.

A number of ministers also observed that their people seemed less easily satisfied with their old culture. In the 1980s Cairns noted that 'in the old days, if you wanted a crowd, you had a prayer meeting. Now if you want a crowd, you need gospel music.' He quickly made it clear that he had nothing against sacred music in its place (a good thing, given William McCrea's position as Britain's best-selling gospel artist), but he was concerned about an apparent decline in the support for more traditional activities such as prayer meetings. Foster elaborated the dangers of musical evenings:

When I was first converted, a 'Praise Service' was a church service where the emphasis was on God's people praising the Lord.... There was prayer offered: there would have been the singing of praise by the congregation with items from soloists or possibly a choir. The preaching of the Word of God would have been central.... Today there are things accepted in a praise service which would not be acceptable to many in a regularly ordered meeting in God's house.[41]

Many gospel events now take place in secular settings such as concert halls, rather than in churches, which allows 'the fashions and innovations from the world of stage and television to be introduced'. Women go with heads uncovered. The songs sung are often devoid of sound scriptural content and, worse, are sung by those from charismatic fellowships that 'propagate ludicrous myths and fancies'. Backing musicians are often secular and can be found smoking backstage in between performances! A true Christian witness may be clouded by evangelicals performing alongside Catholics.

There was also a sense that standards of personal dress and adornment were slipping. In the 1980s a number of ministers observed, as one man put it: 'A number of years ago a Christian would have been stronger against make-up. Now that's slowly creeping in and being accepted. That's only little things but it adds up'. In 2005 make-up, hair styling, and dress were again mentioned among the list of small changes

---

[41] *Burning Bush* (May 1997), 3.

that worried the clergy, especially the older ones. I often replied to such comments that my impression, gained over twenty-five years of studying the Church, was somewhat different. To me young Free Presbyterians still seem unusual in their relatively unadorned appearance, but it is that word 'relatively' that is significant. An outsider comparing young Free Presbyterians to their contemporaries would be struck by their simplicity, unworldliness, and conservative demeanour; a middle-aged evangelical comparing them to the young people of his youth would have an impression of increased laxity and worldliness.

Finally a number of ministers have noted a decline in attendance at Sunday evening services. The sin of 'half-day hearing', which is now commonplace in the mainstream churches, is appearing in Free Presbyterian circles.

A reasonable conclusion is that the general rise in prosperity has offered the young Ulster evangelicals a range of temptations much wider than that faced by their grandparents or parents, and it is no surprise that they have succumbed to some of them, but the Church has largely succeeded in maintaining the principle that worldliness is an evil to be avoided. Things must be given up. Opportunities for sensual pleasures must be rejected. If the benchmark of success in socialization is for each generation to have exactly the same mores as its predecessor, there are small signs of failure. But if we define puritanism, as social policy analysts define poverty, in relative terms, then the Church has maintained its puritanical spirit. Its young people are aware that their faith requires them to incur the disdain of the world and they manage to do that. The slow lane of the M6 is now much faster than it was thirty years ago but it is still the slow lane.

CONCLUSION

When in 2005 I interviewed a number of ministers and elders I had first met in the early 1980s, I naturally found myself opening the conversation by asking some version of: 'what do you see as the main changes in the Church over the last twenty years?' The answers were always long, thoughtful, and complex, and it does not do them justice to force them into just two types, but we can summarize them as optimistic or pessimistic responses to similar stimuli. On one side were those who were pleased with the growth of the church, saw benefits in greater social acceptance, welcomed the reduction of tension with the wider society, saw opportunities in new forms of mass media for spreading the gospel, and had only mild concerns about the decline of radical fervour. On the other were those who saw major signs of declension and of incipient apostasy.

It has happened unto us, as it has to every generation of Christians, we are waxing fat and like Ephraim who waxed fat we kick, we don't want the reproach. We want to be at ease in Zion. With that recognition has come an increasing desire to maintain that status. Not wanting to indulge in those actions and behaviour that brought reproach on us. We have back-sliden!

This seems alarmist, especially when framed as a critique of the clergy. As the list of protests given above shows, even the generation born after the 1970s seems quite willing to incur the wrath and derision of the secular world by public protest. To help make sense of the divergent responses I was given, I went back to my notes from the 1980s and became aware of something I had rather overlooked then. Even among the first generation of ministers, there was a clear difference between those who relished controversy, who revelled in preaching against error, and who took comfort from being a despised minority, and those who felt more comfortable with the pastoral side of the ministry than with prophetic denunciation, who preferred to preach the positive elements of the gospel message, and who felt that constantly being negative was not helpful to their mission. The argument was not (and is not now) over major points of doctrine or even over the extent to which the godly should be separated from the ungodly: it was about tone and about which elements of the ministerial role should be emphasized.

The world has changed a great deal since Ian Paisley began his ministry. That he was raised to his mission by his father and grew up on a diet of texts written in the nineteenth century meant that some of what concerned him had already passed, and since the 1950s even Northern Ireland has changed a great deal. The early Free Church operated in an environment that was still in many senses Christian. Most people were members of Christian churches and had some good acquaintance with the cardinal doctrines of the faith. It made sense to publish long and detailed arguments with apostate ministers. When a large part of the population has only a nominal church connection, a more gentle approach to the world, which presents the basic tenets of the faith without a bitter and argumentative tone, to many ministers seems more likely to be successful. In summary, the Church has changed slightly in tone, but the change is only slight, and it results from a small shift in the relative efforts given to denouncing the sins of other clergy and preaching a positive message. However, I would not present this as evidence that the Church is, like Ephraim, 'waxing fat'. Instead I would suggest that, like most outsiders, I previously concentrated too much on doctrine and in treating ministers and committed church members as if they were just the passive 'carriers' of ideas. I missed the point that they also have personalities and that some are by nature both more pessimistic and more combatative than others. When some described the last twenty years in terms of declining commitment and others chose instead to begin by listing the positive changes, they were not disagreeing about the reality so much as they were displaying their natural character differences. Those who tended to look on the bright side were just the sort of people who were naturally optimistic.

It is not for the social scientist to determine what is pleasing (or otherwise) to God. This account of the FPCU has been concerned only with its mundane this-worldly fate. It has achieved a remarkable degree of success. The general cultural climate has not been helpful. Since the 1950s the presence and popularity of Christian ideas and culture have declined sharply. As it has shrunk, Protestantism has become either liberal or charismatic. The Free Presbyterian movement was slow to take off and until the O'Neill era and the start of the Troubles seemed likely to stagnate. The political insecurity dramatized Ian Paisley's twin critique of unreliable elites in politics and treacherous clergy in the churches and gave Free Presbyterianism a major boost. The FPC success lies in having consolidated that surge in its fortunes. A province-wide structure of congregations has been created, and the recruitment and training of the clergy have been put on a sound footing. Although the expansion overseas has been relatively slight, that the Church is looked to by tiny groups of orphaned conservative evangelicals testifies to its presence.

6

Church and Party

INTRODUCTION

Ian Paisley is such a compelling and forceful leader of church and party that it is easy to suppose that each organization is entirely united in support of his views and that both dovetail neatly into a single cohesive movement. It is certainly the case that the founding principles of church and party are similar and reinforcing: religious elites are not to be trusted with the preservation of the true gospel, and political elites are not to be trusted with the defence either of the character of Northern Ireland or of its place in the United Kingdom. But the political thought of Ulster evangelicals is complex, and, even within the FPCU, there are differences of opinion. Evangelicals wrestle with the tension between the individualistic emphasis of their view of salvation—each person separately has to come to Christ—and the temptation to see the Ulster Protestant people as having some specially favoured status in divine providence. Within the party there are differences about the way an individual's faith should translate into political choices, and there is a tension between a democratic politician's obligation to lead and to represent his electorate. Furthermore, the answers that can plausibly be given to these perennially difficult questions change with the environment in which decisions must be made. Principles may be timeless but actions are always fixed in time and place. What was possible, advantageous, or necessary in 1970 may be none of those things in 2000. This chapter will consider in some detail the relationship between Free Presbyterianism, Ulster unionism, the Orange Order, and the DUP, and will examine changes in the personnel who staff the political wing of Paisleyism.

IS THE FPCU THE DUP AT PRAYER?

The Free Presbyterian Church has such a strong profile that there is little chance of anyone joining it who did not in large part share Paisley's knitting-together of unionism and evangelicalism. As the previous chapter noted, there are some signs of relaxation in the asceticism of the FPCU. Some younger people and some of those who have worked abroad have a broader notion of the threats to their religion, but there has been little change in the core linkage of the need to preserve Northern Ireland as part of the United Kingdom and the need to preserve and preach the gospel.

Ulster's conservative evangelicals are unionists because the inherited religio-ethnic divide in politics—Catholic-Nationalist versus Protestant-Unionist—has been reinforced by the events of the Troubles. Despite the Catholic hierarchy's repeated condemnation of terrorism, there has been plenty of material to sustain the perspective of those who believe the Catholic Church to be at heart the unchanging enemy of Protestant Ulster. *Our Own Heritage*, the closest thing the FPCU has to an official statement of doctrine, effortlessly links the fifteenth-century Spanish Inquisition, the 1572 massacre of French Protestants, the 1641 rebellion in Ireland, the Catholic Church's support for the murderous Ustashe in Croatia during the Second World War, and contemporary IRA violence.[1] The Catholic Church's support for Irish reunification, and its refusal to excommunicate convicted murderers or to condemn for mortal sin the republican hunger-strikers who committed suicide, are taken as confirmation that Rome does not really mind if other people exterminate Protestants. It is difficult to exaggerate the strength of Protestant feeling (for the sentiment spreads far beyond Free Presbyterians) about this issue. The following quotation from Jim Allister articulates views that I encountered very many times in the course of my research:

For those republicans who lose their own lives in advancing their struggle, there is available the full solace of their Church as IRA murderers are buried with no lesser Roman Catholic Church rites than the very priests of

[1] P. Kyle, *Our Own Heritage: Not to be Thrown Away* (Tavistock: Tavistock FP Church, 2002), 314–25.

that church. Glorification rather than the more seemingly fitting ex-communication is the response of the Roman Catholic Church to the IRA terrorist. It is this insoluble marriage of Roman Catholicism to militant Irish republicanism, where the latter is seen as the 'political' expression and promoter of the former, which makes what should other-wise be possible, namely the co-existence of the political expressions of Protestantism and Roman Catholicism, impossible in Ireland.[2]

This view of Rome reinforces Ulster unionism: if this is what happens in the North now, how much worse would things be in a united Ireland? 'The people of Northern Ireland naturally and rightly reason if what they have suffered at the hands of the southern-spawned IRA, they have suffered while a majority, how much greater would that persecution not be if they ever entered a state in which they were a perpetual minority.'[3] The pacific statements of leading Cath-olic clergy are taken as mere rhetoric. When Paisley called Cardinal Cahal Daly 'The Black Pope of Republicanism', he made sure every-one knew what that meant by defining republican thus: 'it includes all those who want to get a united Ireland over the dead bodies of the Protestant people.'[4]

Some ministers fully endorse the Doc's politics. In fact, a number were attracted to the religion and to the ministry by the political conflict. William Beattie, who was raised in a tradition that firmly linked the preservation of a religious culture with the maintenance of a Protestant and unionist polity, sees changes in the political world as the spur to his religious commitment. In his explanation of how he became involved he combines two elements: the appointment of O'Neill as premier and noticing a biblical text that talked of the 'evil to come'. He believed that God was drawing his attention to this particular message from Scripture and that O'Neill was a harbinger of the troubles that lay ahead. So, from the very outset, before O'Neillism was widely recognized as a new force in Ulster politics, Beattie was committed to the politicized evangelicalism that Paisley promoted.

Unlike Beattie, who was steeped in a marinade of evangelism and unionism, Ivan Foster was recruited after a more dramatic conversion.

[2] J. Allister, *Irish Unification Anathema: The Reasons why Northern Ireland Rejects Unification with the Republic of Ireland* (Belfast: Crown Publications, n.d.), 20–1.
[3] Ibid. 16.
[4] *Belfast Telegraph*, 27 Nov. 1984.

Although his uncle was a keen Pentecostalist, his family had a strong Orange background, and his parents were 'saved', Foster had little interest in religion or politics. He was working as a trainee film editor with Ulster Television in Belfast and, like most young men, pursuing an active life of sin when he felt the Lord speaking to him. Once saved, he entered into the life of the Free Presbyterian Church with gusto. Immediately after hearing Paisley, he wanted to become involved: 'I was mad keen. I rang the Big Man up the next day after I had talked to him and said: "When's the next meeting?" I was bursting for meetings, bursting for meetings!' He simultaneously became an enthusiastic supporter of Paisley's politics:

I didn't divorce the spiritual battle in Ulster from the political and I still wouldn't. So I felt that our heritage was basically a spiritual heritage . . . I went to Gaelic matches in Dublin. I went to Croke Park and I had not the slightest interest in Protestantism but I did come from a Fermanagh family where you did live cheek by jowl with republicanism so I had imbibed it undoubtedly and it resurfaced, the inherited knowledge of the heart of controversy in Ulster. It was there all the time but I had turned my back upon it in a sense, so when I got converted and of course I was listening to the Big Man's comments on events and I recognized the validity of what he was saying. I don't come from an evangelical background, I came from a raw environment straight into the contentions of the Big Man and you couldn't have been too extreme. It didn't bother me. Up the Shankill Road in the riots! I had no problem relating to the roughs and whatnot.

For Foster the resurfaced family tradition of unionism and his newly acquired loyalty to Paisley made him an active and enthusiastic supporter of his political activities.

Other early ministers were pushed into politics by hostile reactions to what they saw as legitimate religious activity. John Wylie's experience in Ballymoney is a good example. He saw nothing political about inviting an ex-priest publicly to denounce the Mass as a blasphemy, and took the council's refusal to let him use public property for this purpose as the state interfering in valid religious activity. The liberals wanted to promote a modern secular understanding of religion as a largely private matter that should be pursued in such a manner as not to offend people of other religions. Wylie's desire to maintain a more traditional notion of religion as a matter of truth and falsity (where those with the truth have an obligation publicly to denounce falsity) brought him into conflict with the state, and he responded to that challenge by standing for election to the council.

The experiences of 1966 and the imprisonment of the three ministers politicized a number of ministers and elders in this way. Some, such as Cecil Menary of Crossgar, remained largely detached, but most found themselves becoming involved in public criticism of O'Neillism. Even those men, such as Bert Cooke and John Douglas, who were later critical of ministers becoming professional politicians found themselves acting in the political arena as they tried to explain to an increasingly interested audience why their spiritual leader was being sent to prison. But they were reluctant and preferred to see themselves involved in a spiritual revival. Bert Cooke describes the imprisonment rallies that he addressed with Alan Cairns:

Alan and I took a lot of meetings . . . in Londonderry, Coleraine, Portglenone. We were involved in a large one in the Ulster Hall. Alan set up the legal part of it and the political side and I would come in with the more spiritual side of it: the demand for separation from the Irish Presbyterian Church that was operating in cahoots with O'Neill at that time. Because this was our charge; that the government linked up with leaders of the Irish Presbyterian Church in order to silence Paisley. And so we were involved a great deal in what we would call 'protesting' but as far as political activity, that was never my thing.

The small circle of political enthusiasts provided Paisley with the resources necessary to launch his campaign against O'Neill. When he decided to challenge O'Neill in Bannside in 1969, he asked Jimmy Beggs, the Free Presbyterian minister of Ballymena who had married his adoptive sister, to act as election agent. The minister of the Rasharkin congregation, Gordon Cooke, became the chairman of the Bannside branch of the Protestant Unionist Party. Of the six Protestant Unionists who stood in that election, three were Free Church ministers (Paisley, Wylie, and Beattie) and a fourth was an elder. Nevertheless, Paisley was keen to establish a public distinction between these two roles. At an early election meeting in an Orange Hall in the Bannside constituency he was asked if Protestant Unionism was just Free Presbyterianism by another name. He replied that 'there are those who agree with me politically but who disagree with me religiously' and said he wanted their political support. His reliance on his church was inadvertently demonstrated by the story: the questioner was a local Free Presbyterian elder who had been asked to raise it!

There were some ministers who were positively attracted by the controversy and some of these were unionist before they were 'saved' Protestants. Harry Cairns first met Paisley in 1958 when he was promoting Albert Duff as a Protestant Unionist candidate against Maginnis, the Attorney General, in the rural Iveagh constituency. Although he had recently been converted, it was Paisley's conservative attack on unreliable unionist leaders that first drew him to Free Presbyterianism. When the 1966 imprisonment again gave Paisley a high profile, he attended meetings being led by Beattie in Hillsborough and became a founding member of the Free Presbyterian congregation there. He then felt called to the ministry.

If that is the biography of a rural evangelical Free Presbyterian activist, the following is the urban working variant:

Way back in the 1960s, when the tricolour flew in Divis St, I was only sixteen at the time. I thought the man was crazy really but in 1966 I did develop an interest and started to attend the services … I went to him for the political because I was a red hot loyalist at that time. Doc Paisley was the first man I ever heard preach to me directly that I was sinner, that God loved me and that Jesus died for me … It was shortly after that I was converted, in my own home, 5th November 1966.

He went on to add that, had his interest not been channelled into the evangelical Protestantism of the Free Church, it would probably have led to him getting in with 'a bad crowd' and joining the tartan gangs of loyalist youths.

Of course, it was possible for people to accept both Paisley's political analysis and the need for evangelicals to be politically involved and yet not support the particular organizational expressions of those views that Paisley led. The church was always broad enough to include such people. Cecil Harvey was one of the founding elders of the Free Presbyterian Church. He sat as a Unionist councillor and, when the Unionist Party became dominated by power-sharers, he moved to Vanguard, then to Ernest Baird's United Ulster Unionist Party (UUUP), and only switched to the DUP when the UUUP collapsed. Harvey's position was somewhat unusual in that his involvement in party politics pre-dated the formation of the DUP, but he was not unique. In the 1980s there were at least two committed Free Presbyterians who sat in local government as UUP councillors.[5] My interviews suggest that the scarcity of Free Presbyterians in the UUP is explained less by the church being partisan than by the bitterness of competition between the two unionist parties. Whether we think of it as a very large blind spot or as a character virtue, it is clearly the case that Paisley expects others to 'compartmentalize' his views. So he calls Ulster Unionist MPs traitors at a press conference in the morning and in the afternoon greets them affably when they set off as a joint delegation to meet British government officials. Not surprisingly, most people find such alternation difficult, and disagreements in the political realm have led to Free Presbyterians leaving the church.

The dominant position in the church is that 'God's people need to have a prayerful interest in political affairs and get involved in praying for our political situation. This is especially important in Ulster where there is so much unrest, godlessness and dishonesty.'[6] However, note the stress on prayer: there is no specific injunction to be a member of any political party (and certainly not any one party) or even to vote, though the FPCU has criticized those evangelicals who think that their faith requires a complete retreat from the public world. The Church's statement goes on to say: 'our church does not maintain an organic bond with any political party.... We do not believe that the church of Christ should form any official links with any political party, nor should we preach politics.'[7] For all the FPCU describes itself as Calvinist, most of the ministers and elders I interviewed accepted the modern secular notion of a separation of church and state. One said: 'There is only one organization I join as a Christian and that is the church. Anything else I join as a citizen or as a Protestant.' Another said simply: 'I do not believe in a union of church and state.' In the 1970s a quite senior minister said:

I'm very careful to keep the church as clear of politics as possible because I'm not a politician. I think the clerics have more say in politics than they're

[5] There does not seem to be any problem with Free Presbyterians being active in the UUP provided they always have been. However, where someone has been active in the church and party and falls out with either his Free Presbyterian or his DUP colleagues, the ill-feeling is not compartmentalized but spills over, and tensions are resolved by the person also breaking with the other organization.

[6] Kyle, *Our Own Heritage*, 359.   [7] Ibid. 361.

entitled too. Its o.k. for Paisley, McCrea, Foster and Beattie because they've been elected. They just happen to be ministers of religion but they've been elected so they're entitled to speak on politics. But I'm not. I'm not elected by anybody so in my own congregation I steer clear of political messages. I certainly don't make the pulpit a political platform.

One minister who was an elected councillor in the 1980s said: 'I never mention politics in church or permit them to be mentioned. I don't make any political announcements.' The cynic could say that his political preferences were so well known, he did not need to, but I see no reason to doubt his sincerity. Everything else about him suggested that he would rather have converted another soul than won another election and he feared partisanship would restrict the audience for his gospel message.

The FPCU clergy feel that, like all people in positions of responsibility, they are obliged to take a view on matters of great severity or general application, but they do so sparingly. There was no dissent when the General Assembly issued a statement calling for a vote against the Belfast Agreement. This was seen not as politics but as morality: 'Our opposition to the Agreement stems from the fact that it is unscriptural, unethical and immoral.'[8] There is no disagreement that the clergy should take a public stand on legislation over such matters as the sanctity of the sabbath or gay rights. But most ministers identified a tension between the need for the Christian to comment on public affairs and their critique of the social power of the Catholic Church in Ireland. One reason they were unionists was that Rome exerted far too much influence over the public life of Catholic countries. Interestingly they did not resolve the tension the Islamic fundamentalist way: distinguishing true and false belief. They did not say that the Catholic Church's role in social policy in the Irish Republic is wrong because it is a false church and that Free Presbyterian preeminence would be fine because it is the true faith. Mostly they went down the road of distinguishing between undemocratically exercising power (a bad thing) and making your views known to electors who can then accept them or reject them (and this should not be done from the pulpit if those views are partisan).

[8] *Newsletter*, 20 May 1998.

Although the FPCU clergy accept the need for a Christian voice in public life, they are generally opposed to their own number being politically active. A number of reasons were given for this reluctance.

A common concern was distraction. Time spent on party politics is time stolen from preaching the gospel. Before the Convention elections of 1974, the Presbytery refused to allow ministers other than Paisley and Beattie to stand as DUP candidates. Clifford Smyth, who had been a leading activist in the DUP, believes this was done to prevent the DUP being too closely associated with a particular church,[9] but that would be more plausible had the objections to clerical candidates come from the party. The church wanted to constrain its clergy because it needed full-time workers. The arguments had actually been rehearsed on many occasions. Alan Cairns said:

The Presbytery has not encouraged party political participation and it has only been because we felt certainly that Dr Paisley's position, that the country needs it, that we felt that he should be allowed to go. For years we had requests from political people, parties, you know, around the country, to allow other ministers to go forward and we said 'No'. The Free Church had got its hands full. We are not going to have all our ministers in politics.

When Alan Cairns and other leading ministers opposed the candidacy of William McCrea and James McClelland, they did so to preserve the interests of the church. In the event, permission was given for Paisley and Beattie to go forward because they had been members of the Stormont Parliament before it had been suspended.

A second consideration was the barrier to soul-saving that is created by partisanship. As one man who had begun his ministry in the 1960s reflected in 1985:

There was a time when I felt that the Free Church could present a broader appeal to the Protestant people, while there was greater harmony among the unionist parties as such. Now when you find a lot of political infighting between the Officials [UUP] and the DUP, a lot of people, wrongly in my opinion, suspect that the Free Church is just the religious arm of the DUP. I would like to think

---

[9] C. Smyth, *Ian Paisley: Voice of Protestant Ulster* (Edinburgh: Scottish Academic Press, 1987), 45–6. He has been misled by his wish to prove that the party was not democratic. He cites the Presbytery meeting that debated the issue of ministers in politics as an example of the way in which the church undemocratically affected the policies and direction of the party, when the point is that the Presbytery was trying to withdraw from the party.

that my ministry would appeal to a cross section of the population, that Official Unionists could come to my services and not be insulted by anything I say.

They almost certainly could go to the services of any Free Church and not be insulted, but they could not escape being reminded that the FPCU had been founded by Ian Paisley.

A further set of considerations might be grouped together under the rubric 'politics is a dirty business'. Some of the illustrations that were offered concerned honesty and directness of speech:

Like it or not, and I don't like it, if you're going to succeed in politics, you sometimes have to be a bit economical with the truth. Now I think our men are the most straight-talking of any politicians and they are often criticised for being straight but even they cannot always say what they're up to because that would lose some important advantage and I don't think that's really on for a minister of the gospel.

Even politicians who build their career on their supposed saintliness (Mahatma Gandhi, for example) have to plot and scheme. Few politicians can entirely avoid duplicity. For example, with hindsight most people would accept that Prime Minister John Major was right to engage the IRA in dialogue and also right to deny such contacts so long as he believed such denial was serving the greater good. And we accept that political opponents will make political capital by denouncing such deception while themselves engaging in rather similar behaviour. We can see why David Ervine of the PUP and UVF was infuriated by DUP politicians asserting that there should be no dialogue with terrorists when they had themselves periodically met UDA and UVF men, but we would be surprised if the DUP did not occasionally talk to those who professed to be serving the same cause, if only to find out what they were planning to do. But what is politically expedient and necessary is difficult to reconcile with the straight-line ethics required by puritanical evangelicals. In religion, Free Presbyterians take a 'double separatist' stand. To preserve the purity of your gospel message you must avoid those in error and you must also avoid contact with those who, though correct themselves, are in association with error. Such a fear of contamination would make any sort of political activity impossible. Free Presbyterians hold Paisley in such high regard that they can suppose him above contamination, but they are fully aware that political involvement threatens the clear witness required of a clergyman.

The danger of contamination is not confined to such major consid-erations as the politician's need to be economical with the truth or to mix with undesirables. Many ministers offered mundane examples of the way being in public life threatens the gospel witness. The following concerns the Christian's 'walk with the Lord': 'Now I was told, I didn't see it myself, that [a DUP politician] was photographed for the local paper at a civic reception and there was drink in the picture as well. Wine on the table. Now he wouldn't be taking that drink but it is compromising for a Christian to be photographed in that way.' Being a public figure requires you to mix with a wide variety of people. Almost all politicians have principles that will cause them to avoid certain sorts of contact: one cannot imagine a modern Labour Party politician agreeing to speak at an all-male rugby club dinner, for example. The problem is that the born-again Christian excludes a great deal and the separatist Free Presbyterian excludes even more. A Free Presbyterian elder who was also a councillor mentioned one small incident that had caused him some concern. His unionist-dominated council held a civic event for the local Territorial Army (which is the sort of thing unionists like), but one of the army chaplains involved was a Catholic priest: 'Should I have walked out when the priest started to pray? Well, I didn't!'

In 2002 DUP leaders were invited to a service in St Anne's Cath-edral (so often the scene of FPCU protests) to celebrate the Queen's golden jubilee. Nigel Dodds attended. Ivan Foster thought he should not have done and explained his reasons eloquently in a sermon based on a text from Ezra (9: 13–14):

And after all that is come upon us for our evil deeds, and for our great trespass, seeing that thou our God has punished us less than our iniquities deserve and hast given us such deliverance as this; Should we again break thy commandments, and join in affinity with the people of these abominations? Wouldest not thou be angry with us till thou hadst consumed us, so that there should be no remnant nor escaping.[10]

The original context was the return of the Children of Israel from exile in Babylon. God did not forsake them in bondage but released

[10] This and subsequent quotations are from a sermon by Ivan Foster, 'Should Nigel Dodds MP have attended the ecumenical service in St Anne's Cathedral marking the Queen's Golden Jubilee? Ezra 9: 13–14', Kilskeery Free Presbyterian church, 19 May 2002.

them and gave them a second chance. And instead of obeying his commands, they did not separate them from the heathen of the lands; instead they mixed with them and intermarried.

My subject this evening is one that I never ever expected to have to preach but since it has come upon me, preach it I must. I have entitled my subject 'Should Mr Nigel Dodds MP have attended the Queen's Golden Jubilee ecumenical service in St Anne's Cathedral?' The incident has caused me grief of heart and I stand in the pulpit tonight to perform a duty which I earnestly wished I did not have to perform.

Catholic Archbishop Sean Brady prayed during the service, and, as Foster reminds his audience, Brady is not a Christian minister but a representative of the Antichrist. To dignify such a man by sitting through his prayers is against everything the Church stands for. 'We have sought to call the people of Northern Ireland out of the ecumenical denominations. The Free Presbyterian Church has claimed that the Troubles through which we are passing... over the last 50 odd years is a direct result of the judgement of God on this land.' Foster then lists examples of Old Testament men of God risking death by refusing to conform to public expectations when they clashed with God's command.

The choice of those individuals... was basically the choice faced by our good friend and brother Mr Nigel Dodds. It has to be said that the penalty for refusing to attend the ecumenical service in St Anne's was not life-threatening ... Had he decided not to go to the ecumenical service he would have at worst to endure a little name-calling by his political opponents: something which most politicians in Northern Ireland accept as part of the job [but] Mr Dodds decided to attend the service and consequently disobey God's word and defy the stand and witness of the Free Presbyterian Church.

In fine pulpit style, Foster slides seamlessly from the sins of Nigel Dodds to the responsibilities of his audience. This apostasy is a challenge to all his listeners because:

Within the Free Presbyterian Church there has been a breaking down of the walls of separation for quite some time.... God's people have seen their sons and daughters wandering. They have seen them crossing the line into the camp of ecumenism. They have been encouraged to go to social gatherings and functions within the camp of apostasy so don't be surprised if that leads on then to more obvious breaches such as that which took place on Wednesday night.

The sermon builds to a powerful climax that takes the fate of the Children of Israel as a model for the precarious position of the true gospel in Northern Ireland:

The FPC is a church that God has recently brought out of bondage.... the most of you here can look back on forefathers who were in the darkness of apostasy, raised up in churches where there was no gospel and God brought you out and saved your souls and prospered you and now are we going to go back again? We have enjoyed a little reviving. Do we so despise the blessings that God has poured upon us that we're going to rejoin the apostasy? Has not God built us up?... Are we going to go back to the soul-damning darkness.... Oh weep, Christian! Weep over what is taking place. Weep lest your children do not enjoy what you have enjoyed.

While Foster can reasonably claim that his stance is that of the church in the 1960s, his hard line is probably now a minority position. A number of other ministers thought he overreacted and pointed to recent occasions on which Ian Paisley had attended similar events (such as ecumenical Thanksgiving services to mark the end of the Falklands War and the first Gulf War). That Dodds has not been ostracized by the church in the way we would have expected in its early days suggests there has been a shift towards a slightly more relaxed and tolerant separatism. But the final outcome is less important for my purposes here than the original problem. Civic duties obviously raise difficult decisions for separatists. With greater acceptance (and with the DUP's political success) such hard choices are more common. Which is one very good reason why most of the FPCU clergy remain distant from the party.

The political involvement of Free Presbyterian ministers in the early 1980s can be summarized as follows. No minister had been a member or been active in any party other than the DUP or its Protestant Unionist predecessor. Of forty-nine ministers in Northern Ireland in 1985 (which included one retired man and three students), only six had contested elections. Eleven had held office in the party. Fifteen in total—less than a third of the clergy—were or had been members of the DUP. By 2005 church involvement in the DUP had markedly declined: Beattie and Harry Cairns had retired from active politics and Foster had left the DUP. Apart from Paisley and Willie McCrea, no ministers then held office in the party. While all the younger ministers I interviewed expressed enormous admiration for 'the Doc', none felt drawn to emulate his twin careers. A number of elders and church committeemen were active in the DUP (the party's chief executive was treasurer of the Lisburn church, for example) and nothing in my conversations suggested that church people were less sympathetic to the DUP in 2005 than they had been in 1985: the main explanation for the increased distance was that, with growth, the church and the party had both become more professional. Ministers had enough to do pastoring their churches, teaching in the College, fund-raising for missions, and evangelizing, and the party had acquired a large cohort of highly competent professional politicians.

IS THE DUP FREE PRESBYTERIAN?

In the early stages of his political career, Ian Paisley depended a great deal on the Free Presbyterian Church, largely because it was through his evangelistic work that he had become well known. Most of his friends and close supporters were Free Presbyterians. But there was always a second non-evangelical element in his political support that drew on the independent unionist populist tradition. Especially in the Belfast area, people would work for him, not because he was an evangelical who denounced apostasy and promoted sabbatarianism and temperance, but because he was a strong loyalist who articulated their suspicions that the leaders of the Unionist Party—'the fur coat brigade'—were rather more interested in looking after themselves than they were in protecting working-class Protestants.

Changing the Protestant Unionist Party to the Democratic Unionist Party broadened its electorate but made little change to the composition of the party. Almost half of the DUP candidates for the 1973 Assembly were Free Presbyterians. For the 1975 Convention election, the proportion rose to almost 80 per cent: 14 out of 18. Because seniority reflected both years of service and the trust of colleagues, the FP presence increases as we move up the party hierarchy. Apart from the brief chairmanship of Desmond Boal, the leadership was drawn exclusively from Free Presbyterian circles until the early 1980s, when Robinson started attending a gospel hall and Sammy Wilson, from an Elim Pentecostal background, replaced Allister as press officer. All twelve of

TABLE 6.1. *Free Presbyterian DUP activists, 1973–2005*

Year	Group	Total	% FP
1973	Assembly candidates	17	47
1975	Convention candidates	18	78
1976	Councillors	31	65
1978	Councillors	72	60
1982	Assembly members	35	77
1985	Council candidates	218	57
1996	Forum candidates	54	58
1997	Council candidates	160	52
1998	Assembly members	20	80
2003	Assembly members	33	52
2005	Councillors	171	47

the 1975 constituency party chairmen were Free Presbyterians. Figures for various groups of DUP activists are given in Table 6.1.[11]

The first and last two cohorts shown in the table are somewhat unrepresentative: the first because the party was in its infancy and had to take help where it could find it; the last two because the DUP was then being reinforced by defections from the UUP. The average for the middle eight cohorts is 65 per cent Free Presbyterian. The proportion of Free Presbyterians does not, however, fully describe the presence of evangelicalism. There are only four local districts in Northern Ireland where more than two or three DUP activists do not have a church affiliation and they are those with a large unionist working class: Newtownabbey, Carrickfergus, Belfast, and Castlereagh. Almost all DUP activists are religious people, and a large part of those who are not Free Presbyterians are evangelical Christians. Table 6.2 shows details of the affiliations of two cohorts of activists.

The apparently large increase in those with no church connection may not be significant because it pretty well matches a decline in the number for unknowns. But those rows are of little importance compared with the pooled totals for evangelicals: 65 per cent in 1997 and 60

[11] The information that informs these tables was collected by a detailed reading of election manifestos and newspaper reports and from asking DUP activists and FP ministers to identify church affiliations. It is testimony to the smallness of Northern Ireland, the cohesion of the DUP, and the importance of religion that it was relatively easy to identify the church affiliation, if any, of almost all the hundreds of people on my various lists.

TABLE **6.2.** *Denomination of DUP activists, 1997 and 2005* (%)

Denomination	1997 Council candidates	2005 Councillors
Free Presbyterian	52	47
Irish Presbyterian	16	24
Church of Ireland	5	6
Other mainstream Protestant	3	2
Other evangelical	13	13
None	3	6
Not known	8	2
TOTAL	100	100

per cent in 2005. But even these totals underestimate evangelical influence, because a number of the Irish Presbyterian and Church of Ireland people are born-again Christians and make a point of saying so in their election literature. Phrases such as 'a committed Christian', 'keen interest in youth work within his church', 'maintains strong Christian principles', and 'a Christian from the age of thirteen' pepper the profiles.

We might expect that the major realignment of unionist politics after 2003 would have produced a change in the religiosity of the DUP. There was certainly an increase in Irish Presbyterian representation: 9 out of 33 in the second assembly as compared with only 1 out of 35 in the first. But the change is less significant than denominational affiliation suggests, because, like Jeffrey Donaldson, who shares all the FPCU's principles except that of separation, these newcomers are mostly sympathetic to the party's evangelical background.

IMPACT OF RELIGION ON POLITICS

The final chapter of the book will look at the subtle links between the religious beliefs of DUP people and their unionism. Here I want to consider the issue of theocracy: to what extent is the DUP committed to promoting a specifically evangelical Christian agenda?

In some respects that is a difficult question to answer because the border so dominates Ulster politics that very little else ever becomes significant. The manifesto for the 1982 Assembly elections has fifteen items. The first four concern the Union. The fifth calls for an all-out war against the IRA and the return of the death penalty as 'the only suitable punishment for the heinous murders committed in our Province'. The second section of the manifesto outlines the DUP's social and economic policies, which are moderately Keynesian, calling for 'additional but sensible public expenditure on a sustained jobs creation offensive', cheaper energy through a link to the British mainland's North Sea gas network, and major investment in housing. The strong rural support for the party is recognized by a call for 'a realistic return for the farming community, with special measures to offset the disadvantages especially in the intensive livestock sector, resulting from our isolation from Great Britain'.

The manifesto then proposes more democratic control over education and leisure, an end to the financing of two distinct education systems, an increase in old-age pensions, and more facilities for the handicapped. It is only in the very last paragraph that there is a distinctly evangelical position in the party's platform. Under the heading 'Moral Matters—Morals Matter', the party promises that:

A strong and forthright stand will continue to be taken in accordance with Christian principles on the great moral issues of our day. We utterly deprecate the imposition by Westminster of alien moral standards upon Ulster. The DUP will lead opposition in the Assembly to such matters as the legalising of homosexuality, opening sex shops and Sunday opening of public houses. Ulster should decide its own moral standards and codes of behaviour.

Of the issues specifically mentioned, only the licensing of sex shops and the Sunday opening of public houses have fallen within the remit of bodies on which the DUP has had any significant representation.

The 1985 manifesto shows an interesting change. It demands government action to 'smash Sinn Fein', a rejection of the Anglo-Irish 'sell-out', and an end to cross-border collaboration. Less than halfway through the document is the paragraph headed 'The Republican Sunday':

Recognising the laws of God and the inherent benefits of the Ulster Sabbath as part of our heritage, the DUP is opposed to the introduction or promotion of the Continental and Republic Sunday in Northern Ireland. As it is the rate payer who funds and owns Council facilities, the DUP believes that any change to Sunday opening of Council provisions should only be undertaken following the test of the electorate's opinion in a local poll held for that purpose in the district of the council. If the government seek to deny this facility to a Council, or if other parties successfully oppose such a democratic test of ratepayers' views being held, then DUP councillors will vote, as in the past, against a Republican Sunday.

Some commentators have presented the shift between the two manifestos as a matter of a once-religious party abandoning its principles for electoral purposes.[12] That story is sometimes told with the additional theme of younger, more secular politicians displacing the older evangelicals. This is not a terribly accurate picture. It is certainly the case that some older members of the DUP have sounded like impositionists. One councillor said: 'It's not a case of the DUP enforcing anything. It is God's law. It is the Lord who has told us for to keep the sabbath day holy. It is not the DUP. But I am thankful the DUP believes in that.'[13]

Not everyone did, and the divisions were not between young and old, or Free Presbyterians and the secular. William Beattie, a Free Presbyterian minister and founder member of the DUP, was opposed to sabbatarianism ever being in the DUP manifesto, and his explanation clearly disavows a theocratic intent: 'I made it absolutely clear that I would never support the imposition of Free Presbyterian moral standards on the general public. My biggest reason for not being in the South ... is that reason and I do not want to see this country and the Free Presbyterian Church attempt to do what the Roman Catholic Church has done in the south.' Paisley was equally clear: 'I don't believe you can legislate righteousness. Man has to be changed.' In reply to the point that Calvin and Knox tried to impose righteousness, he went on:

They tried and they failed and I don't believe you can legislate righteousness. I know that the human heart is deceitful about all things and desperately wicked. ... There are standards to preserve society from the worst excesses of man's iniquitous heart but I can't legislate a man into the Kingdom of God. Therefore the Sabbath day, that's an individual matter. If a golf club wants to open on Sunday and they own the golf club and they run it, that's their business. [If the pubs want to open on Sunday?] that brings us into the public place and the public have to have some say about what's going to

[12] J. McAuley, *The Politics of Identity: A Loyalist Community in Belfast* (Aldershot: Avebury, 1994).
[13] N. Southern, 'Evangelical Protestantism within the Democratic Unionist Party', *Irish Political Studies*, 20 (2005), 131.

happen on their land. That's the difference. And that is where I believe we have to make a decision. Now of course I am a 'local option' man. The people of the neighbourhood should have a say in that because that's a public thing and that has always been a view I have advocated.

Like Beattie, Foster did not think sabbatarianism should have been in the manifesto: 'I do not believe that that particular one is something for parties to legislate on. If I had been standing I could have put it in my personal manifesto that I was a sabbatarian but when the Party committed itself to that, it was placing itself in the position of a church.' However, he took the principled but awkward position that, as it had been DUP policy, he was opposed to changing it, even to the extent of the local-option position, because the change would be seen as a weakening, as a change of principle. Gordon Cooke, an FPCU minister who was chairman of a DUP branch, reluctantly accepted the change but only on the understanding that the DUP was not committed to encouraging the local-option votes.

Jim Wells made the same point while offering a secular defence of his religious values: 'I believe that God's laws are not just designed for Christians but they're designed for society, to keep society stable. If everyone, even non-Christians obeyed God's laws, society would be a better place.' He says: 'I believe that the scripture is truth . . . I believe it's incumbent on me to try and live a Christian life.' But what is the mechanism for bringing the non-Christians into line? It is 'to try and influence others to uphold God's law'.[14] And if they are not persuaded, so be it.

To give them their due, most DUP councillors accepted the decisions of local people, and, over the decade following the 1985 elections, council after council allowed their leisure facilities to open on Sundays. The final bastion to fall was in Paisley's heartland. In 1998 the Ballymoney council invited Queen's University to poll residents over the Sunday opening of the Riada Centre. Of 1,200 randomly chosen electors, 700 responded and 70 per cent voted for opening. The DUP councillors could have sulked and allowed the opening motion to be passed by the votes of others, but they did the honourable thing and supported the motion, which was passed unanimously.

---

[14] N. Southern, 'Evangelical Protestantism within the Democratic Unionist Party', *Irish Political Studies*, 20 (2005), 132.

The DUP found a way of reconciling the evangelical principles of most of its activists with the need to serve its electorate: the right of individuals to choose to make mistakes. The important point about the sabbath debate is that it was misunderstood by outsiders who supposed that the evangelicals (especially the FPCU clergy) would be in favour of imposing their religiously inspired values on others. As we saw, the clergy found it very easy to accept that the electors should decide. And, if we go back to the start of this section, we can see why. It is often assumed that only secular liberals wish to separate church and states, or religion and politics, or morality and state law; that the purpose of recognizing two distinct spheres is to diminish the power of the church. But the same divisions can be appreciated by those who view the problem from the other end, whose primary concern is to safeguard religion. As the people faced with the dual responsibility of serving the church and their electors, the clergy who were involved in the DUP could appreciate, better than lay evangelicals, that they had to keep their roles separate.

THE LOYAL ORDERS

The fraternal orders play an important part in bridging religion and politics. Its own myth pushes the formation of the Orange Order back to the 1680s and the battles between the supporters of Catholic James VII and William, Prince of Orange, but a more realistic starting point is a century later, when violence between Protestant and Catholic agrarian vigilante groups become more common and vicious. In September 1795 a large body of Catholics attacked a smaller number of Protestants at Dan Winter's cottage at the Diamond, near Portadown in County Armagh. At a subsequent meeting in Loughgall, the Protestant victors decided a permanent organization was needed to protect their interests, and they fashioned it after the common model of the day: the Freemasons.

Initially the typical Order member was a landless agricultural worker, Church of Ireland in his religion, and somewhat rowdy in his habits. Although successive governments could see the benefit of a mass organization that supported the Crown, the Order's propensity to provoke nationalists made it suspect and its parades were periodically banned. Towards the end of the nineteenth century, when the Irish Home Rule movement gathered strength, large numbers of Presbyterians joined, as did clergymen of every denomination, businessmen, professional men, farmers, skilled artisans, and members of the upper classes.

The Ulster Unionist Party was founded in 1886 by seven Westminster MPs, all of them Orangemen, and, when the Ulster Unionist Council was created, the importance of the Order as a vehicle for binding in the common people was recognized by it being given 122 of the 760 seats. Until the late 1950s the Order was led by the same grandees who led the UUP. In 1954 the Grand Master was the former Prime Minister John Andrews and twenty-six members of its Grand Committee were titled. Its influence on Northern Ireland can be gauged from the fact that all of the six prime ministers from 1926 to 1972 were Orangemen, as were over 90 per cent of UUP MPs at Westminster.

The Order is organized in a pyramid. Members belong to one of 1,400 private lodges, which send representatives to the 126 district lodges, which in turn send representatives to 12 county Grand Lodges. Most private lodges meet monthly, and most meetings involve a religious service at some point.[15] They also deal with lodge finances, initiate new members, install members in their myriad offices, commission banners, and arrange social functions, but most importantly they plan parades. Only a core of members attend meetings regularly, but all members march. The explicit purpose of the Order is to preserve the reformed Protestant faith. Among other qualifications, an Orangeman is required to 'have sincere love and veneration for his heavenly Father; a humble and steadfast faith in Jesus Christ, the saviour of mankind, believing in him as the only Mediator between God and man'. He should also 'honour and diligently study the Holy Scriptures, and make them the rule of his faith and practice' and he should 'love, uphold and defend the Protestant religion'. Moreover, 'he should strenuously oppose the fatal errors and doctrines of the Church of Rome, and scrupulously avoid

[15] For an account of Orange principles, see B. Kennedy (ed.), *Steadfast for Faith and Freedom: 200 Years of Orangeism* (Belfast: Grand Lodge of Ireland, 1995) and *A Celebration 1690–1990: The Orange Institution* (Belfast: Grand Lodge of Ireland, 1990). See also P. Mitchel, *Evangelicalism and National Identity in Ulster, 1921–1998* (Oxford: Oxford University Press, 2003).

countenancing (by his presence or otherwise) any act of ceremony of Popish worship'. In the context of Northern Ireland this personal faith is also a political statement, and the point of the marching season is to dramatize the power of the Protestant people. From the middle of June onwards Orangemen hold a variety of small local parades, but the major event occurs on the Twelfth of July, when the districts commemorate the Battle of the Boyne of 1690.

As with the Masons, there are a variety of degrees of membership within the Orange Order. The Royal Arch Purple is one such; the Black Institution another. The day after the Orange parades, the 'Blackmen' meet at Scarva, where they mount a sham battle between the forces of William and James. The Imperial Grand Black Chapter of the British Commonwealth, to give it its full title, is effectively the senior branch of the Orange Order. All members are Orangemen but they differ in being more respectable and more likely to be Christians. The sovereign grand master for almost thirty years was James Moly- neaux, leader of the UUP from 1979 to 1995.

Quite separate from the main Order is the Independent Orange Order. In the late nineteenth century, the domination of the upper reaches of the Order by wealthy businessmen and landed gentry and the periodic government bans on its parades bred considerable resentment, which, in 1902, flared into rebellion when a march in Rostrevor was banned. At an unruly Belfast County demonstration in Castlereagh, Thomas Sloan, Worshipful Master of St Michael's Total Abstinence Lodge and a prominent member of the Belfast Protestant Association, challenged the County Grand Master, Colonel Saunder- son MP, to say how he had voted on the 'Inspection of Convent Laundries' bill. As the title suggests, this piece of legislation was an attempt to embarrass and annoy the Catholic Church by requiring that its convents (which militant Protestants suspected of exploiting the labour and the sexuality of young girls) be subject to government inspection. The point Sloan wished to make was that Saunderson, like most Unionist leaders, had put government interest before anti- Catholic principle. Although popular enough to win the South Belfast Westminster seat previously held by William Johnston of Ballykilbegs (a Protestant hero since his prison sentence in 1867 for defying a parades ban), Sloan was disciplined by Grand Lodge for embarrassing a grandee and led a breakaway. The Independent Order (independent from the UUP, that is) briefly flirted with left-wing politics before settling down to become the Order of preference for pious evangelicals, strongest in the rural parts of the province and in North Antrim in particular.[16]

The third fraternal organization to which Ulster Protestants may belong is the Apprentice Boys of Derry, which, as its name suggests, exists to celebrate the example of the apprentice boys who closed the gates of Derry city to prevent its surrender to the forces of Catholic King James.

Evangelicals and the Orders

The strong bond between religion and politics in Northern Ireland causes many evangelicals to join one or more of the fraternal orders. The Orange Order is a mass movement in defence of reformed religion that regularly conducts services, appoints chaplains, and requires members to honour and diligently study the Holy Scriptures, but it has always been obvious that many members are Protestant only in the ethnic sense, prefer the social (for which read 'drinking alcohol') to the religious aspects of the organization, and engage in its rituals with little regard for the promises they make. In addition to encouraging dishonest oath-taking, some rituals themselves can offend some evangelicals because, as an evangelical website argues, they supposedly borrow from paganism.[17]

Because its membership is much more obviously pious and God-fearing, the Independent Orange Order causes less anguish for conservative evangelicals. For the opposite reason, the Apprentice Boys of Derry is also likely to be more acceptable than the Orange Order. It is avowedly political rather than religious and thus avoids the problem of improperly claimed piety. However, it has a large working-class membership, which sees its parades as an opportunity for considerable drinking, and it has a close historic tie to the Church of Ireland, whose cathedral in Londonderry is regarded as the spiritual headquarters of the association.

[16] Independent Orange Order, *Why an Independent Orange Order?* (Belfast: Independent Loyal Orange Institution of Ireland, 1961).

[17] www.nireland.com/evangelicaltruth/Q+A.htm.

Generally speaking, evangelical ill ease with the fraternal orders has increased over the twentieth century. There have always been rough elements within these organizations, but the typical Orangeman or Apprentice Boy in 1900 was markedly more likely to be a born-again Christian than his counterpart in 1990, and the private lodge or local club structure meant that respectable Christians could cluster together and turn a blind eye to the extent to which others fell short of the organizations' requirements.

Most Ulster Protestants have some family connections with the fraternal orders. Richard Paisley, Ian's grandfather, was a prominent Orangeman in County Tyrone. William McCrea's grandfather was Worshipful Master of his private lodge for twenty years, and his son inherited the position, which he also held for twenty years. It is thus hardly surprising that McCrea himself joined as a teenager. Paisley was once a member of a North Belfast lodge and then of one in East Belfast, close to his Ravenhill church. After a year in the Order he became a chaplain in No. 6 district, which covered East Belfast and was one of the largest. The formation of the FPCU in 1951 created tension between Paisley and Orange leaders who, because they saw one of the major purposes of the Order as uniting Protestants of different denominations, were not at all happy with Paisley's criticisms of Irish Presbyterians. A few months after the Crossgar split, Grand Lodge formalized its rules for the office of chaplain and in a very deliberate snub determined that the clergy of pretty well every Protestant church except the Free Presbyterian were entitled to be chaplains. Although Paisley continued as a member, the logic of his separatism increasingly caused problems. In the late 1950s he quarrelled with Warren Porter, an Irish Presbyterian minister and respected Orange leader. And in 1962 he resigned from the Order when the County Grand Lodge refused to expel Sir Robin Kinahan, who, in his capacity as Lord Mayor of Belfast, had attended a Roman Catholic funeral Mass. Paisley was also an Apprentice Boy and had been elected chaplain of the Belfast and District Amalgamated Committee, but after the Crossgar split Irish Presbyterians arranged for a popular candidate to stand against him and ensured that he was replaced. He resigned the following year and only rejoined in 1971 when the Dromora Apprentice Boys Club in County Down invited him to join. Although not a member, Paisley has strong links with the Independent Orange Order (which has its strongest support in his North Antrim constituency) and regularly addresses its Twelfth demonstration.

The FPCU does not have an official view of the fraternal associations, but its general attitude is just on the hostile side of neutral; which was pretty much the attitude of the loyal orders to the FPCU until the Belfast Agreement. Of the first generation of FPCU ministers and of those who joined prior to 1985, about half had been members of one or more of the orders, but about half of those had resigned. Of 45 ministers in 1985 whose affiliations are known, 21 had never been members of any fraternal organization, 10 had been members of the Orange Order but 7 had resigned; 3 had been members of the Independent Orange Order and 1 had left; 11 ministers were known to be members of the Apprentice Boys of Derry and 2 had resigned. In 1977 Ken Elliott, the Free Presbyterian minister of Portadown, offended many Apprentice Boys by refusing to take a collection for the restoration of St Columb's Church of Ireland Cathedral in Londonderry. For him, the Church of Ireland was 'poisoned by ecumenism'.

One Free Presbyterian minister in explaining why he had left the Orange Order said: 'Perhaps the main reason was that in 1969 I was saved by the grace of God and therefore felt that I could not sit and be associated with members of the Orange and Black while they consumed alcohol in their meetings on the Twelfth and Thirteenth mornings each July.' Among reasons cited for leaving the Order were: 'religious convictions', 'influence of the World Council of Churches', 'ecumenical clergy as chaplains', and 'left because of II Cor. Ch. 6, 14–18' ('Be ye not unequally yoked together with unbelievers: for what fellowship hath righteousness with unrighteousness? And what communion hath light with darkness'). The most succinct reason given was the single word 'drink'.

The close ties of the loyal orders to the Ulster Unionist Party and to the main Protestant churches gave their hierarchies a good reason to dislike Paisleyites, but it is clear that many ordinary Orangemen and Apprentice Boys sympathized with either the FPCU's evangelical critique of ecumenism or with the DUP's critique of UUP unreliability, and a number of private lodges were supportive. One has had a painting of Paisley's Martyrs' Memorial Church on its banner since 1969. After it had abandoned what Foster called 'the spiritual Siberia' of the Shore Road and before the new church at Corr's Corner was built, the Newtownabbey congregation met in the Mossley Orange Hall. Orange Halls in Lurgan, Bangor, and Ballygawley have been used for missions, as has the Ballyvea Orange Hall, which for a time gave a home to the fledgling Kilkeel congregation. And, despite their misgivings about the piety of Orangemen, many ministers have conducted Orange church parade services (and used the opportunity to hector the nominal Christians!).

Over the course of the Troubles there was a marked change in the attitudes of the loyal orders to Paisley and to Paisleyites that stemmed from a major change in the class composition of the orders and a weakening of their ties to the Ulster Unionist Party. At the high point of unionist unity (in, say, 1926) the Orange, Purple and Black and the Apprentice Boys had a considerable upper- and middle-class presence. By the 1960s this was already changing, with the professional middle classes and the landed gentry withdrawing from the unionist ethnic bloc. The early 1970s saw this process accelerated, and the orders passed into the hands of lower-middle-class people such as James Molyneaux and Revd Martin Smyth. In 1974 the Apprentice Boys broke their formal ties to the UUP. It was not until 2003 that the Orange Order did the same, but long before that many rank-and-file Orangemen had come to prefer Paisley's politics to those of the UUP.

The Free Presbyterian clergy have been slow to respond.[18] In 2005 only eight ministers were members of the Orange, two were members of the Independent Order, and perhaps ten were Apprentice Boys. Without exception Free Presbyterians would have shared the political goals of the loyal orders, but most would not have wished to be associated with the least respectable elements, and they continued to be to the fore. The principles of Orangeism are fine, but the reality is often rioting drunks and attacks on the police.

---

[18] Moloney and Pollak pursue a relentlessly cynical view of Paisley and his followers. In their discussion of FP links with the orders they assume that Free Presbyterians strongly wished to have careers in the orders that would give them influence and were forced out by the unionist elites. For example: 'Since then [1971] Free Presbyterians have flocked to the Apprentice Boys, a much smaller organization than the Orange Order, where they can exercise much greater influence.' E. Moloney and A. Pollak, *Paisley* (Swords: Poolbeg Press, 1986), 53. 'Flocked' is silly. Although the political tide has been running Paisley's way for a decade, core Free Presbyterians have not returned to the loyal orders.

The DUP and the Orders

DUP activists, even those who are committed Free Presbyterians, do not share the FPCU clergy reservations about the loyal orders. Of the 34 Members of the Legislative Assembly (MLAs) in 2005, all but 4 were Apprentice Boys and at least 25 were in the Orange Order. Three people from the north of the province were in the Independent Order. Apart from the obvious point that the DUP and the Orders share common principles, the institutions provide politicians with important networks. As Jim Wells MLA said:

I find being in the Orange—I've been an Orangeman for 27 years—is extremely useful in my own constituency because Orange is very strong within the unionist community in South Down. I get invited to lots of functions and banner unfurlings and hall openings and it keeps me in direct contact with grassroots unionism right across the spectrum.[19]

Those invitations flow because there has been a significant shift in Orange attitudes to the DUP. By 2003 a survey of 293 Orangemen showed that 42 per cent aligned themselves with DUP with only 31 supporting the UUP: which, as compared with the Assembly elections of that year, gave the DUP a greater lead among Orangemen than among unionist voters.[20] When asked how they would vote if there was an election tomorrow, the Orange respondents split DUP/UUP two-thirds and one-third. The survey collected information on a variety of characteristics, so we can compare the profiles of DUP and UUP supporters in the Order. Those who preferred the DUP tended to be poorer. They were more likely to have no educational qualification, to be manual workers, and to describe themselves as working class. There were also less likely to be Church of Ireland. But the biggest difference was in age. Although in 2003 the popularity of the DUP and UUP was similar for Orangemen aged 55 and above, two years earlier—before the great shift—the older respondents supported the UUP by a margin of two to one. This gives statistical

[19] C. Farrington, 'The Democratic Unionist Party and the Northern Ireland Peace Process', paper presented to the Political Studies Association annual conference, Lincoln, 2004.

[20] J. Tonge and J. Evans, 'Eating the Oranges? The Democratic Unionist Party and the Orange Order vote in Northern Ireland', paper presented to the Political Studies Association Elections, Public Opinion and Parties annual conference, 2004.

confirmation of what we would guess from a general acquaintance with this world. Those Orangemen who remember back to the 1960s, when Paisley was seen as a wrecker of all-important unionist unity, were far less keen on Paisley than the younger men whose impressions were formed in the 1980s and later.

THE GENERATION GAME

Much writing about the DUP has been based on two myths. By 'myth' I mean a story that is false but that is believed because the belief serves an important purpose. The first myth is the story of generational conflict. The second, often compounded with the first, is the story of a religious/secular divide. In explaining why the DUP was so keen on making the 1983–5 'rolling devolution' Assembly work, Ed Moloney of the *Irish Times* wrote: 'a large number of those attracted to and recruited into the party through Robinson's efforts were different in a number of important respects from the traditional Paisley follower of the early rabble-rousing days . . .'. An analysis of unionist politics said:

The old guard was largely rural and had a basic education, fundamental Protestantism, and a belief in Ian Paisley, while the new guard, personified by Peter Robinson and Sammy Wilson, was mainly urban, well-educated and less directly connected to the Free Presbyterian Church . . . The conflict within the DUP between secular and fundamentalist factions hampered the party as disagreements began to erupt over tactics such as civil disobedience.[21]

It is generally supposed that, while Paisley, Beattie, Foster, and such people wish to maintain the evangelical ethos, the younger generation of Robinson, Jim Wells, Jim Allister, and others recruited through the Queen's University branch of the DUP wanted to create a mass popular party platform by pursuing more respectable methods of political action.

---

[21] F. Cochrane, *Unionist Politics* (Cork: Cork University Press, 2001), 46, 55. Cochrane is quite good on the documents and the stated policy positions but he does not understand his subjects. It seems highly likely he has never actually talked to leading DUP people.

There is a good reason to expect this sort of pattern. It is common for radical political movements, once they have grown to a certain size and achieved some success, to moderate.[22] Particularly once the movement employs professional managers, the original radical thrust is lost as the professionals redirect the organization to serve their own ends. Keeping the structure going becomes more important than attaining the initial goals of the movement. For members, there is a shift in the main source of satisfaction. They joined the movement because they were inspired by its goals. As it settles down and the chances of attaining the radical goals recede, members find new sources of satisfaction in belonging. For the leaders a dilution of the radical goals is attractive because it reduces the stigma attached to the movement and the tension between it and the wider society. There are substantial rewards for accommodation to the prevailing consensus. Moloney offers such an analysis of the younger DUP activists: 'men like Robinson, Allister and Kane who are at the start of political careers know that the negative politics practised for so long by their leader would deny them the office and power that could be theirs.' Twenty years later the same story is told but with a new reason for moderation. The first generation of DUP had careers and businesses or were at the end of the working lives. The second generation consist largely of professional politicians who have no other life and hence who have much to lose if this one ever dries up completely.

A further reason for expecting moderation is increased prosperity and social status. As we noted in the previous chapter with regard to Free Presbyterians, DUP activists have benefited from the general shift in the economy from primary extraction and manufacturing towards service industries, from manual to professional and technical work. The party's founders were farmers, small businessmen, and manual workers. It is a little difficult to show the increase in social status of the DUP activists because their individual class positions are distorted by them being successful politicians. Of the

[22] The founding text of this field of social science is R. Michels, *Political Parties: A Sociological Study of the Oligarchic Tendencies of Modern Democracy* (New York: Free Press, 1961), which analysed the decline of radicalism in left-wing parties and trade unions, coined the phrase 'the iron law of oligarchy', and spawned a huge literature in the field of social movements. It has many parallels with the Niebuhr thesis mentioned in Ch. 5.

34 DUP members of the 2005 Assembly, a third were full-time politicians and most of them had been for some long time. However, we can see the point from the occupations of those who had worked at an honest trade. The DUP's rural roots were still well represented, with 6 MLAs who farmed (or were something closely allied: haulier, for example). There were 6 businessmen; 3 lawyers; 3 teachers; 5 civil servants or administrators; and 2 clergymen. There were only 3 who had worked at what could be described as manual jobs, and 2 of those were technically skilled. At least 10 MLAs were university graduates and at least a further 6 had attended college beyond schooling.

In brief, the DUP leadership of 2005 had a much greater proportion of well-educated, high-social-status people in it than the cohort of twenty years earlier; which permits the logic of accommodation. These people have more to lose than their parents. They are smarter and so should know better. And they have had (albeit short) brushes with power, and, as one Free Presbyterian critic of the party put it: 'There's something about plush seats and walnut panelling that intoxicates.'

Testing the Myth

The purpose of the generations myth is to keep cheerful those with an interest in negotiating a diplomatic solution to the Northern Ireland conflict. It is the sibling of the myth of the centre: the idea that the extremes of Ulster politics are unrepresentative and that, if the right circumstances can be engineered, then a solid middle ground of Alliance Party, liberal unionists and liberal nationalists will sustain a solution. In the generations version the death of Paisley will liberate the younger men of the DUP to compromise their principles.

There is little or no evidence to support this. Peter Robinson was as happy as Paisley to don the maroon beret of Ulster Resistance and deliver demagogic speeches. He was involved with Paisley and Johnny McQuade in the demonstrations again the invitation of Charles Haughey, then the Republic's Prime Minster, to the enthronement of the Church of Ireland Primate in Armagh in May 1980. In the same year Robinson was invited by Haughey to a reception in Dublin. His wife, Iris (later an MP and MLA), wrote 'No Surrender' in big Orange print on the invitation and sent it back. Robinson rivals Paisley for

serious offences: he was fined £15,000 in connection with his invasion
of the Irish Republic. Jim Wells has his conviction for public-order
offences. Ian Paisley Jr and another young DUP man, Edwin Poots,
were ejected by the US Secret Service from a Washington function for
heckling Republic Prime Minister Bertie Ahern.[23]

Two of those cited by journalist Ed Moloney as young men who
would compromise for office—Jim Allister and Alan Kane—quit the
party when Paisley moderated in the interests of unionist unity.
Robinson's brief departure over Paisley's rejection of the Task Force
report could be seen as evidence of potential moderation, but his
disagreement was concerned more with presentation than with substance. He thought Paisley and Molyneaux were making a presenta-
tional mistake in allowing themselves to be portrayed as the men who
only said 'No'. Because so many commentators in the late 1980s
concentrated on the difference between Paisley and Molyneaux,
with the Doc being seen as the agitator being reined in by the calmer
and more accommodating Molyneaux, they overlooked an equally
telling contrast. Paisley was himself a moderating influence during
the protests against the Anglo-Irish Accord, often trying to restrain
his own party's hotheads.[24] And most of those were precisely the
younger men so often portrayed as the potential compromisers

In sum, the idea of a generational divide does not seem supported
by the evidence. If the DUP now spends less time on the picket line
and the banned parade, it is because its political success has given it
many other (and better) ways of conveying its principles. I have no
doubt that Robinson and Dodds would shout on a picket line if they
thought it worthwhile; that they do it less than Paisley and Beattie did
in 1966 is because as members of the largest party at Stormont and
the largest Unionist party at Westminster they have other pressing
things to do and they have excellent access to the mass media.

The contrast between a religious and a secular wing is also inaccur-
ate. With perhaps one exception, all those who are named as representative of the secular generation are either Free Presbyterians or regular
attenders at gospel halls or the Metropolitan Tabernacle. The latter do

---

[23] *Irish News*, 18 Mar. 2000.

[24] The one analyst who has this right is Paul Dixon; see P. Dixon, *Northern Ireland:
The Politics of War and Peace* (London: Palgrave, 2001), 208–10.

not hold to the separatist line of the FPCU, but they are evangelical Christians. Kane turned down an opportunity to explain his Save Ulster from Sodomy campaign on television because the studio discussion would take place on a Sunday. Wells has been active in opposing the opening of a Bainbridge disco that will operate on the Sabbath. Theatrical illustration of their principles was given by Dodds and Gregory Campbell in 2001 in the way they responded to the returning officer's announcement of their election victories at the count. Paisley has always sung the Doxology (or the Doc's-ology as one party wag dubbed it). Dodds and Campbell made a point of thanking God before giving the conventional thanks to the returning officer.

A more plausible source of change in the DUP than generational differences is the entry of large numbers of former members of the UUP. It is assumed that the DUP's replacement of the UUP as the dominant unionist party will draw in a large number of people who do not share either the religious background of the DUP core or its political obstinacy. The religious underpinning of its unionism will be weakened and the new unionism will become more 'realistic': that is, more amendable to compromise. This seems rather unlikely. Certainly at the level of senior party activists, the new recruits differ from the core of the original DUP only in not accepting Paisley's ecclesiastical separatism. The weight given to seeking divine guidance in Donaldson's biography is much the same as that in Willie McCrea's: the only significant difference is that Donaldson has satisfied his desire for an evangelical ministry by attending Irish Presbyterian and Baptist congregations led by sound evangelical ministers.

There have, of course, been significant changes in the DUP's politics. It now talks to Dublin government ministers in Dublin. It is prepared to accept Sinn Fein in government if republicans can convince unionists that they are thoroughly committed to democratic politics and if the IRA stands down. If republicans cannot make that shift, then the DUP will accept a voluntary coalition with the SDLP. It will accept an 'Irish dimension' to Ulster politics. The hated reforms to the RUC have occurred and most cannot be reversed. The Ulster Defence Regiment has been disbanded despite DUP objections. For all that it wants certain elements of the Belfast Agreement changed, the DUP works to achieve the best result for unionists within the contours first laid down in the hated Anglo-Irish

Accord. But these changes are no surprise. Ulster is not an autonomous political unit. As it proved with the early release of terrorist
prisoners, the reform of the RUC, and so on, the British government is
sovereign. In the absence of a return by the IRA to the sort of violence
that would persuade most unionists to support rebellion, the DUP's
only options are to boycott the political process altogether or constantly to press for the best deal for unionists that the British will
permit. Many conservative unionists would find the former emotion-
ally satisfying, but wiser heads know that such abstention would only
advantage nationalists. So the party has constantly to change to be as
effective as possible in whatever circumstances prevail. The important
point for understanding the DUP is that such realism is not the
monopoly of younger or more secular members.

CONCLUSION

Paisley's church and party were once very close. As each grew, they
moved apart, not so much because either changed but because as
each has grown it has become more demanding and required greater
professionalism and commitment. The casual analyses of church–
party links offered by outsiders generally miss the point because they
simplify to the point of caricature. As I have argued above, the idea
that the growth of the DUP from its tiny Protestant Unionist base to
being the largest unionist party has been accompanied by a dilution
of its evangelical ethos is simply mistaken. Certainly as regards the
character and interests of its core activists, that picture is misleading.
The proportion of committed evangelicals in the core remains pretty
much as high as ever it was.

A more accurate account would start by recognizing that all
Christians (indeed all religious people) have to work out how they
will engage with the world. The simplest solution is to retreat into a
pious ghetto and as far as possible ignore the world. But reformed
Protestants generally disdain that easy solution and feel some obligation both to reform the world and to bear witness to the gospel
within it. Another fairly simple strategy is that of those Islamic
fundamentalists who suppose that they have an obligation to impose

righteousness on the world, whether the world likes it or not. But again the reformed Protestant tradition gives little support to such theocratic principles. It lays too great a stress on the need for individuals to become saved: a society based on God's law will be better than one that ignores divine precepts, but it will not ensure salvation. Outsiders also miss the extent to which Protestants are deeply committed to the principles of liberal democracy. The original Reformers were not democrats; when they spoke of the individual it was always in terms of responsibilities and not rights, but the logic of their core religious beliefs eventually led to a defence of rights. If each of us has to answer to God for our own actions, then we must be free to be responsible, and we must have the wherewithal to acquaint ourselves with the saving faith. Hence the Reformers' interest in promoting literacy and printing. Many early Protestant sects were theocratic impositionists. Most of the early schisms from the Church of Scotland were led by people who saw nothing wrong with the state imposing the true religion on a reluctant people; they objected only to the wrong religion being supported by the state. But, when they failed to become the majority, they gradually came round to seeing the virtue of individual liberty, and by the nineteenth century most reformed Protestants had become enthusiastic supporters of a reality that they had accidentally, reluctantly, and inadvertently created: in a society where a variety of religions competed, the only sensible attitude to diversity was to separate the church and state, to distinguish between what God required of us and what it was possible for the laws of man to require. The logic of their critique of Roman Catholicism led militant Protestants very firmly in the same direction.

Accepting the principles of liberal democracy allows evangelicals to function effectively in the public world. They present their divinely inspired principles to the electors, and it is up to the electors to respond. At the same time they work hard to convert the ungodly so that the number who share their principles increases. However, this leaves the believer with the daily challenge of deciding just how far he or she can go in working with those who reject the true faith. Between the extreme positions of the pious retreat from the world and the radical imposition of God's will, there is a vast territory of more or less difficult decision-making. That we see a clear difference between the attitudes of the FPCU clergy and Free Presbyterian DUP politicians (as illustrated, for example, by the argument between Foster and Dodds about attending an ecumenical service) should not be taken to identify a major clash of principles. What it shows is the rather different point that, even within a consensus over big principles, people have to choose what weight they will give to particular aspects of their roles in this or that setting. With the exceptions of Paisley and McCrea the FP clergy are full-time specialist promoters of the gospel. For them the need for clarity of witness is paramount. Lay Free Presbyterians (and other evangelicals) who are politically active have other imperatives to face.

The next two chapters will pursue this theme in greater detail, but the issue of relations with the loyal orders allows me to draw attention to the important aspect of religion in the politics of Northern Ireland: its ethnic dimension. In Northern Ireland Protestantism is not just a religion of individuals; it is also part of the shared identity of 'the Ulster Protestant people'. There is nothing unusual about a nation or an ethnic group claiming divine approval: few countries go to war without asserting that they have God on their side. But supposing that one's people have a particularly favoured place in the eyes of God is much easier for the Catholic and Orthodox strands of Christianity because they see salvation as a collective property. Religious merit can be transferred from the more to the less pious and a cadre of professionals can worship God on behalf of the entire people. The radical individualism of Protestantism weakens such collectivist visions and that is most apparent to the seriously religious and to those who have a professional obligation to preach the gospel: hence the difference between the FPCU clergy and the DUP activists in attitudes to the loyal orders.

7

Paisley and Trouble

INTRODUCTION

One biography describes Paisley as a 'malign colossus'; another is entitled *Persecuting Zeal*; a third describes him as a 'man of wrath'.[1] Some critics assert that Paisley bears a considerable degree of responsibility for the violence in Northern Ireland. When a Free Presbyterian Bible (almost certainly one of hundreds given by the church to prisoners) turned up in a UVF arms cache in Ballymena, an election opponent of the DUP was quick to extract some advantage:

The Democratic Unionist party has dominated the political life of Ballymena for over three decades and generations of loyalists have grown up looking to that party for leadership.... Is it really surprising, given the political and religious ethos which has been dominant in Ballymena . . . that a Free Presbyterian Bible and firearms should be allegedly found together?[2]

One suspects that 'allegedly' was added to the statement by a nervous journalist.

This chapter will consider the record of Paisley and his associates against accusations that range from the commission of terrorist

[1] Respectively, E. Moloney and A. Pollak, *Paisley* (Swords: Poolbeg Press, 1986); D. Cooke, *Persecuting Zeal: A Portrait of Ian Paisley* (Dingle: Brandon, 1996); P. Marrinan, *Paisley: Man of Wrath* (Tralee: Anvil Books, 1973).

[2] *Irish News*, 10 July 2002. The speaker was Billy McCaughey, who had been convicted for murdering a Catholic shopkeeper in Ahoghill in 1977 while a serving RUC officer and who later became a PUP activist. In retaliation for the IRA removing a dead or dying police officer from a murder scene, McCaughey kidnapped Father Sean Murphy and was inspired to release him unharmed after an impassioned appeal from Ian Paisley; see J. Cusack and H. McDonald, *UVF* (Swords: Poolbeg Press, 1997), 189–90, and P. Taylor, *Brits: The War against the IRA* (London: Bloomsbury, 2001), 286.

crimes to 'stirring things up'. That material will also allow us to consider a bigger issue: are Ulster evangelicals jihadis? In almost every Islamic society there are fundamentalists who believe that the call to jihad (or Holy War) should be interpreted literally; that the pursuit of the Kingdom of God, the repulsion of the infidel, or the overthrow of ungodly rulers justifies violence and that such religiously inspired violence will be rewarded by God.[3] It is not hard to imagine Protestant fundamentalists working up a justification for jihad from their interpretation of Irish republicanism. Northern Ireland is one of the last strongholds of Protestantism in Europe. Therefore the Catholic Church wishes to destroy it. Republicans are Catholics doing the work of the Antichrist. So it is quite proper for the Children of God to fight back; to die in the cause would be proud martyrdom.

THE FORMAL POSITION

Paisley's stated attitude to political violence is clear enough. Although he frequently refers to his Covenanter background with pride and enjoys holidays visiting sites in south-west Scotland associated with the Covenanting days, he does not hold to the Reformed Presbyterian view that, until the state supports the true church, the Christian has no obligation to the state. Instead he holds the commonplace modern position that the state should protect the citizen and the citizen should be loyal to the state. So long as the state delivers, the private citizen has no right to use violence for political ends. The following from Paisley's *Protestant Telegraph* succinctly expresses his view:

it is wrong for Protestants to contemplate taking the law into their own hands and meting out justice to those whom they believe guilty of atrocities . . . 'Avenge not yourselves' is the unmistakable teaching of Scripture. Romans 12, verse 19, goes on to remind Christians that 'Vengeance is mine; I will repay, saith the Lord'. This does not mean, of course, that Protestants ought not be ready to

---

[3] For a good journalistic account of a variety of 'jihadi' movements, see A. Taheri, *Holy Terror: The Inside Story of Islamic Terrorism* (London: Sphere, 1987). For a more scholarly treatment, see M. Juergensmeyer, *Terror in the Mind of God: The Global Rise of Religious Violence* (Berkeley and Los Angeles: University of California Press, 2003).

defend themselves, their homes and their families from attack. It does mean that the punishment of offenders must and should be left to those holding official authority to judge and punish.[4]

If the government completely abandons the citizen, the citizen is released from his obligation and may do whatever is necessary to protect himself, his family, and his country. In the early 1970s Paisley said: 'If any attempt is made to try to put the people of Northern Ireland into a United Ireland the people would fight and I personally would fight.'[5] A decade later, he repeated the sentiment:

It would mean the very same as traditional Unionists did at the start of the setting-up of this state. We know what happened. The Protestants of Ulster armed themselves and said 'We will resist to the death'. I would resist to the death any attempt to subvert the democratic wishes of the Ulster people.[6]

Clearly there is a lot of slack in deciding what circumstance justifies the conclusion that the state has failed the citizen and there is a crucial difficulty of definition involved in just who is the 'Ulster people', the thwarting of whose will legitimates rebellion, but the principle is clearly opposed to vigilante violence and to loyalist terrorism.

Paisley has routinely condemned specific acts of loyalist terror. When a young Catholic barman was murdered by loyalists in Malvern Street in 1966, Paisley was quick to announce:

Like everyone else, I deplore and condemn this killing, as all right-thinking people must. Incitement, direct or indirect, must be treated with the full rigour of the law. Under the Special Powers Act the [Stormont] government has the full authority to act and has failed to do so. If it continues to abdicate its responsibilities then the British government must act immediately in its place.[7]

Forty years later, he was equally clear in condemning a wave of attacks on Catholic houses and chapels in North Antrim: 'There is no excuse for it. It has to stop. And I have made that clear.... I have

[4] *Protestant Telegraph*, 17 Feb. 1973, p. 5
[5] *Irish Times*, 23 Oct. 1972.
[6] David McKittrick, 'Making a Virtue of Extremism', *Irish Times*, 12 Feb. 1981. I might add that other more moderate Unionist leaders such as John Taylor and Robert Bradford concurred with the sentiment: see *Newsletter*, 7 Feb. 1981.
[7] D. Boulton, *The UVF 1966–73: An Anatomy of Loyalist Rebellion* (Dublin: Torc Books, 1973), 51.

no reservation in condemning any attack because that is not the way you fight your democratic programme. In fact, you have lost the argument when you take to strife. That's not democracy. That's anarchy.'[8] It is, of course, possible either that Paisley is a hypocrite whose actions belie his words or that he bears responsibility for the actions of others. These possibilities will now be considered.

COMMITTING CRIMES

Paisley and his colleagues certainly have a long record of civil disobedience. In the 1960s he led illegal demonstrations and banned marches, and some of those turned ugly. There is no evidence he ever assaulted anyone, but some of his political allies did not shrink from confrontation. The Protestants who set upon a Civil Rights march at Burntollet Bridge in County Londonderry in January 1969 were led by an associate, Major Ronald Bunting, and the intention to stop the march had been announced at a Paisley rally in Derry's Guildhall the day before.[9] As he aged and became more successful in electoral politics (and I would not like to guess which of those had the greater effect on his behaviour), the street protests became less frequent. However, as the following examples show, colleagues periodically broke the law on assembly and confronted the police.

In the summer of 1985, as part of their continuing campaign against the Anglo-Irish accord, DUP politicians frequently challenged the RUC by leading marches that had been banned in the interests of public order (the police said); in the interests of the Dublin government (the DUP said). For example, a group of loyalists arranged a band parade through the overwhelmingly Catholic County Down town of Castlewellan. The RUC banned it, and the local DUP councillor Ethel Smyth called for defiance. The RUC surrounded the town with a cordon of riot police. DUP Assemblyman (and Free Presbyterian minister) Ivan Foster announced that the Third Force (of which more below) would take part in the march. The RUC held its lines, and twenty-two people, including Ethel Smyth, were injured and Foster and another DUP Assemblyman,

---

[8] *Newsletter*, 5 Sept. 2005.   [9] Cooke, *Persecuting Zeal*, 160.

George Graham, were arrested. The following night there was a similar confrontation between loyalist marchers and RUC in Cookstown and again the DUP was prominent, this time in the figure of William McCrea, the local Westminster MP.

The worst trouble that summer was in Portadown. There the Orange Twelfth of July parade had been rerouted to take it away from the Tunnel, a part of the traditional route that, with population shifts, had become a Catholic area. This time the Orange Order, which had distanced itself from the Castlewellan and Cookstown incidents, was involved. Senior Orange leaders and UUP and DUP representatives badgered the Secretary of State to have the rerouting order lifted. On 4 July, while the negotiations were still going on, 30,000 Orangemen gathered in Portadown 'to demand the right to march anywhere in Ulster'. This march was not banned. The Chief Constable added confusion to the parades policy by announcing that he would permit an Orange church parade on the Sunday before the Twelfth to pass through the Tunnel because it would be a 'peaceful, dignified, church parade', but insisted that the Twelfth march had to be rerouted. When the first parade passed off without serious incident (but with a massive police presence), the Portadown Orangemen reaffirmed their determination to go through the Tunnel on the Twelfth. At this point, the Orange leadership began to retreat, suggesting that they had made their point with the church parade and calling on the Portadown loyalists not to break the law. While Grand Master of the Order Martin Smyth was trying to persuade the march organizers to relent, Paisley was promising his support. Although committed to speaking at the Independent Orange Order's rally in Ballycastle, at the other end of the province, he announced that he would begin the Twelfth by visiting Portadown to show solidarity.

The marchers did not walk through the Tunnel. The massive police presence prevented them, but over that weekend 53 police officers and at least 19 civilians were injured in serious rioting, which wrecked shops in the town centre. At least 48 loyalists were arrested. To make matters worse, the Dublin government complimented the RUC on its firm stand against loyalist agitation. Over the following weeks, Portadown loyalists harassed the police in retaliation for what they claimed was police persecution. In Portadown and Cookstown,

RUC officers were driven out of their homes in areas that had once been safe because they were loyalist.

All unionist leaders were agreed that Protestants should be allowed to march anywhere in their own country and almost all agreed with the Paisleyite interpretation that the 1985 bans were a sop to a Dublin government enjoying its new role as the approved spokesman for the interests of nationalists in Northern Ireland, but there was a clear difference between the DUP and the Ulster Unionists about how to react. After her Castlewellan protest, Smyth was arrested in Down-patrick while trying to stop a Sinn Fein march and was roundly condemned by the local UUP for trouble-making. Her young colleague Jim Wells, DUP Assemblyman, had a criminal record for 'using threat-ening, abusive or insulting words and behaviour with intent to provoke a breach of the peace' acquired in similar circumstances confronting a nationalist band parade in Kilkeel.[10] That act of martyrdom was easily trumped by the fine imposed on Peter Robinson, the deputy leader of the DUP. In August 1986 Robinson led some 500 men into the Irish Republic, where they blockaded the small village of Clontibret and terrified two policemen. Initially faced with charges of assault and malicious damage, Robinson eventually pleaded guilty to a charge of unlawful assembly and had £15,000 deducted from his bail bond.[11] In 1971 Willie McCrea served four months of a six-month sentence for disorderly behaviour at a banned parade in Dungiven and was arrested for disrupting a Catholic Mass in Canterbury Cathedral.[12]

In defence of his party, Paisley can reasonably claim that its civil disobedience, while not quite in the manner of Mahatma Gandhi, has always been intended to be peaceful and has generally been restrained. As I noted in Chapter 2, Free Presbyterians did not retaliate when stoned at Cromac Square in 1966. The DUP has consistently criticized loyalists who attack policemen or wreck shop fronts. Trying to walk through a line of policemen or refusing to be moved is acceptable;

[10] Less dramatically, DUP councillor (and later MP) Gregory Campbell was sent to prison in June 1987 for refusing to pay his television licence in protest at the Anglo-Irish Accord and the BBC's bias.

[11] S. Elliott and W. D. Flackes, *Northern Ireland: A Political Directory 1968–1999* (Belfast: Blackstaff Press), 428.

[12] Ibid. 327; D. Porter, *In His Pathway: The Story of Revd William McCrea as Told to...* (London: Marshall, Morgan and Scott, 1980), 69.

throwing bricks is not. This is precisely the sort of position one would expect, given the social class, and regional and religious backgrounds, of DUP members. Pious farmers and small shopkeepers are not natural rioters. The rather moderate and bourgeois position of the DUP is often overlooked, not just by its critics (one would expect that) but also by some of its supporters. This is partly because, when condemning loyalist violence, DUP politicians cannot resist the opportunity to make political capital by adding that, of course, none of these unpleasant things would happen if it was not for the treachery of the British government. So the words condemning violence get somewhat lost in a heated denunciation of someone or other who should bear at least part of the responsibility.

Even when the condemnation is crystal clear, audiences can be selective in their hearing. Consider this example from the summer of 1985. About 400 loyalists had gathered in Portadown to voice their grievances over police action in the town and to call to task UUP's law-and-order spokesman Ken Maginnis, who had described loyalist actions as 'orchestrated thuggery' and said those responsible were despicable rebels in the same mould as members of Sinn Fein. It is testimony to Maginnis's personal courage that he turned up at all. For the best part of two hours he listened patiently as members of the audience berated him and the local RUC. He finally lost his patience when a woman announced, to some approval, that she would clap her hands if she heard of an RUC constable's death. As Maginnis was walking out to jeering and catcalls, Paisley arrived and the meeting broke into cheering and clapping. Here was their man! When Paisley was later told about the woman's remark, he sternly rebuked her, but this made little impression on the basic loyalties of the audience or on wider perceptions of Paisley: the thugs liked him and therefore he must really like the thugs.

It is worth adding a point of context here. Over the course of the Troubles there have been hundreds of thousands of disorderly demonstrations and riots and the vast majority of them have not involved Paisley or his supporters. We can list three well-known examples from the post-1994 period: Drumcree, Harryville, and Holy Cross. Although Paisley vocally supported the Orange Order's right to walk down the Garvaghy Road, no Democratic Unionist of any prominence manned the Drumcree barricades.[13] The thuggery came, not from the DUP, but from young Orangemen and from dissident UDA and UVF men unhappy with their organizations' part in the peace process. For two years from 1996, and again for a time in 1999, Ballymena loyalists maintained an at-times-intimidating picket outside a Catholic church in Harryville. This was in retaliation for nationalists blockading the village of Dunloy to prevent loyalists using the local Orange hall. Although this was Paisley's heartland, he and his core supporters were not involved. In 2001 large numbers of loyalists in North Belfast blockaded the Holy Cross primary school. The DUP was not involved, and Nigel Dodds, the local DUP leader, repeatedly condemned the action.[14]

In summary we can say that Paisley and his people have broken public-order laws in order to demonstrate their politics. In fairness we should add that such actions are an accepted part of the political currency of democracies—CND marches, industrial strikes, socialist demonstrations—and it is hard to think of many Northern Irish politicians who have not flirted with such illegality.

Authors such as Marrinan imply that Paisley has been involved in more serious crimes by detailing the actions of people close to him and allowing innuendo to do the rest. The explosions arranged by some of his Ulster Protestant Volunteers in 1969 were detailed in Chapter 2. The crucial question concerns Paisley's knowledge and involvement. Of those charged in four separate cases, only Sammy Stevenson, the prosecution's chief witness, claimed that Paisley had any knowledge of these attacks, and, when his evidence was judged by the court to be unreliable, all the cases, except ironically that against Stevenson himself, collapsed.[15] Noel Doherty, the founder of the Protestant Volunteers, is unequivocal about Paisley's involvement. When journalist Peter Taylor asked him if he had ever mentioned

[13] For a very detailed account of the various Drumcree disturbances, see C. Ryder and V. Kearney, *Drumcree: The Orange Order's Last Stand* (London: Methuen, 2001), and G. Lucy, *Stand-off at Drumcree: July 1995 and 1996* (Lurgan: Ulster Society Publications, 1996).

[14] For a journalistic account, see A. Cadwallader, *Holy Cross: The Hidden Story* (Belfast: Brehon Press, 2004). For the school's perspective, see A. Troy, *Holy Cross: A Personal Experience* (Blackrock: Currach Press, 2005).

[15] The text of Stevenson's statement and details of the court cases are given in Boulton, *The UVF.*

weapons to Paisley, he replied: 'Never. Never. I would never trust him.... Let's put it this way. He was OK as a figurehead whilst we would do the job underneath him. He didn't know. He may have had an inkling. He may have, but certainly we never told him.'[16] Billy Mitchell, who was active in the 1969 UPV conspiracy and in the formation of the Ulster Volunteer Force (which was a real terrorist organization), confirmed Doherty's assertion that Paisley did not know, and Taylor adds a sensible judgement: 'As neither man today has any love for Paisley, and neither knew I was interviewing the other, there is no reason to believe they were being economical with the truth.'[17] Although I never met Doherty, I interviewed Mitchell a number of times, and he was consistent in saying that, as far as he knew, Paisley was never privy to the crimes that he planned and committed with Doherty.

In listing Paisleyites who developed paramilitary ties, we should add the curious group Tara. This was formed by William McGrath, an evangelical Protestant with somewhat odd beliefs and, though it was not known at the time, a secret life as an aggressive homosexual paedophile.[18] The secretive organization issued a number of blood-curdling press releases in 1969 and 1970, and it was infiltrated by UVF men who were keen to see if it had any weaponry they could expropriate. Tara did nothing other than issue bizarre statements and was soon made irrelevant by the growth of the UVF and of a series

[16] P. Taylor, *Loyalists* (London: Bloomsbury, 1999), 37–8.

[17] Ibid. 38.

[18] C. Moore, *The Kincora Scandal: Political Cover-up and Intrigue in Northern Ireland* (Dublin: Marino, 1996). The 'scandal' of the book's title was the failure of the social services to prevent McGrath's abuse of boys in his care and the slowness of official response to initial reports of abuse. The connections with Paisley are slight. A man who was later an elected DUP representative for a short time was a member of Tara (but then so was a man who later held high office in the UUP). Paisley met McGrath a few times because they both moved in Belfast's evangelical and unionist circles and McGrath's two children were married by Paisley. McGrath's Orange lodge used the John Knox Memorial FPCU church in north Belfast for some services. When Paisley was presented with evidence of McGrath's homosexuality, he interviewed the young man who had apparently been 'corrupted' by McGrath and asked him if he would face McGrath with the accusation. When the young man declined, Paisley confronted McGrath and told him that he would no longer be welcome to lead services in an FPCU church. Despite considerable innuendo, Moore offers no evidence that Paisley knew of McGrath's paramilitary fantasies, knew that he was a predatory homosexual, or knew that he worked in a children's home.

of other paramilitary groups that coalesced as the Ulster Defence Association. A more serious link is that formed by John McKeague, who was in Paisley's UPV and went on to lead the Shankill Defence Association, one of the largest components of the UDA. Also sometimes mentioned is Billy Spence, brother of Gusty Spence and one of the founders of the UVF. Billy Spence had worked with Paisley in Ulster Protestant Action and in election campaigns for maverick unionist politicians.[19]

Listing the names of the few people who worked in legitimate political activities with Paisley and who went on to serious terrorism without listing the vastly greater number who did not creates one impression, but it is misleading. Paisley was a radical unionist; his supporters were radical unionists. The UDA and UVF drew their support from the same population as did Paisley. That some people who had worked with Paisley responded to the unrest of the late 1960s and early 1970s by taking up arms is no more surprising or significant than the fact that some republicans who joined the IRA had been radicalized by the Civil Rights marches. The crucial test of Paisley's responsibility comes in how he responded to former associates once their criminality was clear: he denounced them. Even Marrinan, who strongly wishes to convict Paisley of guilt by association, reports that, when McKeague formed the SDA, Paisley issued a press release saying 'the Ulster Constitution Defence Committee and the Ulster Protestant Volunteers wished to state that the Shankill Defence Association was in no way connected with them and John McKeague, its chairman, in no way represented either the views or the policy of the movement'.[20] Marrinan tries to sustain Paisley's guilt by adding: 'It was the end of a long friendship and close political association . . . What the real bone of contention was has never been revealed.' Actually it had been. Unless one starts by refusing to believe

---

[19] Cooke (*Persecuting Zeal*, 184) claims two other leading paramilitary figures as Paisley associates when he says that Davy Payne and Tommy Herron, who were leading lights in respectively west and east Belfast's UDA, had attended Paisley's Martyrs' Memorial Church. This seems unlikely for Herron, none of whose associates ever mentioned any religious interests to me. Payne, whom I interviewed a number of times, said he had been inspired by Paisley's political rallies but denied any interest in his religion.

[20] Marrinan, *Paisley*, 187.

anything Paisley says, the bone of contention was obvious: Paisley did not approve of what McKeague wanted to do.

As an aside, it is worth stressing here that very many people (journalists in particular) have an interest in proving that Paisley was involved in serious crimes. There are thousands of photographs of Paisley with his mouth wide open shouting; there are none of him hitting anyone. Had he done so at all often, we would expect the photographs to exist and to command a high price. Given the financial rewards that the tabloid press would have given to anyone who could produce convincing evidence of more serious crimes, the absence of such evidence is surely telling.[21] Over twenty years I have been offered, in all sincerity, the most bizarre conspiracy stories linking particular evangelicals and terrorism. They have usually been supported by the 'no smoke without fire' justification: because there are a lot of rumours about, some of them must be true. My response, and it strengthens with every year that goes by, is that, with so many people having such a strong interest in finding the fires, were they there, we would have seen the evidence by now.[22]

INCITEMENT

Having considered the evidence that Paisley was involved in serious crimes and found it wanting, we can move to the lesser charge of incitement. Did Paisley deliberately encourage others to commit terrorist acts?

The first documented claim that Paisley encouraged others to commit acts of violence dates from the very start of the current violence. In 1966 Hugh McClean, one of the three men convicted with Gusty Spence of the murder of a young Catholic barman in

[21] It is worth noting that S. McPhilemy's *The Committee: Political Assassination in Northern Ireland* (Niwot, Colo.: Roberts Rinehart, 1998), which claims to have discovered an elaborate terror conspiracy linking the RUC, unionist politicians, and the UVF, does not implicate Paisley or the DUP.

[22] The only documented case of a clergyman being involved in terrorism during the Troubles concerns a Catholic priest. In 1972 Father James Chesney planted bombs in Claudy that killed nine people; D. McKittrick, S. Kelters, B. Feeney, and D. McVea *Lost Lives* (Edinburgh: Mainstream, 2004), 241.

Malvern Street, is reported to have said: 'I am terribly sorry I ever heard of that man Paisley or decided to follow him.' This statement has been endlessly recycled as evidence of Paisley's influence[23] without anyone either considering if that statement sounds like an ill-educated Shankill Road Protestant speaking or checking the newspapers for details of the trial. In court, McClean denied making this and other statements attributed to him by the police. In Roy Garland's biography, Spence is clear that the police, under political direction from O'Neill's government, wanted to implicate Paisley in the murders and in the formation of the UVF: 'Gusty was asked about Ian Paisley and what connection he had with him. He told them he did not agree with Paisley and had no connection whatever with him.'[24] This accords with what Spence and one of the others involved, Robert Williamson, told me in interviews in the 1980s. Twenty years after the events, Spence said, when pressed about Paisley's role: 'I have no time for Paisley's type of religious fervour or his politics but he had no involvement in re-forming the UVF though he stirred up a lot of tension at that time for his own ends.'[25]

In his defence against the charge of incitement, Paisley could assert that he has been unequivocal and consistent in denouncing vigilante murder. In particular he has repeatedly accused loyalists of betraying the Protestant people.

What really stuns the decent Ulster Protestant is that a section of his own community would engage under the guise of Protestantism and Loyalty in crimes just as heinous and hellish [as those of the IRA]. As a Protestant leader I once again totally, utterly and unreservedly condemn these atrocious crimes and those who perpetrated them or planned to perpetrate them.[26]

Or to quote his reaction to a sectarian murder in 1986: 'To take the word Protestant and use it as a flag under which this bloody deed was done reeks of the foulest hypocrisy.'[27] Other Free Presbyterians and DUP leaders have been as clear. In responding to one of the especially vicious murders committed by Lenny Murphy, the leader of the

---

[23] Boulton, *The UVF*, 54. That statement has been repeated endlessly but uncritically. See, e.g., Cooke, *Persecuting Zeal*, 149, and Moore, *Kincora*, 42.

[24] R. Garland, *Gusty Spence* (Belfast: Blackstaff, 2001), 62.

[25] *Shankill Bulletin*, 31 May 1985.   [26] *Protestant Telegraph*, 29 Mar. 1975, p. 8.

[27] *Glasgow Herald*, 18 Sept. 1986.

'Shankill Butchers' gang, Ivan Foster said: 'Protestants must never believe that murder is an answer to murder' and that he 'utterly repudiated murder as a means of defeating the IRA'.[28] When in 1997, as part of the peace discussions, the UVF asked for Scottish sectarian killer Jason Campbell to be transferred to a prison in Northern Ireland (where he would have become eligible for early release), one of the first and strongest condemnations came from the DUP's Gregory Campbell, who described the proposal as 'grossly offensive.'[29]

TACIT APPROVAL

A DUP councillor once memorably said that those who walked behind the coffins of IRA killers were showing support for their actions.[30] Critics have turned the same claim on the Free Presbyterian Church and cited speaking at the funerals of paramilitary activists as evidence of tacit approval. There have certainly been a few such cases: William McCrea and Ivan Foster conducted funerals for Wesley Somerville and Harris Boyle, members of the notorious Portadown UVF cell led by Robin Jackson in the 1970s. Foster gave a graveside oration for Sinclair Johnston, a Larne UVF man shot by the RUC during rioting in 1972. McCrea buried Benjamin Redfern, a UDA lifer who was crushed by a bin lorry while trying to escape from the Maze prison. Robert 'Basher' Bates, convicted of a number of vicious murders committed by the 'Shankill Butchers', was murdered by a loyalist in June 1997 and was buried by Free Presbyterian minister Alan Smylie. Roy Metcalfe, a Lurgan businessman who sold army surplus clothing and loyalist memorabilia, was murdered by the IRA in October 1989, purportedly because he was active in Ulster Resistance and in the UVF. He was buried by Free Presbyterian minister David Creane. Revd David McIlveen buried UDA man Raymond Elder in 1994. When Billy Wright, the UVF man who founded the

[28] BBC Northern Ireland News, 26 Oct. 1982.   [29] *Herald*, 9 Oct. 1997.
[30] *Sunday World*, 17 Mar. 1985.

breakaway Loyalist Volunteer Force, was buried, McCrea spoke at the family home and the Revd John Gray preached at the graveside.[31]

Although this list may sound impressive, it shrinks under closer examination. Foster buried Sinclair Johnston because he was a relative; McCrea buried Redfern because some of the Redfern family were Free Presbyterians. 'I was asked by a family to bury their son: my answer was very clear and definite. I was making no mention of what he'd done. I was only going on one condition and that was that I would preach the gospel to those who were around the open grave. I took that opportunity and I preached Christ.' Basher Bates had long repented of his terrorist activities when he was killed.

Anyway, that conducting funerals signifies support for the actions of the dead is not a terribly persuasive argument, especially for Protestants, who, unlike Catholics, do not believe that any sacramental power is involved in such activities. Ministers of all denominations have taken part in the funerals of loyalist paramilitaries. Almost every republican terrorist has been buried by the Catholic Church, and the republican Maze hunger strikers were given the last rites despite being unrepentant.

A better case for the charge of implicit legitimation can be made from examples of keeping bad company. In his early days in Belfast Paisley courted John Nixon, an independent unionist Stormont MP who was widely suspected of having led a murder squad in Belfast's violence of 1922. In his defence, Paisley could, as Trimble did thirty years later, insist that Nixon was never charged with any offence, but many other Protestants would not have welcomed the connection.[32]

When he was young, McCrea very briefly acted as spokesman for the short-lived United Loyalist Front. In July 1972 he shared a platform with masked UDA men. Although by then the UDA had a reputation for sectarian murder, McCrea issued a press statement saying:

We call on all Loyalists to give their continued support to the Ulster Defence Association as it seeks to ensure the safety of all law-abiding citizens against the bombs and bullets of the IRA. As the Catholic population have given

[31] BBC News, 'The Gospel Singing MP', http://news.bbc.co.uk/1/northern_ireland/936685.stm.
[32] See Ch. 3, n. 2.

their support to the IRA throughout this campaign of terror so must Loyalists grant unswerving support to those engaged in the cause of truth.[33]

In 1974 Paisley, along with every other Ulster unionist politician, supported the Ulster Workers' Council strike that brought down the power-sharing executive. Paisley was not particularly active. He was in the USA when the strike began, and even after he had returned played little or no part in coordinating the action. Nonetheless he sat at a table with leading paramilitaries, at a time when there were no illusions about who was responsible for the many sectarian murders of Catholics and bomb attacks on bars in nationalist areas.[34] The DUP was more centrally implicated in the attempt in 1977 to repeat the strike in that it was planned by Paisley and leaders of the UDA and did not involve the Ulster Unionist Party. In both cases, Paisley could insist that he was not formally associating with the UVF (which was banned) and that the UDA was a legal organization, but had a Catholic offered a similar justification Paisley would have dismissed it as 'Jesuitical' and he would have needed to be remarkably unobservant not to notice that the UDA banners often also displayed the initials 'UFF'. This represented the Ulster Freedom Fighters, the *nomme de guerre* that UDA gangs used to claim their murders and thus protect the legal status of the parent organization. Anyway, he had already described the crimes of the UDA as being 'just as heinous and hellish as those of the IRA'.[35]

Billy Wright, the leader of the UVF in Portadown, was expelled from the organization in 1996 for rejecting its political direction. He and the dissident south Belfast Brigadier of the UDA, Alex Kerr, formed the Loyalist Volunteer Force. Both were threatened with death unless they left Northern Ireland. Wright's supporters organized a rally in defence of 'free speech'. Because he did not want to pass over an opportunity to criticize the political parties associated with the UDA and UVF, McCrea accepted an invitation to address the meeting and found himself on a platform with Wright, who was greeted as

[33] Statement phoned to BBC Northern Ireland, 25 Aug. 1972. The public meeting was reported in the *Irish Times*, 15 July 1972.
[34] For details of Paisley's involvement in the UWC strike, see Taylor, *Loyalists*, 133–5, and D. Anderson, *14 May Days: The Inside Story of the Loyalist Strike of 1974* (Dublin: Gill and Macmillan, 1994), 74–5.
[35] *Irish Times*, 20 Mar. 1975.

a hero by the crowd. McCrea later said he did not know that Wright would be there. In response to the predictable outcry that the DUP was supporting terrorism, the party issued a somewhat half-hearted defence: 'William McCrea's attendance last night, at a legal rally, in his personal capacity, was to stand for the fundamental principle of the right to freedom of speech without the threat of being murdered.'[36] Given Wright's record of sectarian murder and the wish of the UVF leaders to keep the ceasefires intact, their spluttering annoyance at the DUP's opportunism was understandable, and many in Northern Ireland thought McCrea's involvement was reprehensible.

THE RECORD OF PAISLEY'S PEOPLE

One way of trying to assess the consequences of Paisley's rhetoric (and of the impact of the religion that inspires him) is to examine the behaviour of the members of the Free Presbyterian Church. If Paisley has incited others or if evangelical Protestantism encourages political violence, we might see this is in the denominational affiliations of those convicted of serious offences. This is not easy. Courts and newspapers do not regularly record the denomination of those charged and convicted. However, where someone was known to be a Free Presbyterian, this seems to have been reported, presumably because the reporter wished to expose the hypocrisy of the pious. Hence my information, compiled by carefully reading the papers for twenty-eight years and asking respondents in the Free Presbyterian Church about names I thought I recognized, probably falls not far short of the complete tally. It is also difficult to know what proportion of Free Presbyterians *should* have been involved in terrorism if their religion or Paisley's preaching had had no effect. Knowing what is remarkable requires knowing what is normal or what we should expect. Most terror has been the work of young adult males. Allowing for turnover by defection or death, the FPCU has probably had about 10,000 adult male members since 1966. Apart from the 1969 UPV

[36] *Belfast Telegraph*, 5 Sept. 1996.

explosives men, I can find only three Free Presbyterians who have been clearly involved in terrorism. Membership of other evangelical sects is probably less likely to be mentioned in press reports, but, as most terrorist activity has been the work of the UDA and UVF, data on the religion of their members (given below) can stand as a fairly complete assessment of the violence of evangelicals. We can reasonably conclude that committed evangelical Protestants have not been as involved in political violence as their proportion in the general population would lead them to be if their religion was irrelevant. For all that Paisley is supposed to have been whipping his audiences into a militant froth, the people who heard him and his message most often were less likely than the typical Ulster male to get involved.

What is the record of Paisley's party? Again it is hard to know how many adult male members the DUP has had over the course of the Troubles, but, even if we confine our attention to those active enough to have stood as candidates in elections, we would have to set a figure of at least 500, and, given the turnover as people move in and out of parties, the cadre could be larger. I can find only six DUP activists who have been implicated in serious crimes.

One was Eddie Sayers, a small businessman from Omagh, who stood as a DUP candidate in elections in 1973 and 1977. He later left the DUP for the UDA and became its Mid-Ulster Brigadier. Another was Billy Baxter, a Bangor DUP councillor who was arrested in 1993 and convicted for soliciting funds for the UVF; he was expelled from the party. In 1986 a DUP councillor pleaded guilty to three counts of arson: he set fire to a digger, a primary school, and a GAA club.[37] And there are the three Ulster Resistance cases mentioned below.

We might also add George Seawright, a DUP councillor for North Belfast and Free Presbyterian elder (he later switched to attending a gospel hall) who refused to retract an outburst at a meeting of the Belfast Education and Library Board. One agenda item concerned complaints from Catholic parents that, when their children took part in joint concerts at state schools, they were obliged to listen to the national anthem. Another concerned the installation of a new incinerator at a Catholic school. Seawright said something to the effect that the incinerator should be used on the Catholic parents and their

---

[37] Ibid. 2 June 1986.

priests and refused to withdraw or apologize. The party later insisted that he apologize. He refused to do so and was expelled.

There may have been more subtle exclusions. It is sometimes difficult to distinguish the various reasons why a person was not adopted as a candidate for particular elections or frozen out of party councils. Someone might be shunned because he was insufficiently pious or inarticulate (and both of those characteristics were involved in two of the three cases I have in mind), but it is noticeable that two working-class party activists who were founder members of the party but who happened to have relatives in the paramilitary organizations were gradually sidelined.

In summary, we can say that there is no evidence that Paisley has deliberately encouraged others to use political violence. He has used mild civil disobedience in pursuit of goals that others have pursued in more violent ways and he has twice worked in general strikes with the main loyalist terror organization, but he has also consistently denounced UDA and UVF terrorism.

CREATING A CLIMATE CONDUCIVE TO VIOLENCE

A more compelling charge against Paisley and his supporters is that, despite their condemnation of those who murder, riot, and assault, the way in which they have pursued their political goals has created a political environment in which others have found it easy to see terrorism as acceptable.

Among the evidence that would be presented for such a charge is the number of times Paisley has tried to mobilize popular militia. Although he insisted that his UPV was intended as a political rather than a paramilitary organization, it was obviously intended to revive memories of the 1912 UVF. In August 1969 Paisley reacted to the disbanding of the Ulster Special Constabulary by saying: 'I say to all B-Specials, "Don't let anyone disarm you". We will take whatever action we think fit to stop the B Specials being disbanded,'[38] and by calling for the founding of a People's Militia. Two years later he called

[38] *Irish Times*, 18 Feb. 1981.

for the B Specials to be re-formed. In 1981, after the British and Irish governments had signalled a new closeness in their relationship, Paisley launched the largest of his 'third forces' (the police and the army being the first and the second forces). The initiative was heavily backed by DUP members. In February, Paisley took five journalists to a secret location near Ballymena to see 500 men in combat jackets wave what were purported to be certificates for legally held firearms. While addressing a crowd in Portadown, he 'brandished the bandolier which his father had worn as a member of Carson's UVF, an act which impressed upon those gathered the seriousness of the present situation and just what the price could be'.[39]

In November of that year, when the political temperature had been raised by the IRA's assassination of MP and Methodist clergyman Robert Bradford, Paisley inspected a parade of 6,000 men in Newtownards. As usual there was much militant rhetoric. At the Newtownards rally, Paisley said: 'We demand that the IRA be exterminated from Ulster...there are men willing to do the job of exterminating the IRA. Recruit them under the Crown and they will do it. If you refuse, we will have no other decision to make but to do it ourselves.'[40] At a rally in Belfast shortly after, he said: 'I believe the time has come when all Lundies [i.e. traitors], yellow bellies and all the cowards must leave our ranks—and we shall fight to the death.'[41] But that pulpit rhetoric was quickly qualified when he later said: 'This force proposes to act entirely within the law and will in no way usurp either the work or the activities of the crown forces.'[42] But there was no fighting. The rallies gradually got smaller: fifty men in Enniskillen and only twenty in Portadown. In a few places, small groups of Third Force men made a display for journalists of 'patrolling', but the initiative petered out. When three Enniskillen Third Forcers were charged with usurping the power of the police and with action likely to cause a breach of the peace, the DUP allowed the matter to pass. In fairness to the DUP we should note that UUP politicians shared its sense of crisis. Even the normally log-like James Molyneaux thought that 'something had to be done', and John Taylor called for a volunteer defence force.[43]

[39] S. Wilson, *The Carson Trail* (Belfast: Crown Publications, 1981), 40.
[40] Cooke, *Persecuting* Zeal, 192.   [41] *Magill* (Dec. 1981), 21.
[42] *Irish News*, 18 Dec. 1981.   [43] *Irish News*, 17 Nov. 1981.

In 1986, after the signing of the hated Anglo-Irish Accord, which signalled a deeper involvement of Dublin in Northern Ireland, Paisley, Robinson, and other DUP leaders accepted an invitation to lead a new third force called Ulster Resistance. There were large rallies in Larne and Ballymena, addressed by Paisley and other DUP leaders. Paisley's deputy Peter Robinson made the following hyperbolic assessment at an Enniskillen rally: 'Thousands have already joined the movement and the task of shaping them into an effective force is continuing. The Resistance has indicated that drilling and training has already started. The officer of the nine divisions have taken up their duties.'[44]

The reality was quite different. There was no mass movement. This third force dribbled away to leave a small handful of County Armagh loyalists who collaborated with the UVF and UDA in a bank robbery in Portadown in July 1987 to fund a large purchase of arms from South Africa. Two DUP activists from the area, Noel Little and James King (both Free Presbyterians), were arrested in Paris apparently trying to arrange the exchange of a Shorts missile system for small arms with the South African state company Armscor. A third member of the group was part of a Territorial Army (TA) missile unit that trained with a replica of the Shorts weapon; three of his colleagues were drummed out of the TA.[45] Peter Robinson campaigned on behalf of the 'Paris Three', and Dr Paisley sent them Bibles. One of them, James King, told a reporter: 'that made a difference, with God's word to read every day.'[46] All three were fined and given suspended prison sentences.[47] By now the DUP leadership had divorced itself from the rump Ulster Resistance, but when, in November 1988, part of the South African arms shipment was found in an arms dump with five maroon Ulster Resistance berets, one of the men convicted of possession was a long-serving DUP member and Free Presbyterian elder.

In *Loyalists*, Taylor offers a relatively benign view of Paisley's initiatives. Of the 1981 initiative he writes: 'He was thinking more of a Home Guard than a UDA or UVF.'[48] In a number of interviews with men involved in Ulster Resistance, Taylor deliberately sought evidence that Paisley had been involved in the plan to acquire

---

[44] *Irish News*, 10 July 1986.   [45] *Sunday World*, 29 Mar. 1992.
[46] *Newsletter*, 27 Aug. 1989.   [47] Elliott and Flackes, *Northern Ireland*, 486.
[48] Taylor, *Loyalists*, 177.

weapons and reports: 'Paisley, I am told, was never present at any meetings where arms were discussed.'[49]

THE POWER OF THE METAPHOR

In addition to these grand martial gestures, Paisley and his associates have repeatedly used apocalyptic and militant language. His early associate Ronald Bunting is reported to have said of Paisley that 'he uses words to create violent situations but never follows the violence through himself'.[50] To all the examples above we can add a couple from the hot summer of 1985. The otherwise normally mild-mannered DUP Assemblyman George Graham responded to one confrontation with the RUC by telling a crowd: 'The day has come when we see that the country has gone to the dogs. We have lost everything that we cherish and hold dear. Our backs are to the wall and we must fight.'[51] Ivan Foster added: 'We are declaring war. If we didn't do what was done at Castlewellan we would have had a complete sell out.'[52] Paisley himself has been given to bad-tempered outbursts. On 23 June 1986 the 'rolling devolution' Assembly, which Jim Prior had launched in 1983 but which had been boycotted by every party except the Alliance and the DUP, was formally prorogued. Rather than go quietly, DUP members barricaded themselves in Stormont and had to be ejected by the RUC. That was the summer that a number of RUC officers had been intimidated out of their homes in what had previously been safe Protestant areas. When Paisley was dumped outside the Stormont building, he snapped at the officers: 'Don't come crying to me when your homes are attacked. You will reap what you sow.'[53] Paisley told a press conference: 'There could be hand-to-hand fighting in every street in Northern Ireland. We are on the verge of civil war because when you take away the forum of democracy, you don't have anything left.'[54] He also called on RUC officers to 'follow the example of the British Army officers at the Curragh'. He later denied he was inciting them to revolt against the

[49] Ibid. 189.   [50] *Belfast Telegraph*, 20 Nov. 1981.
[51] *Newsletter*, 29 June 1985.   [52] Ibid.   [53] *Guardian*, 25 June 1986.
[54] Ibid.

government and said that he was encouraging them to resign, which is what the Curragh officers threatened to do in 1917 if they were asked to serve in Ulster against the potentially rebellious unionists. In his address to the Independent Orange Order rally on the Twelfth of July, Paisley told his audience that his father had shouldered a rifle in Carson's 1912 UVF and he would do the same. 'They can call it sedition if they like, and they can call it incitement to violence if they like. But I want to say that it will be over our dead bodies if they ship us down the river.'[55]

There are a number of separate things going on here. First there is the repeat of the contractarian idea that, at a certain point, citizens are free to oppose the government because it has betrayed them. So, in the aftermath of the failure of the various protests against the Anglo-Irish Accord, one finds DUP politicians saying, in effect, we have tried democratic politics and we have won a majority of seats in elections but still we do not get our way. As Jim Allister, DUP Chief Whip, in 1985 put it: 'If we have done all that and we are still ejected [from the UK]...then I would act in concert with hundreds of thousands of other individual loyalists in arming ourselves. No self-respecting individual is going to do anything but resist.'[56] Gregory Campbell, DUP member for Londonderry, talked of setting up a provisional government: 'that provisional government must have a defence; and that defence must be armed.'[57]

In most of these statements there is both a philosophical and a pragmatic alignment of the individual's likely actions with those of others: the DUP men would take up arms if that was the popular wish of the Protestant people. There is a prediction that there will be lots of violence, usually because other people, less level-headed and thoughtful, will commit it. When looked at closely, few of these statements are a direct incitement to violence. Most are the proposition that violence will be justified 'soon' and that some other group of people will lead the resistance. Nonetheless, it is possible to conclude that the speakers will be rather pleased if that is the result. However, we should remember they would have been even more pleased if the government had changed its policy!

---

[55] *Newsletter*, 14 July 1986.
[56] F. O'Toole, 'Fire and Brimstone', *Magill*, 9 (1985), 27.   [57] Ibid.

One particular way in which Ulster evangelicals could be accused of exacerbating the political conflict is through their use of violent language. Like the cartoon thug whose knuckles read 'love' on one hand and 'hate' on the other, almost every religion holds in tension the two themes of love and justice: the God of Love and the God of War. Alongside the pacifist symbolism of Christ's death on the cross and the injunction to turn the other cheek, popular Protestant hymns encourage the Christian to 'fight the good fight'. When the ladies of the Hampshire Women's Institute sing William Blake's *Jerusalem*, we know that the threat not to let 'the sword sleep in my hand' is metaphorical, but when sung by a population engaged in an actual war it takes on a new resonance. Similarly, the language of the Old Testament that promises salvation to a small people beset on every side by its enemies acquires a new sharpness in the context of the Troubles.

Liberal Christians criticize Paisley for his Old Testament religious language on the grounds that it appears to encourage violence and that, even when it does not, by stressing the radical division of the world into the saved and the damned, the good and the evil, them and us, it needlessly polarizes. Paisley can reply that he is doing no more than preaching the Christian gospel and singing the hymns that have been part of the Protestant canon throughout the English-speaking world for 200 years. This does not exhaust the charge of using inflammatory language because it can be argued that Ulster evangelicals are unusually or unnecessarily harsh in the terms they use in their own speeches and sermons. Paisley has described himself as a 'bluff Ulsterman'. In replying to the charge that his language 'could inflame other people to violent acts', he said:

No, I don't accept that because people who say that don't know the Ulster temperament. All Ulster people speak strong... and I mean that's done on the Republican and Roman Catholic side, it's done on the unionist side, it's done in business as well... That is the language, the trademark of an Ulster man. He's blunt, he's straight.[58]

Even allowing for the bluntness of Ulster speech, there are two features of Paisleyite rhetoric that can reasonably be thought to

---

[58] BBC interview, 22 Nov. 1981.

stimulate conflict. The first is the elision of enemies. Ulster evangelicals believe that the conflict really is a religious war. They believe
that, in Paisley's words: 'The Provisional IRA is in reality the armed
wing of the Roman Catholic Church. Its real aim is to annihilate
Protestantism.'[59] Secular analysts see religious rhetoric as a cover for
essentially secular motives. Evangelicals take an inverted view. They
suppose that secular motives (Irish Republicanism, for example) are
a cover for an essentially religious struggle that is centuries old: since
the Reformation the Catholic Church has sought to destroy Protestantism. That in turn is just one historical embodiment of the eternal
struggle between good and evil. Christian critics such as Cooke,
Mitchel, and Brewer and Higgins[60] suppose that conflating the IRA
and Catholicism has the effect of dehumanizing all Catholics in the
eyes of potential loyalist terrorists. Journalist Susan McKay makes the
same point stylistically by interweaving accounts of Loyalist Volunteer Force murders in Mid-Ulster with quotations from DUP politicians such as Sammy Wilson calling the Gaelic Athletic Association
'the IRA at play' and Willie McCrea describing the loss of his
Westminster seat to Sinn Fein as nationalists 'voting for murder'.[61]

   The second connection concerns the apocalypse. The political
rhetoric of Paisleyites is often metaphorically apocalyptic in that it
supposes things are very very bad and are about to get very much
worse. It is easy to mistake predicting doom for wishing it. The
response of many, and this is important for understanding Protestant
views of the conflict, is that they genuinely believe in the imminence
of the real Apocalypse. All Christians suppose that God began the
world and will at some time bring it to an end. Christians differ in
how they interpret the biblical passages that are interpreted as scen-
arios of that end of the world. Although evangelicals (even within the
Free Presbyterian Church) do not all share the same view, many read
the dire evidence of murders, bombings, and political betrayal as
proof that the end is probably nigh and that the world will become

   [59] Cooke, *Persecuting Zeal*, 58.
   [60] Ibid.; P. Mitchel, *Evangelicalism and National Identity in Ulster, 1921–1998*
(Oxford: Oxford University Press, 2003), 211; J. Brewer with G. Higgins, *Anti-
Catholicism in Northern Ireland, 1600–1998: The Mote and the Beam* (London:
Macmillan, 1998).
   [61] S. McKay, 'He was Just Another Catholic', *Sunday Tribune*, 18 Jan. 2004.

ever more violent as the Day of Judgment approaches. Those who do not share this vision may explain Paisley's constant doom-saying as a secular political device for increasing electoral support. However, to one large strand of evangelical thought, Paisley is simply expounding biblical prophecy.

What critics of Paisleyite apocalyptic rhetoric fail to notice—and this is a significant point—is that Ulster's 'end times' Protestants do nothing to hasten the end. They are not like the millenarians of the English Civil War period who believed that killing the aristocracy would speed the arrival of miraculous justice and that catastrophe was a vehicle for national or religious redemption. Unlike some Jewish and Islamic messianic movements, Ulster's evangelicals do not take the next step from predicting impending Judgment to believing that, if they kill republicans, God's cosmic punishment of wrongdoers will come sooner rather than later.[62]

It is always impossible to prove that the words of one group of people did not stimulate another group to act in a particular way, but we can test these claims about the impact of Paisley's rhetoric with a simple question of weight of influence. On the one side, we have Paisley's sometimes extravagantly militant rhetoric. On the other, we have large IRA car bombs that kill and maim. Which is likely to have been the better recruiting sergeant for the loyalist terrorists? Paisley is certainly not the peacemaker some Christians would wish and much of his language can sound like warmongering, but to give his commentary on the Troubles as much weight as real bombs and bullets is a strange displacement.

CONDUCT UNBECOMING

The best-founded accusation against Paisley is also the weakest. A recurrent theme of criticism is that he and his followers behave in a manner that is not 'Christian'. After one protest the following letter was sent to a Belfast newspaper:

[62] On Jewish messianic terrorism, see E. Sprinzak, 'From Messianic Pioneering to Vigilante Terrorism: The Case of the Gush Emunim', in D. C. Rappaport (ed.), *Inside Terrorist Organizations* (London: Frank Cass, 1988), 194–216.

I often wonder what sort of Bible Mr Paisley and co. read. Surely it cannot be that of the 'Gentle Christ' who was so kind, considerate, understanding and even forgiving to those who nailed him to a cross to die and whose teaching was 'Love one another as I have loved you'.... Can these people call themselves Christian while insulting others by calling them 'Popish pigs' and 'No peace with Romans'?[63]

In response to Paisley calling Bishop Daly 'the Black Pope of republicanism', an SDLP politician said:

Dr Daly is a man of God, a peace-maker, who rarely misses an opportunity of showing his respect for the Protestant and Unionist tradition and who at the same time works tirelessly for peace and understanding between our traditions ... if [Paisley] really believed himself to be a Christian, he should put some serious effort into promoting reconciliation.[64]

The SDLP has been viciously critical of unionism, of the Stormont-era Unionist government, and of the British state. SDLP leaders have often led demonstrations and marched despite bans. Clearly the SDLP man, in drawing the comparison between Daly and Paisley, is assuming that behaviour that is acceptable for politicians is unbecoming in a man of the cloth.

It is certainly the case that, in a secular society such as contemporary Britain, the judgemental or prophetic aspects of Christianity have been forgotten. 'Christian' is taken to mean inclusive, tolerant, and forgiving, and clergymen are expected to be decorous morally neutral bringers of solace in times of need. A good example of what the public expects of a Christian can be seen in the figure of Gordon Wilson, whose daughter was one of eleven people killed in the Enniskillen bombing of 1987. He told BBC news reporters that he had prayed for the bombers and had no ill-feeling towards the IRA.[65] In response to Free Presbyterian criticism that repentance must precede forgiveness, the *Sunday Times* said: 'If Mr Wilson can forgive what right have others to call for revenge? Not for the first time, it's the Rev Ian Paisley who is out of touch with the public yearning for peace, not Mr Wilson.'[66] When Wilson, who had been commended

---

[63] *Sunday News*, 2 Feb. 1986.   [64] *Belfast Telegraph*, 27 Nov. 1984.

[65] BBC TV 6 o'clock News, 9 Nov. 1987. For a detailed analysis of media coverage, see A. F. Parkinson, *Ulster Loyalism and the British Media* (Dublin: Four Courts Press, 1998), 50–70.

[66] *Sunday Times*, 15 Nov. 1987.

for his forgiving attitude by the Queen in her New Year message, attended a Catholic Mass for the souls of those killed, DUP councillors in Ballymena denounced him for blasphemy.[67]

Free Presbyterians would argue that true Christian charity requires that they confront people with the gospel truth: 'If a man's house is burning down, who is his real friend: the man who screams at him and hits him round the head till he wakes up or the man who says "We'd better not disturb him"?' But, for all their good intentions, Ulster evangelicals of Paisley's prophetic stamp can sound simply mean-spirited. And here the tension between the standards required of a cleric and those expected of a politician becomes obvious. When McCrea was replaced as chairman of Magherafelt District Council by an SDLP man, he dramatized his assertion that this represented a victory for republicanism by presenting his opponent with a miniature coffin.[68] When Paisley was asked to condemn the Harryville picket, he condemned violence but pointed out that the police had escorted worshippers into the church, which was more than they had done for Protestants in Dunloy.[69] From politicians, such point-scoring would be unremarkable. In men who are also gospel preachers, it confirms the views of many that Paisley's people are just not very nice.

However, that we might want to fault Paisley and his associates for putting doctrinal purity before secular notions of charity and good manners is a very long way from finding them guilty of encouraging violence.

THE RELIGION OF THE LOYALIST PARAMILITARIES

Having searched for a wide road to take us from Paisley to the paramilitaries and found at best a few sparse tracks, we can now pursue the search for connections from the other end. What can we infer about the influence of Paisleyism (and evangelical Protestantism more generally) from those whose responsibility for the Troubles is not in any doubt?

---

[67] *Sunday World*, 10 Jan. 1988.   [68] *Belfast Telegraph*, 6 June 1983.
[69] *Burning Bush* (Jan. 1997).

Since 1978 I have interviewed hundreds of UDA and UVF men and noted the biographies of many more. I can think of only a handful who claimed to be Christians before or during their paramilitary involvement. In addition to Noel Doherty, Thomas McDowell, and the others involved in the 1969 bombings, there was Billy Mitchell, who was on the UVF Brigade Staff in the mid-1970s and who wrote for the UVF's magazine *Combat* under the pseudonym 'Richard Cameron'—a name chosen to signify his attachment to the Scottish Covenanting tradition. The UVF's political spokesman Ken Gibson was, some time before his involvement with the UVF, involved in the FPCU, but unlike Mitchell he never explained or justified his paramilitary activity in religious terms. And there was Billy Wright, of whom more later.

Among the first generation of loyalist paramilitaries there were many who, although not personally pious, were happy to acknowledge the historical and social importance of evangelical religion by maintaining the elements of religious ritual and symbolism that they had learnt either in the Orange Lodges or in the British Army. If pushed they would claim that Protestants were better people than Catholics because they had the right religion. Many had a household division of religious labour, and, though they admitted that religion played no part in their lives, they would tell me proudly that 'the wife is God-fearing' and good-living and took the children to church.[70] The next generation, the men who reached adulthood and commanding positions in the UDA and UVF in the late 1980s and 1990s, had no time at all for religion. Presumably because they could not think of anything else that would add a bit of solemnity to the ritual, they used a Bible in administering membership oaths, but, that apart, they were openly scornful of even the limited borrowing of Christian symbolism and rhetoric from Orange Lodge or Army ceremonies. No one who knows anything of the character of Johnny 'Mad Dog' Adair can think that C. Company of the West Belfast UDA was in the slightest inspired by religious principles.

Critics spend so much time trying to establish links between Paisley and the paramilitaries that the reality of their relationship

---

[70] In quoting an extract from *The Red Hand* where I say something similar, McGarry and O'Leary, *Explaining Northern Ireland* (Oxford: Blackwell, 1995), 181, use an inserted '*sic*' and exclamation marks to imply that I am guilty of sexism. I am merely reporting the sexism of working-class loyalist paramilitaries.

gets missed. In all my years of interviewing members of the UDA and UVF I have yet to meet one person who did not dislike Paisley intensely and this should be no surprise if we remember that Paisley and his people have repeatedly described loyalist paramilitaries as being no better than republicans, have demonized their political initiatives as 'communist', and have tried to have them hanged. In the mid-1990s, when the details of the Belfast Agreement were being developed, the DUP was as opposed to loyalists gaining political representation as it was to Sinn Fein being allowed into the talks, and it consistently opposed the early release of prisoners from both sides of the divide. In this period Michael Stone, as 'officer commanding', invited a variety of politicians to the Maze to address UDA prisoners: 'The only people who did not get an invite were Sinn Fein and the Democratic Unionist Party—Sinn Fein because they were the political wing of our enemy and the DUP because they had repeatedly called for the death penalty.' He adds: 'Loyalist prisoners never referred to...Ian Paisley by name. They called him "cow head".'[71]

Colin Crawford's study of the UDA contains long interviews with a number of UDA men. Of the seventeen biographies presented, only two mention religion at all in their explanations of how they become involved in terrorism. Stone notes that his family were church people and that as a boy he regularly attended Sunday school and was in the Boy's Brigade, but the church in question was not Free Presbyterian. It was the mainstream Church of Ireland.[72] Another man mentions a church background but does so to draw a before-and-after contrast. There was the respectable church life of his family that he consciously rejected and there was his involvement in the UDA. In the seventeen case studies of convicted loyalist paramilitaries, there are only two mentions of Paisley. One is an off-hand reference to having voted for him. The other criticizes him for not supporting the campaign for the segregation of loyalist and republican prisoners. Almost every biography identifies republican violence as the cause of his violence. Typical is the man who said: 'I suppose the event which changed my life was the murder of a good friend of mine...The IRA murdered

---

[71] M. Stone, *None Shall Divide Us* (London: John Blake, 2003), 277.
[72] C. Crawford, *Inside the UDA: Volunteers and Violence* (London: Pluto, 2003), 144.

Billy on the Crumlin Road just outside Everton Girl's School. I was
distraught when I heard he'd been murdered.'[73]

In my many interviews with loyalists over the years I have sometimes found a very weak (and somewhat inconsistent) assertion that
Paisley should take some of the blame because 'he marched us up to
the top of the hill and marched us down again', but the stress is always
on the second command and not the first. When they were taking risks
to save Ulster, 'that fat bastard did nothing'. When they were serving
life sentences, 'the self-righteous Bible-bashing creep was trying to
have us executed'. More often, when I have deliberately pressed the
issue of whether others encouraged them to become terrorists I have
found a simple honesty. One serial killer from the 1970s said in
response to my probing for Paisleyite influence: 'That's all bollocks.
Paisley did not make me go out and kill people. I done that.'

A clear sign that evangelical religion is alien to the world of the
paramilitary is that, when loyalists have become born-again Christians, it has been as part of withdrawing from terrorism. Within
loyalist circles, 'getting saved' is widely accepted as a good reason for
leaving the UVF or UDA. Buried in the general scorn for those who
become 'good living', there is often a hint of respect. Conversion can
even offer protection. One East Belfast brigadier of the UDA was
deposed for supposedly informing on the organization and stealing
its funds. Conventionally he would have been murdered or at least
seriously wounded for either offence. He was not, and the explanation
given was that he had become a Christian and was now an associate
pastor of a Pentecostal church. As one of his former men put it: 'I never
trusted that lying bastard. He's safe for now but if we ever find out he's
faking he's booked into Roselawn [the local cemetery].'

THE ROUGH AND THE RESPECTABLE

Those who are familiar with the UDA and UVF know that their
members are not Paisley's people. To the evangelical they are scum
who blaspheme, fornicate, drink alcohol, smoke, take drugs, and kill

---

[73] C. Crawford, *Inside the UDA: Volunteers and Violence* (London: Pluto, 2003), 159.

people. The evangelical and paramilitary worlds barely touch, let alone overlap. The slight exceptions only make the contrast clearer. In the early 1970s there were a number of very small organizations that employed some of the trappings of militia organization without actually engaging in violence. Tara has already been mentioned. The Down Orange Welfare (DOW) recruited primarily from farmers and respectable small businessmen in County Down. The 1970s Orange Volunteers (OV) was a planning and marching organization within the Orange Order that collected some weapons but appears not to have done anything with them. Bill Craig's Vanguard movement within the Ulster Unionist Party had its Ulster Vanguard Service Corp, but it did little more than parade as a ceremonial bodyguard for Craig. When Vanguard folded, it retained its initials (after all, it would have been a shame to scrap all the badges) by becoming the Ulster Volunteer Service Corp. There was also the Ulster Special Corp, an attempt by former RUC B Specials to retain some sort of organizational structure in rural areas west of the Bann after they had been stood down. Like Paisley's various third forces, these groups saw themselves as creating a structure and a capacity that would allow effective defence in the case of all-out war; the vast majority of their members never became terrorists.

In brief, we can say that Ulster unionists divided by class and region in their response to political threat. The paramilitaries recruited primarily from the urban and secular working class. Rural and middle-class evangelicals expressed their opposition largely within conventional democratic politics. The first proposition needs to be qualified by two observations about the scale of support for violence. First, the vast majority even of urban working-class Protestants did not get involved in paramilitary organizations. Secondly, unlike a large part of the Catholic population that voted for Sinn Fein even when the IRA was active, working-class Protestant voters repeatedly declined to vote for their self-appointed defenders.

There are two very small exceptions to this division between the rough and the respectable. In the 1960s the working-class Christian population of Belfast was still big enough to produce ten or twenty Noel Dohertys and Johnny McKeagues: men with church connections whose nostalgic fondness for the old UVF shaded into vigilante violence. And there was a similarly small number of rural evangelicals (mostly to be found in County Armagh) who flirted with the fringes of terror. These were the UPV men who took the martial rhetoric literally; later they were to be found in the Ulster Clubs and in Ulster Resistance. In the main, however, and all of the above may seem like a very long way to get to this simple point, the vast majority of Ulster evangelical Protestants (even those closely associated with Paisley) have not engaged in politically motivated violence, and they have not encouraged others to do it for them.

BRITISH ISRAELISM AND THE DISSIDENTS

After the UDA and UVF ceasefires of 1994, a number of small loyalist splinter groups were formed to continue the armed struggle: the Loyalist Volunteer Force (LVF), the Orange Volunteers (OV), and the Red Hand Defenders (RHD). A UVF leader memorably described the dissidents as 'a motley collection of scum-bags and Bible-bashers', and he is right. A few of the dissidents resented the ceasefires because they felt too much of principle had been conceded to republicans. Some simply wished to continue to murder. Others were ambitious men who felt they were undervalued in the UDA and UVF. Some were professional criminals (mostly drug-dealers) who resented the half-hearted attempts of the paramilitary leaders to constrain their activities. But that point about Bible-bashers is intriguing. Although we are talking about no more than ten people, they are worth pursuing for what they tell us about the kind of Protestant religion that *might* support violence.

Billy Wright, the Portadown UVF leader whose expulsion from the UVF started the breakaway, had been a born-again Christian. During a five-year absence from the organization, he sometimes acted as a gospel preacher in the County Armagh area. Always a man for the grand gesture, the code word he gave the LVF for claiming its murderous acts in statements to the media was 'Covenant'. The man who led the Orange Volunteers in 1998–9, Clifford Peeples, was a keen but peripheral UVF man who later became a Pentecostal pastor. One of the OVs first actions was a synchronized arson attack on eleven Catholic churches, which Peeples defended on the grounds that they are the bastions of the Antichrist: 'We are defenders of the reformed faith. Our members are practising Protestant worshippers.'[74] A close colleague of Peeples is a former Paisley supporter, an evangelical Christian lay preacher, and a British Israelite. Although there is no evidence that he has been involved in any crimes as a result of this association, the man who acted as the link between the LVF and the wider world was an Elim Pentecostal pastor. Four is not a large number, but to have four evangelicals out of at most 200 dissident loyalists, when you have none among 2,000 loyal UDA and UVF members, is suggestive.

What they all had in common was a hyper-ethnic unionism, tinged with British Israelism. This creed argues that the British race (exemplified now by Ulster Protestants because the rest of Britain has proved itself unreliable) is descended from one of the lost tribes of Israel and hence is not just metaphorically but actually the people of God. With local variations in just who is held to compose this lost tribe, British Israelism was popular in the heyday of the Empire, especially in places such as the USA, Canada, Australia, and New Zealand, where British settlers competed with the Irish and other Catholic peoples. Evangelical Protestantism has long been a major component of the ethnic identity of Ulster unionists, many of whom are tempted to think that, even if they are not quite God's chosen people, then they are still pretty special in his eyes. They suppose that God practises a form of ethnic favouritism.[75] Paisley and his supporters often speak of 'the Protestant people of Ulster' as if they were a people of whom God particularly approves, but they do not confuse a nation and the people of God. For Protestants, salvation is an individual burden. It cannot be inherited by being born into the right family or tribe or people. That Ulster Protestants as a whole might be more godly than the Italians, for example, does not mean that all Ulster Protestants will be saved or that the property of being pleasing to God is passed on at birth. Each of us must get saved. Which is why Paisley will flatter an Orange Lodge dedication service by reminding the members of the godly principles that the Order supposedly maintains, but he will also point out that those principles

---

74 *Irish News*, 28 Nov. 1998.
75 I am obliged to Neil Southern for this felicitous expression.

mean nothing at all unless the individual Orangeman gets saved and lives a godly life.

British Israelism offends most evangelicals because of its negative view of those who are not descended from the lost tribes of Israel. Free Presbyterian minister Ron Johnstone, normally a very mild man, concludes a lengthy critique of the biblical interpretation behind British Israelism by saying:

Some of the communications I have received have made me righteously indignant. How shocking it is to receive literature defending Sheldon Emery as a man of God. In one of his books the Negro is described as 'the beast of the field' and Christianity as being a religion ONLY FOR THE WHITE MAN.... We believe that the Bride of Christ is the Church made up of some out of *every tribe, tongue, people and nation*. We in the Free Presbyterian Church have no room for those who teach the blasphemy that Adam is the father of the white race only.[76]

British Israelism also offends Ulster evangelicals because its offers an unwarrantedly positive view of Ulster. Unlike Peeples, Wright, and the unnamed former Paisleyite, Paisley subordinates the political fate of Northern Ireland to the will of God. Though he hopes they may be closely linked, they are not the same thing. Outsiders who see only Paisley's anti-Catholicism miss the point that the vast majority of his protests have been directed at the Church of Ireland and the Irish Presbyterian Church. He has also frequently denounced 'those who are Protestant in name only'. In politics he appeals to the Protestant electorate, but he does not believe that they are God's chosen people. It is common to find Free Presbyterian ministers praying for Ulster but also recognizing that it may be in God's will to 'test' the people of God by forcing them into a united Ireland. Some can even see some value in that; it will test the people of God. As Ivan Foster put it in a sermon:

The spiritual health of the church is not dictated by the political health of the nation. This is something we in Ulster need to learn. We have become used to the cause of Christ being allied to the political cause of our Province, so that we have begun to think that the well-being of the Church of Christ is indissolubly linked with the political entity of Northern Ireland. That is not the case.... God's Kingdom is a superior land unaffiliated to the kingdoms

[76] R. Johnstone, 'British Israelism Examined and its Errors Exposed', *Burning Bush* (Mar. 1970), 3. This was the last of four long articles.

of men....God's cause may flourish, irrespective of who sits upon the throne of government.[77]

CONCLUSION

The rise of violent Islamist movements such as Al-Qaeda has reminded us of what political movements and actions informed by religious beliefs can look like. We are now familiar with the cleric who encourages suicide bombings by assuring the intending martyr that his or her actions have divine approval and will be rewarded with a special place in heaven. Far from encouraging the use of violence, Paisley and his supporters have consistently condemned it, and the record of his church and party offers good evidence for a conclusion quite the opposite of what is commonly supposed: far from encouraging vigilante violence, evangelicalism inoculates people against its appeal. At times, some evangelicals, like most other unionists, have been tempted by the idea of reviving the 1912 UVF—a respectable disciplined body of patriots who defend their country against a treacherous government—but the overwhelming majority have never gone beyond contemplating a 'Dad's Army' of the last ditch. Aside from a tiny handful of men, none has argued that a holy war will justify their attacks on Catholics.

Even Billy Wright did not claim divine approval. On the contrary. In one interview shortly before he formed the LVF, when I pressed him about how he reconciled his professed faith and his sectarian murders, he told me: 'See, I know this is wrong. I am going to have to answer for it, to be punished for my sins. But somebody has got to do it.' I should add that, as with much of Wright's thinking, that moment of lucidity was brief. Later, in prison, he summoned a Free Presbyterian minister and announced with pride that he had finally understood why republicanism was winning. It was because it had three strands: the IRA was the military wing, Sinn Fein the political wing, and the Catholic Church was its spiritual arm. Ulster unionism needed the same three strands: his LVF would be the military wing,

[77] *Burning Bush* (Jan. 2000).

the DUP could be its political front, and the Free Presbyterian Church would provide its spiritual base. The disappointed minister said: 'Billy, you haven't really understood, have you?' and walked out of his cell.

Not only does Paisleyism not claim a spiritual justification for terror. It does not even assert that its religious principles trump secular ones. As I have tried to demonstrate at various points in this story, for all their claims to the heritage of Calvin and the Covenanters, Free Presbyterians are actually entirely conventional in their political philosophy. They do not claim that their political preferences trump all others because they are God-mandated. Instead they defend unionism on the secular grounds that it is the expressed preference of the majority. They do not assert that they should be protected by the state because they are doing God's will. Instead they claim that their secular human rights should be protected. When they have flirted with third forces, they have not claimed divine approval for a holy war. Instead they have claimed the secular principle of self-defence in the last resort. And, even when they use the language of a 'covenant', they are not thinking like the seventeenth-century Scots Covenanters. Instead they are reasoning like secular liberals: our obligation to allow the state a monopoly of the legitimate use of violence is conditional on the state accepting its obligation to protect us.

The Paisleyite fondness for Old Testament language and imagery has obscured the real nature of the movement's politics, possibly from Free Presbyterians almost as much as from their critics. It is common for states to claim divine approval. Especially when a people of one religion is at war with those who worship a different God, the temptation to assert divine 'favoured nation' status is difficult to resist, and the majority of most populations readily give in to temptation. The resistance to such blasphemy comes from the committed believers who may hope that they are indeed favoured by God but who are also only too aware of how far short of God's ideals they and most of their compatriots fall. Because Free Presbyterians are fiercely critical of ecumenical clergymen who preach peace through the erosion of difference, it is easy to suppose that they are uncritical supporters of everyone on their side of the Protestant–Catholic divide. The waters are sometimes muddied by the requirements of the political wing of

Paisleyism. When speaking to the electorate or an Orange rally or when recruiting for Ulster Resistance, Paisley uses 'the Protestant people of Ulster' to mean 'unionists', but in his religious teaching he is clear that, as Johnstone put it, the true church is made up 'of some out of every tribe, tongue, people and nation'. It is this awareness that we stand before God each of us alone that explains why evangelicals have been much less likely than other Ulster unionists to resort to vigilante violence.

8

With God on his Side

INTRODUCTION

The Northern Ireland conflict is a religious conflict. Loyalist killer Michael Stone did not have 'In the name of God the Avenger' inscribed on the barrel of his automatic pistol and Sinn Fein voters do not go to the polls muttering about the correct number of sacraments or the status of the mother of Jesus, but religion is deeply implicated in the Troubles. We cannot hope to understand the durability of the historic divisions in Ireland if we fail to see that religious differences helped create those divisions in the first place and played an important role in sustaining them. Ian Paisley created a political party and a church. In displacing the Ulster Unionist Party, which had dominated unionist politics for most of the twentieth century, Paisley exceeded everyone's expectations but his own, and we have no chance of understanding that success if we ignore Paisley's religious beliefs and rhetoric. This concluding chapter will examine in detail the impact of Paisley's religion on his own behaviour and on his electoral appeal.

WHAT RELIGION DOES FOR PAISLEY

A useful starting point is to eliminate the charge of cynicism. It is tempting (and his critics often give in to this temptation) to suppose that Paisley is opportunistic in his use of religious ideas and symbols: to the fore when needed and dropped when awkward. It is true that there is something a little too neat and knowing in the symmetry of him using his time in prison to write a commentary on Paul's Letter to the Romans—the New Testament book written by the apostle Paul when he was in prison. And we could see the DUP's dropping sabbatarianism from the party platform as the party putting votes ahead of religious rectitude. But over Paisley's career as a whole there are far too many instances of him pursuing his gospel mission in a way that was sure to lose him political support to suppose him guilty of much opportunism, and the point made in the previous chapter about the potential market for scandal can be made again here. So many people have had such a powerful interest in finding proof that his actions betray his words that its scarcity must be significant. I see no reason to doubt Paisley's own self-image as a man driven by a wish to discover God's will for him and his people in these troubled times and to do it.

In the next section I will consider how others—unionist voters in particular—have responded to Paisley's religion. First I want to examine the effect his religion has had on him and his core supporters.

Fortitude and Hope

That he is doing the will of God has been a powerful source of sustenance for Paisley and his core supporters. Since the 1970s nationalists have been convinced that the Union is doomed and a united Ireland merely a matter of time. This view has been shared by most commentators and not a few unionists. It formed the justification for the 1974 power-sharing proposals and for the Belfast Agreement: unionists are bound to lose and they might as well strike the best bargain while bargains can still be struck. Such pessimism was common even in right-wing unionist and loyalist circles. Probably half the loyalist paramilitaries I interviewed in the 1980s thought a united Ireland likely in their lifetimes and few thought their actions would prevent it. What many were doing was less a campaign to change the future and more a product of frustration at their own impotence; what rationality their violence possessed was to be found in winning the best possible terms for the inevitable armistice negotiations.

Even when the province's place in the United Kingdom was not being doubted, Paisley's place in Ulster politics was. Rereading the press coverage of Paisley from the 1960s to the 2003 elections, I found that journalists, political commentators, and politicians repeatedly wrote him off. He was an oaf, a charlatan, or a buffoon. His insistence on taking seriously such arcana as the sovereign's coronation oath only showed how out of touch he was and the Ulster electorate would soon rumble him. We might have thought that twenty years of winning elections might have won Paisley some degree of political credibility, but in 1990 the *Guardian* managed to headline a story 'Are his crowd-pulling days over' and answered its own question in the affirmative.[1] Four years later (and still wedded to the rhetorical question) it asked: 'Does anyone still listen to the Rev Ian Paisley?'[2]

What kept Paisley going for fifty years was the belief that he was doing God's will and the hope that, if it was part of God's inscrutable providence to reward his loyalty, he would eventually triumph. This 1980s sermon neatly encapsulates Paisley's vision and the fortitude he derives from his faith.

I was reading...the seventh chapter of the prophecy of Micah. In this chapter I realized that there was a description here of the sad and terrible plight into which our land has fallen. In verse two we read 'The good man is perished out of the earth, and there is none upright among men. They all lie in wait for blood'...As we read we are told that they do evil with both hands earnestly. There is a dedication today in the doing of evil. There is a revival of evil. There is a resurgence, a renaissance of evil, and it seems that the whole world has become polluted with a confrontation against the truth, righteousness and godliness of God's law, of God's standards and of God's commandments.

Then this old prophet asks 'What will I do?' All the props on which I have leaned, the foundations on which I ought to rely, the confidences I ought to have, the supports on which I ought to rest, they are all swept away. On whom will I rely? Where shall I find a sanctuary, a refuge for my soul? He turns and draws his conclusion in verse 7: 'Therefore will I look unto the Lord.' He lifts up his eyes away from the turmoil, away from the deceit, away from the lying, away from all the programme of confusion, and he lifts up unto the Lord.

That is what we need to do in this day. If ever there was a day that God's people needed to look up and put their confidence in the Lord, it is now.[3]

---

[1] *Guardian*, 15 Apr. 1990.   [2] Ibid. 26 Nov. 1994.
[3] This and subsequent quotations are from the sermon 'A prime text for the Prime Minister', Martyrs' Memorial Free Presbyterian Church, 15 Dec. 1985.

Paisley goes on to consider the lesson of the Children of Israel in Egypt. A mighty power oppressed the Lord's people but he delivered them from out of bondage. The mighty Pharaoh chased after them with his army. Moses asked for deliverance and the God of Heaven parted the waves. The Children of Israel passed to the other side. The chariots of Egypt were dashed. In the tenth verse of the chapter— 'Then she that is mine enemy shall see it, and shame shall cover her which said unto me, Where is the Lord thy God? Mine eyes shall behold her: now she shall be trodden down as the mire of the streets'—Paisley sees God's judgment on Margaret Thatcher:

The Protestantism of Ulster is an embarrassment to her. The old way of thinking that the Bible is true, that men need to be changed by the power of that Holy Word, that there is a separation demanded between God's people and those that live for the devil and sin, she does not like. So she takes Ulster and puts Ulster in a marriage bond with the Republic in order to destroy the identity of the Ulster Protestant people...I have news for the Prime Minister. God is in Heaven. You may have no respect, Mrs Thatcher, for praying people. You might laugh at their religion, laugh at their Bible, and laugh at the Day of God but 'He that sitteth in the heavens shall laugh at you, the Lord shall have you in derision'...

God has a people in this province. There are more born-again people in Ulster to the square mile than anywhere else in the world. This little province had the peculiar preservation of divine Providence. You only have to read the history of Ulster to see that time after time when it seemed humanly impossible to extricate Ulster from seeming disaster, that God intervened. Why? God has a purpose for this province, and this plant of Protestantism sown here in the north-eastern part of this island. The enemy has tried to root it out, but it still grows today, and I believe, like a grain of mustard seed, its future is going to be mightier yet. God who made her mighty will make her mightier yet in His Divine will.

Paisley and his people are sufficiently orthodox Christians that they do not take divine approval for granted. He has often reflected that it may not be any part of divine providence to save Ulster's Protestants. After all, God punished the Children of Israel by allowing them to be dispersed into an exile that lasted until the twentieth century. But the righteous can hope.

The belief that he is doing God's will means that Paisley and his core supporters do not play politics with the same deck of cards as the rest of those involved in negotiations. Of course, he is not blind to this-worldly realities. His long career amply demonstrates that he and those around him are extremely skilful political analysts. But he has the trump card of divine encouragement. The detailed accounts of the final hours of the negotiations that led to David Trimble instructing the UUP delegation to accept the Belfast Agreement show just how hard he was pressed by the US President and the British Prime Minister into accepting a position on disarmament that did not persuade him and that he knew would not persuade many other unionists. Instead of making Sinn Fein entry to government conditional on the IRA disarming and disbanding, he took a post-dated cheque and he did so because of political pressure. In his calculations, Trimble had only secular considerations. In similar circumstances, Paisley has been able to resist coercion because he has God on his side. In the words of the hymn, 'hobgoblins nor foul fiends shall daunt his spirit'.

Clarity of Purpose

Paisley's divine mission has given him a clarity and certainty of purpose. We can think of a few statesmen who have been extremely effective because their indifference to (or ignorance of) political realities has prevented them being deflected from their chosen course: US President Ronald Reagan is good example. But dogmatism is more often a hindrance than a help to a politician who is responsible for managing affairs of state. However, to someone in opposition it is a major advantage. Opinion polls and focus groups need not hinder the man of God.

Party Cohesion

As we saw in Chapter 6, despite the DUP's growth, its core of activists remain united by their shared faith. The majority are members of the FPCU, and almost all the others are members of a few small evangelical sects. They speak the same language and draw on the same stock of examples and illustrations. They think the same thoughts.

They socialize with each other. They marry into each others' families. It is this rather than Paisley's overbearing personality that allows the DUP to speak quickly and almost always with a single voice. Clifford Smyth, who was close to Paisley for a short time in the 1970s, gets this wrong when he says 'critics of DUP policy or those who privately questioned the leader's approach have invariably been isolated, quarantined, and then expelled'.[4] Smyth is actually one of the very few senior people who have been pushed out of the party, and his departure was concerned more with personal qualities than with policy. The cohesion of the DUP does depend a lot on Paisley's person, but it is his role as interpreter of an ideological canon that is central.

The contrast with the UUP could not be greater. It divided in 1970s over power-sharing, in the 1980s over devolution and integration, and again in the late 1990s over power-sharing. The UUP was not helped by its structure. Its governing council of 860 members had been designed to incorporate the largest number of Ulster unionists into one broad movement, not to produce an agreed policy that could be imposed on members. That its 'executive' committee consists of 124 people justifies its description by one of Trimble's advisers as being 'run on the lines of Presbyterian anarchy'.[5] Over 150 of the Unionist council seats were allocated to the Orange Order and the Young Unionist council, both bodies that were increasingly dominated by people whose views were closer to those of Paisley than to those of Trimble. That structure allowed dissidents repeatedly to force Trimble to defend his actions and to prove that he enjoyed the confidence of only a slim majority of delegates. The structure would not have been a problem if the party activists had shared common goals and values: they patently did not.

These three observations add up to this: Paisley and his small core of highly committed supporters were able to address the Ulster people with a single voice and with perpetual confidence that theirs was not a lost cause. Various sections of the Ulster Protestant people reacted in different ways.

[4] C. Smyth, 'Paisley Plays a Moderate Game', *Fortnight* (Feb. 1993), 4.
[5] G. Walker, *A History of the Ulster Unionist Party: Power, Pragmatism and Pessimism* (Manchester: Manchester University Press, 2004), 262.

RELIGION IN PAISLEY'S APPEAL

It may seem obvious but it is worth saying that Paisley and his evangelical DUP activists do not hide their faith. On the contrary, candidates were always keen to advertise their piety in their election leaflets. The couple who said 'Roger is married to Frances and as a family they acknowledge the sovereignty of God in all matters, placing their lives in his care and keeping' were a little extravagant, but the following are typical of the many routine citations: 'evangelical Christian', 'a committed Christian', 'active in his church', 'a Christian from the age of thirteen', and 'maintains strong Christian principles'.

The Ulster electorate has always known what drives Paisley but how has it responded? To answer that, we need to distinguish different unionist populations.[6]

Core

The core of Paisley's support is to be found in his own church and only a little beyond it. Those who joined in the early 1970s and before were people who shared his twin vision of elite betrayal in religion and politics. As Chapter 6 demonstrated, FPCU ministers have worked hard to avoid being party-political, and their congregations are by no means slavish followers of a line. Polls repeatedly show small numbers of Free Presbyterians deviating slightly by, for example, saying they hoped the Belfast Agreement would succeed even as they voted against it! Still, Paisley's presence in the Church is such that it is hard to imagine many people staying for long if they positively supported alternatives to DUP policy such as Faulknerite power-sharing in 1974

---

[6] As a methodological aside, it is worth noting that much attitude survey political science work on Northern Ireland looks for too simple a connection between religious and political values. It is not likely that we will find a direct correlation between, for example, evangelicalism and ultra-unionism because, as I note here, a number of different political agendas can be derived from evangelical theology, and the political views of even those evangelicals minded to be conservative unionists are influenced by other considerations such as denominational loyalty.

or the UUP's talks position in 1998. But the FPCU and similar sects are small and probably number no more than 15,000 voters. So arithmetic tells us that the DUP always had support from beyond its narrow evangelical core. Surveys confirm this. Generally they have shown that DUP voters come from two very different worlds: rural evangelical and 'secular' working class. But we can also identify churchgoers who voted DUP who did not like Paisley's church. When asked if they were in favour of joint worship services with a variety of churches other than their own, respondents in a major survey of Belfast Protestant church members showed a distinct frost for Free Presbyterianism.[7] Two-thirds of UUP and Alliance supporters (who were overwhelmingly Irish Presbyterian or Church of Ireland) said they were opposed to joint services with the Free Presbyterians, but a third of DUP supporters also objected! In brief, any explanation of Paisley's political success must take us beyond his conservative evangelical base.

Periphery

What needs explaining is why those Protestants who did not share Paisley's religious beliefs were prepared to support him rather than other right-wing unionists. It is important to add an aside here. The explanation of a party's long-term success need not positively explain every gain. Party success occurs in competition, and it is often the case that the overall explanation depends as much on the failures of others as on the positive virtues of the victor. To be specific, we need not suppose that every victory rested on Paisley converting people who might have voted for someone else. Often his victories were won because his competitors failed to mobilize those who had previously voted for them and who might still sympathize but who were sufficiently disillusioned on this or that occasion to stay home. Even in electoral systems that use proportional representation, small shifts in sentiment may be enough to deliver large swings in voting. Part of

---

[7] F. Boal, J. A. Campbell, and D. N. Livingstone, 'The Protestant Mosaic: A Majority of Minorities', in P. J. Roche and B. Barton (eds.), *The Northern Ireland Question: Myth and Reality* (Aldershot: Avebury, 1994), 119.

Paisley's triumph is simply the failure of his competitors. The UUP's long stranglehold on power created a culture that did not encourage talent, and the alternative route to prominence through the loyal Orders rewarded those who painstakingly attended the years of meetings that would promote them through the endless degrees and ranks of 'Worshipful' this and that. Harry West was a dull and plodding farmer who was uninspiring at best, and even his supporters had to search long and hard to find much to praise about James Molyneaux. William Craig was a conceited but unsure man who changed tack frequently without taking the trouble to persuade those close to him of the need for change. The one unionist who might have provided serious competition, Robert McCartney QC, was so difficult that he was unable to remain within an organization or hold together the one he formed himself. Five years after winning an election for the UUP he was expelled from it. His own UKUP won five seats in the first Belfast Agreement Assembly, but within a year the other four representatives had abandoned him to form their own party.

Undoubtedly part of Paisley's success is due entirely to the secular fact of him being an effective spokesman for right-wing unionism. He established his credentials early on with his work in the National Union of Protestants and Protestant Action, and in his early campaign against O'Neill. But Paisley did not have the right wing to himself. In the 1970s his party was one of three components in the anti-power-sharing coalition, and, until William Craig surprised his power base by suggesting a voluntary coalition with the SDLP, he looked like the more effective champion of the right. Not only did Paisley face severe competition, but he started with the disadvantage of not having ready access to the powerful networks of influence provided by the Orange Order.

The next step in the analysis is to see what features of Paisley's religious persona might have roundabout appeal to voters whose reasoning is based primarily on secular considerations. In hundreds of conversations with ordinary unionist voters, I have been offered some version of the following comment from an East Belfast former Labour party activist: 'To be honest, I have never had any time for all that gospel rubbish and I used to dislike him, but at least you know where you are with Paisley.' And we can add the following:

At least I feel that the DUP are there, at least I know that when they come out and say this is what's going on here, this is what's going to happen, that this is going to happen....I feel that when the [Ulster] Unionist Party talks they speak with a foreign tongue, with their fingers crossed behind their backs at the same time. I would rather someone would...give it to me straight between the eyes.[8]

This quotation is from a post-ceasefire study of unionists:

Over the years I've been with the Ulster Unionist Party and Tony Blair and Bertie Ahern and Bill Clinton and all the rest. The lies and deceitfulness that's been told and done—I wouldn't trust any of them....I would always vote DUP now. Because I believe...that they've come out and [what they've said] has turned out to be right....Some of the things they would say and do, I wouldn't agree with, to be honest. Sometimes I think Ian, he speaks before he puts his brain in gear but I would give him a fool's pardon on that. He'll never change.[9]

These reasons for supporting the DUP combine assumptions about constancy, reliability, and trustworthiness. Looking back on the press coverage of Paisley's long career, I see a regular failure by journalists to appreciate what matters to some unionist voters. Often press coverage concentrates on the failure of Paisley's initiatives: the 1977 strike that failed to reproduce the success of 1974, the failure of the 'Ulster Says No' campaign against the Anglo-Irish accord, the farcical petering-out of his various third forces. What is less often noticed is that these failed attempts to shift British government policy were rarely punished by the electorate. Less than two years after the abortive 1977 strike, the DUP won two Westminster seats and Paisley topped the poll for the European parliament. In 1982, while the pointless 1981 Third Force was still fresh in people's minds, the DUP recorded a very healthy 23 per cent of the votes for the rolling devolution assembly. A reasonable conclusion from the chronology of DUP initiatives and election performance is that many voters understood that Paisley did not have the power to change British policy but appreciated his efforts. He was at least trying to do something.

[8] C. Mitchell, *Religion, Identity and Politics in Northern Ireland* (Aldershot: Ashgate, 2006), 100.

[9] Rural Antrim Presbyterian quoted in G. Ganiel, 'Changing Northern Ireland: Religion and Identity', unpublished paper 2005.

Of course there is no reason why a secular right-winger could
not have shown the same obstinate doggedness and dogmatism.
Pig-headedness is not the preserve of the religious zealot, but many
of the observations of the form 'You know where you are with the
DUP' made explicit reference to the DUP's religious attitudes, often in
the form of a contrast and with grudging respect: 'I don't like the
religious fanaticism but at least they're honest', 'You may not agree
with Paisley but you know what he is going to say', and 'I know it's a
cliché, but at least his heart's in the right place'.

Heritage and Nostalgia

One of the features that outsiders find most striking and frustrating
about Ulster unionists is that they are persistently backward-looking.
When Ulster Protestants talk about being British, it is clear that the
Britain they have in mind is no more recent than the 1950s, and often
their points of reference are positively Victorian. In the 1970s, cinemas
in Protestant parts of Belfast still finished the bill with the National
Anthem and the audiences stood. London in the Swinging Sixties used
the Union Jack ironically; in Northern Ireland the flag was displayed
with no irony at all. That unionists often seem mired in nostalgia is
not, as some commentators think, because they cannot accept reality:
it is because they dislike the reality. For a conservative unionist the
glory is all in the past: the formation of the 1912 UVF, Carson and
Craig saving Ulster from a united Ireland, the opening of the Stormont parliament buildings, the calm of the 1950s. Since the start of
Troubles, every major change has weakened the position of Northern
Ireland within the Union.

While Catholics bore the brunt of physical suffering, their beliefs about themselves, their sense of identity, and their conviction that their demands were
justified, was more often strengthened than weakened by the events triggered by
Civil Rights. In contrast, many Protestants found their political world collapsing
around them. Their beliefs, their very political and social system, were being
questioned on a world stage, while every political reform ... seemed to remove
another plank from the structure they were defending.[10]

---

[10] S. Nelson, *Ulster's Uncertain Defenders* (Belfast: Appletree Press, 1984), 11.

In this environment, being able to remind people of the past, being old-fashioned, is a positive advantage, and Paisley has built a career on claiming continuity with the glorious past. His refusal to accept bans on marches is portrayed as a reminder of the great William Johnston of Ballykilbegs. His speeches are littered with references to such great religious figures of the past as Henry Cooke and 'Roaring' Hugh Hanna. Before Gusty Spence and his colleagues reformed the UVF, Paisley attempted to claim that inheritance with his Ulster Protestant Volunteers. A series of political rallies was billed as 'The Carson Trail'. When O'Neill and Faulkner talked of modernizing, Paisley countered with a reassertion of the past.[11] Again, as with obstinacy, there is no necessary reason why a secular right-winger should not lay claim to the same heritage, but being a gospel-preaching minister gave Paisley a head start in appealing to nostalgia because the past was more religious than the present. Even those people who wished to use leisure facilities on a Sunday understood the point of the Bangor councillor who frequently wrote to the papers to defend her membership of the DUP by saying that, when she moved from England in the 1940s, Ulster was 'a great wee place' because it kept the Sabbath and did not have the 'republican Sunday'.

There is also a very personal nostalgic resonance of Paisley's religion. Very many of those who by the 1980s would have described themselves in surveys as having 'no religion' had been raised with a church connection. Their parents would have been Bible-believing Christians, and many would themselves have attended church and Sunday school. While Paisley addresses them in a language that they no longer speak, he talks in terms that they have heard before, both often enough, and in such circumstances, as to instil a strong respect. The Grand Master of the Orange Order, the Revd Martin Smyth MP, may have been overstating the case when he once said

[11] Some unionists tried to find a non-religious past to justify their politics. John McMichael and Andy Tyrie of the UDA heavily promoted the work of Ian Adamson, a historian who argued that the Scots who colonized Ulster were actually the original inhabitants, driven out of Ireland by the late-coming Celts, returned to their ancestral lands. Whatever truth there is an Adamson's accounts of the Cruithin, the story did not work as a mobilizing myth, probably because its prehistoric date meant it lacked human detail and made sympathetic association difficult. And it used the sort of artwork that had already been claimed for Celtic mythology!

that Shankill Road Protestants were Bible-lovers even if they were not Bible-readers, but he had a point.

In brief, by exemplifying the pious Protestant, Paisley, with his clerical garb and archaic language, tapped into unionist nostalgia and thus acquired a small but important symbolic advantage over his rivals.

Anti-Cosmopolitan

We can understand Paisley's appeal to small farmers and to parts of the urban working class if we consider the tension between cosmopolitan and local sources of identity. For O'Neill and his supporters, nothing that mattered to them would have been lost had he succeeded in transforming Northern Ireland. The O'Neillites were cosmopolitan, drawing their values more from London and international circles than from provincial Ulster. Very firmly upper middle class and university educated, they could see the advantages in abandoning traditional discriminatory practices: greater international respectability and a greater ability to attract multinational capital. When O'Neill was elevated to the House of Lords, he moved to England. The other Stormont MP who resigned his seat at the same time as O'Neill, Richard Ferguson QC, moved to London to practise at the English Bar. Largely anglicized, O'Neillites looked beyond Northern Ireland for their identity. In the long run, O'Neillism threatened to remove those parts of the Protestant identity that justified Ulster's refusal to become part of a united Ireland. In the short run, it meant abandoning claims to cultural superiority and related status privileges.

The same point can be made about support for the ecumenical movement. The people who most readily participated in the ecumenical movement were those whose reference group was the 'first-world' Christian community. They were religious cosmopolites who took their values from Lausanne, Geneva, and New York rather than from the streets of Belfast, Fermanagh, and Tyrone. Although they defended their rewriting of Protestantism as essential for the continued survival of any Christianity in a hostile secular environment, they were proposing fundamental changes in the traditional faith. Such changes may have seemed necessary to the cultured, mobile, middle classes who wished to preserve something of their Protestantism while adjusting to the pluralistic culture in which they moved; it offered no benefits to the farmers of Down and Armagh or the artisans of East Belfast. When the liberal Irish Presbyterian cleric David Armstrong was driven out of his Limavady congregation, he moved to England and joined the Anglican Church. His childhood friend and Free Presbyterian opponent Wesley McDowell is still in Limavady.

The Troubles saw a major shift in political power and ethos within unionism. There was a marked decline in deference as the gentry and the affluent business class were replaced in the high offices of the fraternal orders and the UUP by farmers, small businessmen, and white-collar workers. Some of the cosmopolitans shifted to the Alliance Party; others just kept their heads down. They became what one frustrated UUP worker called 'the garden centre unionists'.[12]

Paisley's religion located him firmly in the anti-cosmopolitan fringes. If he ventured outside Ulster, it was to Wales, the Western Isles of Scotland, and South Carolina—the places where isolation had preserved evangelical religion. In a context where the common touch was important for dispelling suspicions of elite unreliability, Paisley's evangelicalism gave him an important head start over competitors in signifying that he was an Ulsterman. His faith might be universal, but its expressions were very firmly located in Ulster's soil.

Justifying Claims to Virtue

Perhaps the greatest advantage that Paisley's religion confers on him as a political leader is that it justifies Protestant claims to virtue. We can see the point if we start by recognizing that people who share an ethnic identity that marks them off from some other ethnos need some grounds for maintaining that identity. Identities such as Serb and Croat or Ukrainian and Russian are not just empty labels. They are not just the coloured bibs that footballers of the same club wear when playing practice games against each other. Ethnic labels do not just show which side you're on; they also include claims to superiority. These may

---

[12] M. Kerr, *Transforming Unionism: David Trimble and the 2005 General Election* (Dublin: Irish Academic Press, 2006).

be elaborated with various degrees of sophistication and they may be more or less explicit, but if the competing identities are to survive for any length of time they need to be there. Ask a not-especially religious 'Protestant' why he objects to being forced into a united Ireland or why he sees himself as different from a Catholic and he can list a variety of secular virtues that carry implied contrasts. We are loyal, honest, hard-working, temperant people with small families. They are treacherous, dishonest people who drink too much, have too many children, and live on social-security handouts. Such stereotypes need have no factual basis for them to be well embedded in ethnic images. They are obviously necessary for a privileged people, but, even if there are no material differences between two competing ethnic groups, such invidious comparisons will be commonplace. Catholics think they are better people than Protestants: Protestants think they are better than Catholics. And whatever extent people are aware of it, it remains the case that such competing claims to virtue need some kind of philosophical underpinning. Biology provides a source of justification for *racially* different groups. Whites in the southern states of the USA or in South Africa justified their superiority with claims to racial advantage: the genetic material of white people is better than that of black folks. But such a defence is not available in Northern Ireland. What distinguishes Protestants and Catholics and explains their distinctions? The only answer is the shared faith. The thing that unites Protestants and separates them from Catholics is their reformed religion. For many, that reformed religion is a communal memory rather than a personal faith, but the memory is powerful enough to give those who exemplify the faith an advantage in the competition for the leadership of the Protestant people.

The non-Catholic, non-nationalist people of Northern Ireland have a choice. They can become Irish nationalists. They can adopt the Alliance party position of 'for-the-time-being' unionism: supporting the Union because that is what most people currently want. Or they can become principled unionists. If they are in favour of the Union, they can defend their politics on entirely rational grounds. They can, like David Trimble and Robert McCartney, make a secular case for the superiority of the British polity and its associated public culture over that of the Irish republic. But, to the extent to which any such comparisons involve a criticism of Roman Catholicism, they will be drawn back to implicit claims for the virtue of Protestantism and to religious differences. 'Protestants believed that having access to the "Open Bible", being free from priestcraft and superstition and adhering to a progressive and enlightenment faith were at the heart of Ulster's cultural and economic superiority over the rest of Ireland and, equally important, of Protestant Ulster's superiority over Catholic Ulster.'[13] In one early 1970s survey of Ulster Protestants, only 9 per cent described themselves as evangelicals, but 74.5 per cent gave 'fear of the power of the Roman Catholic Church' as their reason for being unionist.[14] If unionists derive their politics from a sense of belonging to a distinctive ethnic group, then they will draw even more strongly on the major source of difference between the competing ethnic groups. They might not be personally pious, but what identifies them and justifies them is their common religion. And that gives an important advantage to Paisley and his core followers.

Popular Religion

I have just tried to explain why even not particularly religious Protestants might implicitly recognize that evangelicals represent something that lies at the heart of their heritage. In taking the hypothetical case of the 'secular' Protestant I exaggerated the difficulty of what needs to be explained. Ulster popular culture is still thoroughly pervaded by religious rhetoric and symbolism. At least 50,000 people belong to the Orange Order, and all the loyal orders draw heavily on biblical imagery and language in their rituals and ceremonies. 'Although the precise form of the degrees have altered over time, the over-riding theme has remained constant and runs through the Orange, Arch Purple and Black rituals. It is the struggle of God's chosen people in a hostile land, contending against alien peoples and false gods eventually to reach, with faith, the Promised Land and the blessing of God.'[15] As Paisley and his like frequently remind them, many Orangemen do not personally

---

[13] D. Hempton and M. Hill, *Evangelical Protestantism in Ulster Society 1740–1890* (London: Routledge, 1992), 182.

[14] E. Moxon-Browne, *Nation, Class and Creed in Northern Ireland* (Aldershot: Gower, 1983), 38.

[15] P. Mitchel, *Evangelicalism and National Identity in Ulster: 1921–1998* (Oxford: Oxford University Press, 2003), 154.

live up to the standards set down in the membership requirements. But do we really imagine that spending a large part of their lives giving verbal assent to evangelical principles and repeating Bible stories has no effect on Orangemen?

ALIENATING VOTERS

So far I have been considering ways in which Paisley's evangelical religion has appealed to voters and given him an advantage over other right-wing unionists. However, we know that these benefits were limited. If we leave aside the elections for the European parliament (which gave the DUP an advantage by emphasizing personality) and Westminster elections (in which the DUP often contested far fewer seats than the UUP), electoral support for the DUP peaked in 1981 and then fell back and platteaued at about a third of unionist voters. And there it was stuck.

Some of the reasons why two-thirds of unionists did not vote for the DUP are largely secular. Some preferred greater integration with Britain to the restoration of devolution. Some preferred the search for accommodation over the refusal to negotiate. Within the realm of those who shared his broad principles, the UUP enjoyed privileged access to the Orange Order's network of contacts and influence. Through the 1980s and early 1990s, the Grand Master of the Order, Martin Smyth, was a UUP member of parliament, and the leader of the Blackmen, James Molyneaux, was also the leader of the UUP. Undoubtedly many voters were alienated by the DUP's associations with demonstrations and disorder. But, all secular considerations aside, it is also clear that Paisley's religion was a disincentive for many unionists.

DUP councillors certainly report that their sabbatarianism and their temperance principles cost them votes. Even the switch to a policy of supporting 'local options' did not free them from the disapproval of those who disliked their Puritanism. But the greatest cost of DUP evangelicalism was the loss of support from other conservative evangelical Christians.

Commentators have not paid enough attention to the target of Paisleyite criticism. A few of his demonstrations—hiring an ex-priest to mock the Mass or barracking the Pope—were anti-Catholic, but most of Paisley's ire has been directed not at the Church of the Antichrist but at the other Protestant churches. In the weeks before the January 1986 by-elections, which unionist MPs had organized as a referendum on the Anglo-Irish accord, the DUP was committed to a united unionist front. Paisley toured the province arm-in-arm with Molyneaux and Jim Kilfedder (the independent unionist MP for North Down). Yet, only two days before the crucial poll, more than fifty Free Presbyterians disrupted an ecumenical service in the Church of Ireland's St Anne's Cathedral in Belfast. The Belgian Cardinal Leon-Joseph Suenens had been invited to take part in a service to celebrate the 'Week of Prayer and Christian Unity'. Three times the Cardinal's words were drowned out, and, as each group of Free Presbyterians was ejected from the cathedral, they were cheered by a crowd of some 200 supporters outside. The Dean later said: 'These were the sort of bully boy tactics we have come to associate with Paisley. I think Paisley will lose hundreds of votes over this.'[16] That the demonstration had Paisley's blessing is clear from the fact that William Beattie and Paisley's daughter Rhonda and son Ian were involved. The next day Paisley described himself as being pleased with the protest. The Dean was probably wrong about that particular demonstration costing the DUP votes, but only because Paisley's thirty-year-long record of accusing the Church of Ireland of apostasy had already done that job.

Paisley's self-righteous piety alienated three distinct groups of mainstream Protestants for different reasons. Obviously liberal Protestants disagreed with his interpretation of the key doctrines of the Christian faith. Someone who supported the ecumenical movement in church relations and a liberal interpretation of the Christian gospel would find it hard to vote for Paisley. There was also a distinct evangelical voice that disagreed with Paisley's linking of reformed religion and ethnic politics. The Evangelical Contribution on Northern Ireland (ECONI) represented this position.[17] In the late 1980s, under the slogan 'Resourcing

---

[16] *Newsletter*, 22 Jan. 1986.
[17] The following paragraph draws heavily on Mitchel's discussion of ECONI, which is excellent in its description but exaggerates the scale of support for ECONI and its impact; Mitchel, *Evangelicalism*, 260–98.

Christians for a biblical response', ECONI argued that 'the apparent identification of Protestant and Roman Catholic churches with Loyalism and Nationalism is a contradiction of Christ's affirmation of the primacy of the Kingdom of God'. For all that ECONI tried to liberate evangelical Protestantism from its associations with unionism, it remained very small, and the claims made for its influence are unconvincing. A founding advertisement published in the *Belfast Telegraph* was signed by twenty-four Presbyterian ministers. Over 200 prominent evangelicals endorsed the statement of principles published as *For God and His Glory Alone* and over 9,000 copies were distributed. But it is hard to see that it had any lasting impact on the majority of Ulster evangelicals and it was certainly unable to prevent the increased polarization of unionist politics that followed the 1994 ceasefires. In 1997 ECONI sponsored a series of Christian Election Forum meetings intended to help 'Christians to respond biblically to the 1997 elections' and its importance can be gauged from attendance: it attracted only twelve people to its North Belfast meeting, and only the SDLP, Green Party, and Alliance candidates turned up.

Both the ecumenical and the 'anti-ethnic' evangelical rejections of Paisley were small and confined largely to intellectuals. The greatest cost of Paisley's religion was the offence that his advocacy of separatism caused to middle-of-the-road Presbyterians, Episcopalians, and Methodists. Over twenty years of casual conversations with ordinary members of the main Protestant churches, I was repeatedly told that they disliked 'that man Paisley' because of the way he spoke of them and their ministers and their church. People who shared Paisley's condemnation of theological liberalism and ecumenism would agree that there were people in their denomination with whom they differed but add that 'my minister is a saved man' or 'our church preaches the full gospel'. From the formation of the Crossgar Free Presbyterian congregation in 1951, Paisley and his ministers banged on endlessly about 'sell-out' in the main Protestant denominations. By 1974 they had recruited all those who responded positively to that message. From then on, and for almost thirty years, all their persistent criticism and denigration were doing was deepening resentment among those who otherwise might have voted DUP. The separatist clergyman can relish being despised and see it as a mark of virtue. When that clergyman is also a politician, he is alienating potential voters.

WINNING THE MAJORITY

To summarize so far, Paisley's religion gave him certain small but important advantages in presenting himself as the surest guardian of unionist orthodoxy, but it also alienated a lot of potential supporters. Through the 1980s and 1990s the DUP could rely on about a third of unionist votes. There was a small core who shared the dual vision of apostasy in religion and treachery in politics and a large periphery of mostly secular people who, for a variety of reasons (some of them an implicit recognition of the importance of evangelicalism in the historical identity of the Protestant people), preferred the DUP to the UUP.

The rapid transformation that saw the DUP trounce the Ulster Unionist Party owed nothing to religion and everything to a rational response to British government policy. At the time the Belfast Agreement was being negotiated, a number of sceptical commentators (myself included) argued that its foundational approach of treating the voters of Northern Ireland as members of ethnic blocs would destroy the middle ground and strengthen the extremes. The parallel of the Lebanese constitution is instructive. When Lebanon was carved out of the Ottoman Empire, it was given a polity that divided power between the representatives of its various ethno-religious groups. The President was to be a Maronite Christian, the Prime Minister a Sunni Muslim, the Speaker of the House a Shiite Muslim, the vice-Speaker Greek-Orthodox, the Chief of Staff Druze, and so on. Parliamentary seats were similarly divvied up. The consequence was that the citizens of Lebanon had every incentive to continue to act as members of their blocs and to seek advantage by supporting the most extreme representatives of those blocs. It could reasonably be argued that the Belfast Agreement did no more than recognize the divided nature of Northern Ireland, but it did so in ways that entrenched antagonistic positions and encouraged nationalists and unionists to favour the extremes. An SDLP voter might be tempted to vote Sinn Fein because the obvious way to increase the advantages for Catholic nationalists is to strengthen the hand of the most aggressively nationalist party. If nothing else it would allow the SDLP to argue that the British government should make more concessions to nationalists because, if it does not, then the nice nationalists will be displaced by the nasty ones. Similarly a unionist who was in favour of Trimble's policies could be tempted to vote for the DUP because, while that would weaken Trimble vis-à-vis the DUP, it would strengthen him vis-à-vis nationalists.

The reasons why very many unionists did not like the Belfast Agreement were discussed in Chapter 4. It is possible to imagine success. If the IRA had completely disarmed and renounced the armed struggle in the first year, if the SDLP had more enthusiastically embraced the settlement, if Trimble had possessed the power radically to restructure his party and crush his dissidents, and if the leadership of Sinn Fein had changed so that Adams and McGuiness had been replaced by people less obviously associated with terrorism, then the first assembly might have run its course and the narrow and grudging unionist majority in favour of 'giving it a go' might gradually have increased. Instead, circumstances reinforced the perception that Trimble had conceded too much too early for too little and the UUP vote collapsed. Some voters just stayed at home, but a large number swung behind Ian Paisley and the DUP.

Trimble gambled his party on the Belfast Agreement and it failed him. Paisley's final triumph was largely a secular victory. But those who persist in denying that the evangelical Protestantism at the heart of the DUP has played a major part in the party's unlikely success might rerun tapes of the television coverage of the dramatic scenes at the 2005 election. They will see evangelicals Donaldson, Campbell, McCrea, and Dodds thanking God for their victories. They will see David Simpson, a man barely known outside gospel-singing circles, defeating David Trimble in Upper Bann. And they will see a now-stooped and aged Ian Paisley, thirty-nine years after he had first won an election in North Antrim, yet again crediting God with his election victory. After the 1969 result, he had prayed: 'Save Ulster from being sold down the river. Oh, God, give us a great deliverance.' When his 2005 vote was announced, Paisley was able to sing 'Praise God from whom all blessings flow' with the enthusiasm of a man who knows that almost fifty years of resolute political campaigning had finally given him what he had always claimed he had: the mandate of the Ulster Protestant people.

APPENDIX

The Free Presbyterian Church of Ulster

Congregations in Northern Ireland

Table A1 lists the congregations of the FPCU by date of formation (which is usually defined by the start of regular weekly services) and gives an indication of size; Table A2 lists the congregations by size in 2002. Tables A3 and A4 list the congregations outside Northern Ireland. In Tables A1–A4 the last column uses the estimates of regular attendance given in P. Kyle, *Our Own Heritage* (Tavistock, 2002).

Table A5 shows the distribution of Free Presbyterians across Northern Ireland using data from the censuses, and, to highlight patterns of growth since the early 1970s, Table A6 presents the data for 1971 and 2001 with the council areas ranked in order of Free Presbyterian numbers. Note that in official census publications Free Presbyterians are buried in the 'Other Protestant' category. I am grateful to the staff of the Registrar General (Northern Ireland) for the 1971 and 1981 data and to the staff of the Northern Ireland Statistics and Research Agency for the 1991 and 2001 figures.

There is limited value in using statistical analysis to try to go beyond the observations made in the text about the growth and spread of Free Presbyterianism. Geographical analysis works best for some phenomenon that is popular and widespread (so that it may be explained by something other than the activities of one or two proselytizing individuals or the preferences of a few rare people) but not yet so widespread that we cannot extract it from the background. Free Presbyterians are such a small part of the population that detailed statistical analysis is not terribly revealing but a few features can be mentioned.

As we know from congregational histories and the biographies of those involved in the FPCU, there is a connection with rurality. For 1971, the Spearman's *r* statistic for the link between rurality and the proportion of the non-Catholic population that is Free Presbyterian is 0.66. Testing only those districts in which Catholics are not a majority raises it slightly to 0.69.

Other possible connections fail to produce statistically significant results. In part this is likely to be because the sorts of conditions that conduce to FPCU growth cancel out. We might imagine that Protestants in areas with large Catholic majorities feel especially threatened and are thus attracted to

TABLE A1. *Congregations in Northern Ireland in order of foundation*

No.	Start date	Place	Local District Council	Size 2002
1	1946	Ravenhill Road	Belfast	500
2	1951	Crossgar	Down	120
3	1951	Cabra (later Ballymoney)	Ballymoney	280
4	1951	Rasharkin	Ballymoney	100
5	1952	Mount Merrion	Belfast	60
6	1953	Whiteabbey (later Newtownabbey	Newtownabbey	70
7	1954	Ballyhalbert (later Portavogie)	Ards	170
8	1957	Coleraine	Coleraine	175
9	1957	Dunmurry	Lisburn	75
10	1959	Antrim (ceased 1963)	Antrim	—
11	1964	Sandown Road	Belfast	260
12	1964	Limavady	Limavady	40
13	1964	Armagh	Armagh	270
14	1966	Ballymena (founded 1931)	Ballymena	500
15	1966	Moneyslane	Banbridge	200
16	1966	Hillsborough	Lisburn	400
17	1967	Lisbellaw (later Enniskillen)	Fermanagh	170
18	1967	Tandragee	Armagh	280
19	1967	Lurgan	Craigavon	270
20	1967	Londonderry	Londonderry	90
21	1967	Portadown	Craigavon	300
22	1967	Dungannon	Dungannon	200
23	1967	Kilkeel (Mourne)	Newry + Mourne	240
24	1968	Lisburn	Lisburn	250
25	1968	Magherafelt	Magherafelt	330
26	1968	Randalstown	Antrim	300
27	1969	Omagh	Omagh	200
28	1969	Larne	Larne	75
29	1969	Cloughmills	Ballymena	70
30	1970	Clogher Valley	Dungannon	140
31	1970	Castlederg	Strabane	75
32	1970	Banbridge	Banbridge	200
33	1971	Newtownards	Ards	120
34	1991	Mullaglass	Newry + Mourne	200
35	1971	Ardaragh	Newry + Mourne	80
36	1971	Garvagh	Coleraine	65
37	1972	John Knox Memorial	Belfast	85
38	1973	Cookstown	Cookstown	110
39	1973	Portglenone	Ballymena	100
40	1974	Kilskeery	Omagh	80
41	1974	Antrim	Antrim	35
42	1975	Dromore	Banbridge	100
43	1975	Sixmilecross	Omagh	85
44	1976	Bangor	North Down	90
45	1976	Mulvin	Strabane	70
46	1976	Kesh	Fermanagh	45
47	1976	Tullyvallen	Newry + Mourne	85

No.	Start date	Place	Local District Council	Size 2002
48	1978	Ballynahinch	Down	100
49	1979	Ballygowan	Ards	170
50	1979	Carrickfergus	Carrickfergus	80
51	1982	Auchnacloy	Dungannon	85
52	1985	Markethill	Armagh	100
53	1987	Gilford	Banbridge	60
54	1988	Comber	Ards	100
55	1988	Ballymagerny	Armagh	130
56	1990	Annalong	Newry + Mourne	60
57	1990	Donaghadee	Ards	30
58	1992	Tyndale Memorial	Belfast	35
59	1995	Bushmills	Moyle	35
60	1996	Carryduff	Ards	50
61	1999	Aghalee	Lisburn	40
		TOTAL		8,835

the most conservative expressions of their faith (hence the strength in Armagh), but we also know that Free Presbyterianism is more likely to attract Presbyterians than Episcopalians (who will find its religious culture and service forms less familiar). Hence those areas with small Protestant populations where the Protestants are predominantly Church of Ireland are likely to be difficult territory for the FPCU. But even those simple propositions are compromised by another consideration. Protestants whose minority status leads them to feel vulnerable may well feel a greater pull to remain loyal to their historic community church and so be less likely to defect. And the political pressures that might encourage Protestants to desire a very conservative version of their faith may cause congregations to call conservative clergy whose orthodoxy prevents their congregants being attracted by the Paisleyite critique of ecumenical treachery. There may also be local cultural influences. Although he was not sure of the reasons for it, one minister who had served in a number of congregations around the province had a clear impression that the north and north-west (Moyle, Coleraine, Limavady, Londonderry) were poor ground for his gospel.

Some changes in the distribution of Free Presbyterians obviously reflect the wider demographic changes that can be discerned from the pattern of church formation: like other Protestants, Free Presbyterians have moved out of Belfast to North Down and Ards. But, generally speaking, the small numbers involved make it impossible to separate broad social change from such local effects as the attractions of a popular minister, the recruitment efforts of a particular family, or even just the variations in family size that come with differential age distribution.

TABLE A2. *Congregations in Northern Ireland by size in 2002*

No.	Start date	Place	Size 2002
1	1946	Ravenhill Road	500
14	1966	Ballymena (founded 1931)	500
16	1966	Hillsborough	400
25	1968	Magherafelt	330
26	1968	Randalstown	300
21	1967	Portadown	300
3	1951	Cabra (later Ballymoney)	280
18	1967	Tandragee	280
19	1967	Lurgan	270
13	1964	Armagh	270
11	1964	Sandown Road	260
24	1968	Lisburn	250
23	1967	Kilkeel (Mourne)	240
22	1967	Dungannon	200
32	1970	Banbridge	200
15	1966	Moneyslane	200
34	1991	Mullaglass	200
27	1969	Omagh	200
8	1957	Coleraine	175
7	1954	Ballyhalbert (later Portavogie)	170
17	1967	Lisbellaw (latter Enniskillen)	170
49	1979	Ballygowan	170
30	1970	Clogher Valley	140
55	1988	Ballymagerny	130
2	1951	Crossgar	120
33	1971	Newtownards	120
38	1973	Cookstown	110
4	1951	Rasharkin	100
42	1975	Dromore	100
39	1973	Portglenone	100
54	1988	Comber	100
52	1985	Markethill	100
48	1978	Ballynahinch	100
20	1967	Londonderry	90
44	1976	Bangor	90
51	1982	Auchnacloy	85
47	1976	Tullyvallen	85
37	1972	John Knox Memorial	85
43	1975	Sixmilecross	85
50	1979	Carrickfergus	80
35	1971	Ardaragh	80
40	1974	Kilskeery	80
9	1957	Dunmurry	75
31	1970	Castlederg	75
28	1969	Larne	75

No.	Start date	Place	Size 2002
6	1953	Whiteabbey (later Newtownabbey)	70
29	1969	Cloughmills	70
45	1976	Mulvin	70
36	1971	Garvagh	65
5	1952	Mount Merrion	60
56	1990	Annalong	60
53	1987	Gilford	60
60	1996	Carryduff	50
46	1976	Kesh	45
12	1964	Limavady	40
61	1999	Aghalee	40
58	1992	Tyndale Memorial	35
41	1974	Antrim	35
59	1995	Bushmills	35
57	1990	Donaghadee	30

TABLE **A3.** *Congregations and extensions in the British Isles outside Northern Ireland*

Start date	Place	Country	Size 2002
1972	Coragarry, Co. Monaghan	Ireland	70
1982	Liverpool	England	30
1985	Oulton Broad, Suffolk	England	30
1987	Convoy, Co. Donegal	Ireland	30
1987	Lewes, East Sussex	England	20
1988/94*	Rutherglen, Glasgow	Scotland	25
1990	Loughor, South Wales	Wales	2
1992	Burry-Port, South Wales	Wales	6
1994	Bryn, South Wales	Wales	6
1998	Gardenstown, Aberdeenshire	Scotland	60
1999	Tavistock, Devon	England	25
1999	South London	England	30
2000	Stranraer	Scotland	25
2000	Bridlington	England	35
2000	Rhiwderin, Cardiff	Wales	10
2000	Dundee	Scotland	15
2001	Merthyr Tydfil	Wales	10
2002	Bristol	England	20
2002	Isle of Man	Isle of Man	10

* Work ceased and restarted.

TABLE A4. *Congregations outside the British Isles*

Start date	Place	Country	Size 2002
1976	Toronto	Canada	300
1977	Greenville, South Carolina	USA	300
1977	Newtown Square, PA	USA	80
1978	Port Lincoln, South Australia	Australia	40
1980	Calgary, Alberta	Canada	130
1983	Perth, Western Australia	Australia	25
1984	Cloverdale, Vancouver	Canada	100
1985	Manchester, New Hampshire	USA	50
1988	Winston-Salem, North Carolina	USA	*
1988	Decatur, Alabama	USA	35
1988	Orlando, Florida	USA	50
1990	Indianapolis, Indiana	USA	40
1991	Barrie, Ontario	Canada	30
1991	Fredericton, New Brunswick	Canada	35
1992	Boston, New York	USA	35
1994	Port Hope, Ontario	Canada	35
1995	Prince George, British Columbia	Canada	60
1995	Lock, South Australia	Australia	*
1995	Phoenix, Arizona	USA	*
1996	Penticton, British Columbia	Canada	25
1997	Korean Church, Greenville, South Carolina	USA	100
1998	Lehigh Valley, Pennsylvania	USA	80
1999	Kansas City, Missouri	USA	20
2000	Summers (later Siloam Springs) Arkansas	USA	10
2000	Littleton, Colorado	USA	25
2001	Margate, Tasmania	Australia	10
2002	Columbia, South Carolina	USA	*
2002	Greer, South Carolina	USA	*

* Those congregations for which Kyle does not give attendance figures.

Note: In addition in 2004 there was one minister in Jamaica and in Kenya and three in Spain, and eight missionaries were supported to work abroad.

Free Presbyterian Ministers

Some insight into the appeal of Free Presbyterianism may be gained from examining the family backgrounds of those in the ministry in 1981—those whose recruitment predates the point when most clergy were recruited from FPCU families. Where they are known, the previous denominations of Free Presbyterian ministers and their parents are presented in Table A7. Five people who had regularly attended more than one denomination are entered twice.

The final column of Table A7 gives the percentages of major Protestant groups in the 1951 census, and comparison with the other columns makes

TABLE A5. *Distribution of Free Presbyterians by Local District Council, 1971–2001*

Local District Council	1971	1981	1991	2001
Antrim	160	230	352	237
Ards	203	444	785	744
Armagh	471	710	1,016	1,095
Ballymena	430	728	791	753
Ballymoney	351	399	419	518
Banbridge	349	471	722	716
Belfast	1,360	785	835	714
Carrickfergus	55	134	138	115
Castlereagh	429	519	503	444
Coleraine	159	321	340	340
Cookstown	119	223	391	402
Craigavon	562	962	1,245	1,222
Down	204	250	281	263
Dungannon	265	399	481	532
Fermanagh	263	291	378	377
Larne	110	180	212	105
Limavady	69	87	91	97
Lisburn	641	723	984	871
L'Derry	128	102	118	130
Magherafelt	157	537	719	665
Moyle	10	7	23	36
Newry + Mourne	278	387	609	684
Newtownabbey	153	166	194	173
North Down	120	177	265	237
Omagh	243	268	332	338
Strabane	60	121	139	140
TOTAL	7,349	9,621	12,363	11,948

two obvious points: the Church of Ireland is considerably under-represented and 'Other Protestants' (in particular the Reformed Presbyterians and the Baptists) are over-represented. Although the numbers involved are too small to be definite, the explanation probably combines personal elements (Paisley and his earliest supporters were Presbyterians and Baptists and tended to get the best hearing from co-religionists), geography (the early FP ministers evangelized least those areas where the Church of Ireland was strongest), and social class (the Church of Ireland being relatively strong among the landed gentry and their workers and least strong among the small farmers and the urban working class that provided the foundations for the FPCU).

The appeal of the FPCU to rural people is clear from Table A8's listing of the occupations of the parents of FPCU clergy: over a third were farmers. Of the ten skilled manual workers, four lived in Belfast and they were a painter, an electrician, a baker, and a wood turner. The other six were a

TABLE **A6.** *District Council areas by number of Free Presbyterians, 1971 and 2001*

No.	1971	2001
1	Belfast	Craigavon
2	Lisburn	Armagh
3	Craigavon	Lisburn
4	Armagh	Ballymena
5	Ballymena	Ards
6	Castlereagh	Banbridge
7	Ballymoney	Belfast
8	Banbridge	Dungannon
9	Newry + Mourne	Newry + Mourne
10	Dungannon	Magherafelt
11	Fermanagh	Ballymoney
12	Omagh	Castlereagh
13	Down	Cookstown
14	Ards	Fermanagh
15	Antrim	Coleraine
16	Coleraine	Omagh
17	Magherafelt	Down
18	Newtownabbey	+ Antrim
19	Londonderry	+ North Down
20	Cookstown	Newtownabbey
21	North Down	Strabane
22	Larne	Londonderry
23	Limavady	Carrickfergus
24	Strabane	Larne
25	Carrickfergus	Limavady
26	Moyle	Moyle

stonemason, an electrician, two machinists, a painter, and a gardener. Not one Free Presbyterian clergyman had a father in a management position in non-agricultural industry. Of the seven white-collar workers, there were two full-time Christian workers, a grocer, a salesman, two civil servants, and the manager of the creamery.

Ordination Vows

The following is the text of the prescribed questions which ministers (and with some slight modification) elders are required to answer.

Do you believe the Scriptures of the Old and New Testament not merely to contain, but to be, the verbally inspired word of the Living God, the only infallible rule of faith and practice?

Appendix   275

TABLE A7. *Previous denominations of Free Presbyterian clergy, and parents, 1981*

	Clergy		Parents	Non-Catholic population, 1951
Denomination	n.	%	%	%
Irish Presbyterian	24	64	46	46
Church of Ireland	7	14	13	39
Baptist	5	5	10	—
Reformed Presbyterian	5	9	10	—
Methodist	3	5	6	7
Faith Mission	3	—	6	—
Independent Evangelical	2		4	—
Elim Pentecostal	0	2	0	—
Pres. Church of S. America	1	—	1	—
Salvation Army	1	2	1	—
'Other Protestant'			32	7
TOTAL	51	101	99	99

Note: Percentages may not total 100 because of rounding in calculation.

TABLE A8. *Occupations of parents of FPCU clergy, 1981*

Occupation	n.	%
Farmers	15	34
White-collar workers	7	16
Non-agricultural self-employed	3	7
Skilled manual workers	10	23
Unskilled manual workers	8	18
Security Forces	1	2
TOTAL	44	100

Do you sincerely receive and believe the Articles of Faith and the Westminster Standards as containing the system of doctrine taught in the Holy Scriptures?

Are you firmly resolved through divine grace to adhere to the doctrine in the said confessions and teach and defend it to the utmost of your power against all error?

Will you subscribe the said confessions as a confession of your own faith?

Will you maintain at all costs to personal reputation and vain worldly popularity the three great fundamentals of the faith as set out by Dr Henry Cooke: (i) The Trinity; (ii) The Virgin Birth and vicarious atonement of

Christ; (iii) The necessity of the work of the Spirit to originate faith and repentance in the heart of man?

Will you maintain with all the strength God shall give you the truly Scriptural separation position of the Free Presbyterian Church of Ulster and vigorously withstand the apostasy of Irish Presbyterianism, exhorting God's people to obey the teaching and commandment of 1 Timothy 6: 3–5?

Do you believe the Presbyterian government and discipline of the Free Presbyterian Church of Ulster to be founded on and agreeable to the Word of God, and do you promise to adhere to it and support it and to yield submission and be in subjection to your brethren as is taught in the word of God?

Have you the experience of the New Birth and do you believe that it is only by the power of the infilling of the Holy Spirit that you can make full proof of your ministry?

Will you publicly denounce the great public vices of drinking, dancing and gambling and the pleasure crazes of this present evil world and by example live righteously, soberly and godly before all men?

Will you ever maintain the purity of the Communion feast and by all Scriptural and lawful means resist any attempt to weaken the testimony of the church in her stand for the born-again communicant membership?

Do you promise to be zealous and faithful in maintaining the truths of the gospel against modernistic apostasy, and in working for the purity and peace of the church, whatever persecution or opposition may arise unto you on that account?

Do you engage to be faithful and diligent in the exercise of all private and personal duties which become you as a Christian and minister of the gospel; as well as in all relative duties and the public duties of your office, endeavouring to adorn the profession of the gospel by your conversation and walking with exemplary piety before the flock over which God shall make you overseer; and are you now willing to take charge of this congregation, promising to discharge the duties of the pastor to them, as God shall give you strength?

Social Characteristics of Free Presbyterians

Tables A9–A12 use census data to describe the social class of Free Presbyterians.

In Table A9 we can see very clear differences between Irish Presbyterians and the early generations of Free Presbyterians. Free Presbyterians are under-represented in the professions (rows 1 and 2) and in manufacturing (rows 4, 12, and 13) and over-represented in farming (row 10).

Table A10 shows changes in the distribution of Free and Irish Presbyterian males between the various sectors of employment over the two decades between 1981 and 2001. The most obvious changes refer to the economy as a whole: manufacturing has declined and service industries have expanded. The greatest change was the growth in the final service category, which includes the health service, education, and public administration. But the differences between Free and Irish Presbyterians remain much the same.

Table A11 shows the 2001 census divisions by social class, with the cases divided into three age cohorts so that we can see change over time. In these data we can see a very clear difference in social class between Free and Irish Presbyterians. If we draw a line between classes III and IV, above that line Free Presbyterians lag behind Irish Presbyterians in all three age cohorts. For the lowest two social classes and for those not economically active, Free Presbyterians lead Irish Presbyterians. Part of that class difference is explained by a cultural choice. For the middle-age cohort, there is a marked difference in the proportions of women who are not economically active (82 per cent of Free Presbyterians and 69 per cent of Irish Presbyterians) and much of that reflects the evangelical Protestant preference for full-time mothers. But that difference is diminishing. For the age cohort 18–34 the economically inactive figures are 34 and 31 per cent respectively.

Table A12 displays the extremes of educational qualification for Free and Irish Presbyterians divided into three age cohorts. Level 1 includes those with a university degree or above. Level 7 indicates those who have no formal

TABLE A9. *Occupations of male Free Presbyterians and Irish Presbyterians, 1981 (%)*

No.	Occupation	FP	IP
1	Professionals/top managers	1.5	4.5
2	Doctors/teachers etc	2.9	5.2
3	Writers/artists/sports	0.3	0.4
4	Professional engineers	2.0	4.4
5	Managers	19.5	18.3
6	Clerks	4.6	7.3
7	Salesmen	3.9	4.6
8	Policemen/soldiers, etc.	6.6	6.6
9	Cooks/cleaners/other services	2.6	2.2
10	Farmers/fishermen	4.1	2.3
11	Agri-industrial workers	12.1	8.6
12	Metal and electrical workers	14.6	16.2
13	Painters/assemblers	0.9	2.2
14	Building workers	6.7	4.2
15	Transport workers	12.1	8.4
16	Unclassifiable others	5.8	4.7
	TOTAL	100.2	100.1

Note: Percentages do not total 100 because of rounding.

TABLE A10. *Industries of male Free Presbyterians and Irish Presbyterians, 1981 and 2001 (%)*

No.	Industry	1981 FP	1981 IP	2001 FP	2001 IP
1	Agriculture/forestry/fishing	16.5	11.4	8.9	6.3
2	Energy/water supply	2.4	3.0	0.9	1.6
3	Mineral extraction	4.2	3.8	2.0	1.6
4	Metal engineering	8.0	10.6	5.6	6.6
5	Other manufacture (e.g. textiles)	13.5	11.6	15.1	10.4
6	Construction	14.3	10.1	8.3	6.3
7	Distribution/hotel/catering	14.4	14.7	18.9	18.3
8	Transport/communications	4.1	5.4	3.8	4.2
9	Banking/finance/insurance	2.7	5.6	4.1	7.6
10	Medicine/education/public admin	17.8	22.7	29.1	34.6
	TOTAL	98	99	97	96

Note: Percentages do not total 100 because of rounding.

TABLE A11. *Social class of Free Presbyterians and Irish Presbyterians, 2001 (%)*

Class	Age 18–34 FP	Age 18–34 IP	Age 35–54 FP	Age 35–54 IP	Age 55 + FP	Age 55 + IP
I	1.2	2.6	2.0	3.1	0.5	1.5
II	12.2	15.9	17.4	24.7	8.1	11.4
III	39.1	39.7	29.8	32.0	11.3	14.9
IV	15.9	13.8	13.0	10.9	7.6	6.6
V	4.9	3.6	7.9	5.9	5.3	3.6
NEA/NPJ	26.7	25.0	29.8	23.5	67.2	61.0
	100	100	100	100	100	99
n.	3,170	78,852	2,838	80,666	2,209	93,904

Note: Percentages do not total 100 because of rounding.

Key: Class I: professional occupations; Class II: managerial and technical occupations; Class III: skilled occupations; Class IV: partly skilled occupations; Class V: unskilled occupations; NEA: not economically active or retired; NPJ: no paid job in the previous ten years.

qualification, not even a CSE. The disparities are considerable. For those aged at least 55 (who reached university entrance age in 1964 or before), 3.6 per cent of Irish Presbyterians but just under one-third of 1 per cent of Free Presbyterians went to university. The gap is smaller for the middle-age cohort (university entrance between 1965 and 1986) and smaller yet for the youngest group, but the difference is still considerable: 3 per cent to 8 per cent.

The data on social class, sector of employment, and educational qualification all fit neatly. Overall there has been a decline in the primary extraction

TABLE A12. *Educational qualifications of Free Presbyterians and Irish Presbyterians, 2001 (%)*

Level	Age 18–34		Age 35–54		Age 55 +	
	FP	IP	FP	IP	FP	IP
1	3.3	8.2	1.8	8.8	0.3	3.6
2	1.8	2.7	1.2	2.4	—	0.7
3	7.9	12.0	2.1	4.3	0.3	1.3
4	2.7	3.5	1.0	1.5	—	0.4
5	29.6	29.4	10.2	14.0	1.5	4.0
6	9.4	8.9	1.3	1.1	—	0.3
7	45.4	35.3	82.4	67.9	97.9	89.8
TOTAL	100.1	100.0	100.0	100.0	100.0	100.1
n.	3,257	81,646	2,887	81,993	2,227	94,437

Note: Percentages do not total 100 because of rounding.

sector (farming, mining) and in manufacture, and a considerable growth in the service sector (especially in the welfare state). This is work for which educational qualifications are required and the Free Presbyterians lack such credentials and are thus unable to enter the better paid sectors of white-collar work at the same rate as Irish Presbyterians. It is impossible from these data to untangle causation. While it might seem obvious that educational credentials explain entry (or otherwise) to certain kinds of work, for some families the link is the other way round: the family's possession of a farm or agriculture-related business (such as drainage contractor) provides ready employment for its children and thus discourages the pursuit of higher qualifications. There may well also be a cultural component to the patterns. Universities are rightly seen by conservative evangelicals as a threat to their beliefs. Staff and students are unlikely to be Christians and, if they are, they are unlikely to be conservative Christians.

The Democratic Unionist Party

Elections

The electoral fortunes of the DUP are summarized in Table A13. The early 1970s elections are omitted because the DUP contested them as part of a coalition with the conservative wing of the UUP and Vanguard. Much of the fluctuation relative to the UUP is explained by the nature of the election. The European elections, which are conducted on a single transferable vote (STV) form of proportional representation, treat Northern Ireland as a single constituency with three seats. Paisley easily won the first election in

1978 and repeated his victory in 1984, 1989, and 1994. In 1999 he was replaced by Jim Allister, and, as part of the general swing to the DUP, the DUP margin over the UUP increased. The Westminster election results are relatively uninformative because they are fought on a first-past-the-post system and, where there was any danger of a split unionist vote allowing a nationalist to take the seat, the DUP usually deferred to the senior party and allowed the UUP incumbent a clear run. The difference between the two sorts of elections explains why, in 1979, the DUP could be both 8 points ahead of the UUP and 26 behind.

As they were fought on an STV system and involved province-wide competition between the DUP and the UUP, the various assemblies and the council elections provide the best general indicator of popularity. They show the DUP peaking in 1981, then falling back to trail the UUP through the 1980s and 1990s, until disillusionment with the peace process saw a steady shift in unionist preferences, so that in 2003 and 2005 the DUP recorded clear victories over the UUP in all types of election.

TABLE A13. *DUP and UUP percentage of total vote, 1977–2005*

Year	Election type	% of total vote DUP	UUP	DUP advantage
1977	Council	12.7	29.6	−17
1979	Westminster	10.2	36.6	−26
1979	European	29.8	21.9	+8
1981	Council	26.6	26.5	+1
1982	Assembly	23.0	29.7	−7
1983	Westminster	20.0	34.0	−14
1984	European	33.6	21.5	+12
1985	Council	24.3	29.5	−5
1987	Westminster	11.7	37.8	−26
1989	Council	17.7	31.3	−14
1989	European	29.9	22.2	+8
1992	Westminster	13.1	34.5	−21
1993	Council	17.3	29.4	−12
1994	European	29.2	23.8	+5
1996	Forum	18.8	24.2	−5
1997	Council	15.9	27.8	−12
1997	Westminster	13.6	32.7	−19
1998	Assembly	18.1	21.3	−3
1999	European	28	18.0	+10
2000	South Antrim by-election	38.0	35.3	+3
2001	Westminster	22.5	26.8	−4
2001	Council	21.4	22.9	−1
2003	Assembly	25.7	22.7	+3
2005	Westminster	33.7	17.7	+16
2005	Council	29.6	18.0	+12

Religion in the Democratic Unionist Party

Free Presbyterians have always formed a major part of the activist core of the DUP.

As Table A14 shows, although the proportion of Free Presbyterians in the non-Catholic population is generally about 1 per cent, the proportion of Free Presbyterians in eleven groups of activists, identified at various points over almost thirty years, never falls below 47 per cent. The first group sampled, the 1973 Assembly members, are the least typical, because the party was then in its infancy and some candidates were chosen more because they would stand and were well known than because they were typical of the party's inner circle. For the other groups, there is a general principle that, the smaller the group, the more likely they are to be Free Presbyterians. This reflects length of service and closeness to the leadership. The 18 members of the 1975 Convention and the 35 members of the 1982 Assembly were almost all senior figures in the party drawn from Paisley's closest supporters. To assemble over 200 candidates for the 1985 council elections, the party had to cast its net much more widely. There is also a change over time. The change between the 1998 and 2003 Assemblies from 80 to 52 per cent Free Presbyterian is explained by the DUP attracting defectors from the UUP, and this is continued with the 2005 council pool.

As we can see from Table A15, the presence of Free Presbyterians among DUP activists varies considerably across the province. Attempts to correlate the variations with other differences such as proportion of Free Presbyterians in the population or relative size of DUP vote do not produce any statistically robust relationships. In part this is because in some areas the number of DUP councillors or candidates is small and hence it needs only one non-Free Presbyterian to be replaced by a Free Presbyterian for the proportion to change enormously: Moyle and Newry and Mourne, for example, in 2005 each had only two DUP people. The search for patterns probably also defeats statistical analysis because some underlying relationships cancel out.

TABLE A14. *Free Presbyterian percentage of DUP activists, 1973–2005*

Year	Group	Total	% FP
1973	Assembly members	17	47
1975	Convention members	18	78
1976	Councillors	31	65
1978	Councillors	72	60
1982	Assembly members	35	77
1985	Council candidates	218	57
1996	Forum candidates	54	58
1997	Council candidates	160	52
1998	Assembly members	20	80
2003	Assembly members	33	52
2005	Councillors	171	47

TABLE A15. *Free Presbyterian percentage of DUP activists by area, 1978, 1985, and 2005*

Area	1978 Councillors	1985 Council candidates	2005 Council candidates
Antrim	33.3	50.0	50.0
Ards	100.0	60.0	25.0
Armagh	100.0	80.0	100.0
Ballymena	58.3	88.0	57.0
Ballymoney	66.6	75.0	62.5
Banbridge	100.0	85.7	85.7
Belfast	71.4	63.0	35.7
Carrickfergus	x	11.0	0
Castlereagh	x	25.0	23.0
Coleraine	100.0	45.5	33.3
Cookstown	100.0	100.0	100.0
Craigavon	100.0	60.0	85.7
Down	y	100.0	33.3
Dungannon	y	50.0	75.0
Fermanagh	y	66.6	50.0
Larne	33.3	33.3	80.0
Limavady	100.0	50.0	0
Lisburn	66.6	75.0	46.0
Londonderry	100.0	43.0	40.0
Magherafelt	66.6	80.0	100.0
Moyle	0	0	100.0
Newry and Mourne	100.0	75.0	0
Newtownabbey	25.0	36.4	16.6
North Down	0	50.0	0
Omagh	y	75.0	66.6
Strabane	x	33.3	66.6

Note: An *x* means that a proportion has not been calculated because I knew the denomination of less than half the sample; a *y* signifies no DUP councillors or candidates; '0' means that none of the DUP people was a Free Presbyterian.

In so far as we can make some guesses from these data, we can begin with the obvious point that the DUP draws a different sort of support from urban and rural areas. As we can see from the distribution of 2005 DUP activists who claim no religious affiliation (see Table A16), in the areas with a large working-class vote such as Belfast, Castlereagh, Newtownabbey, and Carrickfergus, the proportion of evangelicals and of Free Presbyterians is low. But there are still considerable differences between predominantly rural areas. In Cookstown and Magherafelt the party core is strongly Free Presbyterian, but in Omagh and Strabane it is less so. One might expect that personalities would play a large part in shaping the party core. In Magherafelt, for example, Willie McCrea, the local Free Presbyterian minister, has dominated the party since its foundation; hence the fact that all the DUP activists are Free Presbyterians is no surprise. But then Banbridge DUP has a very strong Free Presbyterian presence and its equally long-serving senior DUP figure is not a Free Presbyterian (though he is a committed Christian).

Simply counting the proportion of DUP activists who are Free Presbyterians underestimates the presence of evangelicals, because many of those who are not Free Presbyterians belong to other small conservative evangelical sects and denominations. This is illustrated by the figures in Table A16, which shows the denominational affiliation of the 2005 councillors.

The broadening of the party that resulted from attracting former UUP activists can be seen in the Irish Presbyterian presence (24 per cent of DUP councillors as compared to about one-third of the Protestant population), but the Church of Ireland remains grossly under-represented (6 per cent as compared to about 30 per cent in the Protestant population). The 'other evangelical' proportion, at 11 per cent (as compared to about 6 per cent of all Protestants) is a considerable over-representation.

TABLE A16. *Council candidates' denominations, 2005*

Area	FP	IP	C. of I.	Meth. + Cong.	Baptist	Other Evan.	None	Not known	Total
Antrim	3	2				1			6
Ards	3	5		1	1	1	1		12
Armagh	5								5
Ballymena	8	4	1			1			14
Ballymoney	5	3							8
Banbridge	6					1			7
Belfast	5	4				2	3		14
Carrickfergus		4	2	1			1		8
Castlereagh	3	3	1			5	1		13
Coleraine	3	3	1				2		9
Cookstown	3								3
Craigavon	6					1			7
Down	1				1		1		3
Dungannon	3							1	4
Fermanagh	2		1			1			4
Larne	4							1	5
Limavady		3							3
Lisburn	6	3	1	1		2			13
Londonderry	2	3							5
Magherafelt	4								4
Moyle	2								2
Newry + Mourne		1						1	2
Newtownabbey	2	2	1		1	2	4		12
North Down		1	1						2
Omagh	2		1						3
Strabane	2		1						3
TOTAL	80	41	11	3	3	17	13	3	171
% OF TOTAL	47	24	6	2	2	10	18	2	101

Index